The author gratefully acknowledges the invaluable assistance of Ms. Maria Breitschopf, Mr. Steve Lovett, Ms. Linda Perez, Ms. Erika Sipiora, and Ms. Sherry Barnash in the preparation of earlier editions of these materials.

© All rights reserved, 2021, David A. Schlueter. Reproduction of any portion of this text is not permitted without the express permission of the author

TABLE OF CONTENTS

CHAPTER ONE

INTRODUCTION TO EVIDENCE; ROLES OF THE PARTICIPANTS PRESERVATION OF ERROR

§ 1-1. Introduction to This Text.

This text collects a variety of cases, materials, problems and questions which are designed to provide the student with not only the substantive rules of evidence, but also with the opportunity to apply those rules. It is important to note that the text does not always provide an in-depth discussion of every evidence topic. That material is left to more complete evidence treatises and manuals. *See, e.g.*, MCCORMICK ON EVIDENCE (8th Edition 2020); Mueller & Kirkpatrick, EVIDENCE (4th ed. 2012). The focus here is on the basics.

The text is divided into ten chapters, which are designed to track the ten articles of the Federal Rules of Evidence. For example, this chapter, Chapter One, focuses on general evidence topics, how the rules of evidence fit into the trial setting, the role of the participants, and preservation of error. Those topics are generally covered in Article I of the Federal Rules of Evidence.

At the end of each chapter the student will find questions and problems on the subjects covered.

§ 1-2. An Overview of the Law of Evidence

§ 1-2(A). Evidence, Procedure and Substantive Law

What is the law of evidence? And how does it differ from, or relate to, the procedural rules and substantive law?

Substantive law, which is normally defined by legislation or case law, focuses on the rights of persons or limits on their behavior. The substantive law, for example, defines criminal conduct and what constitutes a valid contract, or a tort. *Procedural law*, in the context of a trial, sets limits and requirements on how and when the parties may, or must, take certain actions. For example, most jurisdictions have detailed procedural rules for pleading and pretrial discovery. Some procedural rules include sanctions and thus, failure to follow the procedural rules may limit a party's ability to introduce evidence at trial.

Evidence law, on the other hand, determines to a large extent what a judge or jury may hear and consider in deciding a case. Like the rules of procedure, they are "rules of engagement" for the participants involved in the adversarial process of presenting information to the fact finder. Evidence may take the form of oral testimony from a witness who appears in court, recorded oral testimony of a witness who has since died, private and official documents, tape recordings, physical objects, computer printouts, and photographs.

Read together, the substantive, procedural, and evidence rules operate in the following way: The substantive law defines the elements of the crime or the civil cause of action. The procedural rules in turn dictate, inter alia, how the crime or cause of action will be pleaded, timing requirements, and pretrial discovery procedures. The procedural rules may also govern certain trial procedures as well. The evidence rules, on the other hand will indicate what, if any, evidence is admissible at trial to prove the alleged crime or civil cause of action.

Evidence rules operate like multi-level screening devices or sieves, through which each piece of evidence must pass. Consider for example the admissibility, in whole, or in part, of a letter written by a criminal defendant to her friend. The letter must be shown to be *relevant* to an issue in the case. *See* Rule 401. And it must be shown to be *authentic*. *See* Rule 901, et seq. If a witness is used to lay the foundation or predicate for the letter, the witness must be *competent*. *See* Rule 601. Because it was written out-of-court it may be inadmissible *hearsay* (depending on why it is being offered and by whom it is being offered). *See* Rule 801, et seq. Even assuming it successfully passes through those various potential objections, the trial judge may still exclude the evidence because it is cumulative or unduly prejudicial. *See* Rule 403. If the court admits the letter for a limited purpose, then a *limiting instruction* under Rule 105 may be required. Thus, it is critical to understand first, that more than one rule may come into play on any given piece of evidence and second, the rules of evidence are often interrelated.

§ 1-2(B). Reasons for the Law of Evidence.

Why do we need rules of evidence? Why not simply let the judge and jury hear all of the available evidence, as in some other legal systems, and then decide what and whom to believe?

Commentators and courts often cite a number of reasons for evidence law. Although scholars may disagree on the most important reasons for evidence law, the list can generally be shortened to include the following:

First, the rules of evidence seek to insure that only reliable, trustworthy evidence is admitted. This is reflected in the rules requiring that evidence, such as a document, be authenticated, i.e., shown to be the real thing, and not a forgery.

Second, evidence law imposes important limits on the scope and duration of trials, which might otherwise be needlessly extended. Federal Rule of Evidence 403, for example, permits the judge to exclude otherwise relevant evidence if he or she believes that the introduction of the evidence will be a waste of time.

Third, evidence law represents some mistrust of the jurors' ability to disregard untrustworthy evidence or to place too much weight on certain evidence. For example, the hearsay rule recognizes that the jury may be unable to adequately judge the reliability of statements made out of their presence, where they could not see and hear for themselves what was being said. And the rules governing the admissibility of character evidence reflect the concern that if the jury hears that a person has particular propensities they may jump to judgment without considering the facts in the case.

And fourth, evidence law reflects important extrinsic policies, e.g., the need to promote confidentiality in relationships as reflected in the rules governing privileged communications between an attorney and a client or between a husband and wife.

§ 1-3. Identifying the Traditional Sources of Evidence Law

For almost two centuries, trials in America were governed mostly by the common law rules of evidence. Occasionally, a jurisdiction would rely on statutory enactments to determine what evidence was admissible, or inadmissible. While that system reflected local concerns or approaches to evidence, it certainly did not lend itself to national uniformity or consistency.

There are a variety of potential sources for evidence law. First, the Fourth (unreasonable searches and seizures), Fifth (the right against self-incrimination), and Sixth (right to counsel) Amendments to the United States Constitution (and state counterparts to those provisions) may serve as the basis for excluding evidence wrongfully obtained from a criminal defendant. Although those constitutional provisions do not explicitly exclude evidence, the well-known exclusionary rules adopted by the Supreme Court are designed to promote faithful application of the constitutional principles by those charged with administering a criminal justice system.

A second source of evidence law is statutes, at both the national and state level. As noted in the following discussion, Congress adopted the Federal Rules of Evidence as a statute in 1975. Some states have codified similar rules of evidence through statutory enactments and still others have permitted the judiciary to adopt rules of evidence. Some states, like Texas, have permitted courts to promulgate rules of evidence (subject to legislative changes) and also recognized the ability of the legislature to independently promulgate rules of evidence in other non-evidence codes. For example, the Texas Code of Criminal Procedure contains specific rules governing the admissibility of certain types of evidence.

Still another source of evidence law is the common law, a body of judicial decisions which set out rules of evidence. Although the role of the common law has been greatly diminished in the last two decades by the enactment of specific and uniform rules of evidence in most jurisdictions, the common law may still impact on the admissibility of evidence. Congress, for example, declined to adopt specific rules of evidence governing privileges. Instead, Federal Rule of Evidence 501 provides that privileges in federal cases "shall be governed by the principles of the common law as they may be interpreted by the courts of the United States in the light of reason and experience."

The following section discusses the formulation of the Federal Rules of Evidence, which have now been adopted in most of the States.

§ 1-4. The Federal Rules of Evidence

§ 1-4(A). The Road to Codification

Until very recently, the law of evidence in both state and federal courts derived mostly from judicial decisions—the common law. Few attempts were made at synthesizing or codifying the massive and often conflicting rules governing the admissibility of evidence, probably due in large part to the resistance to, and difficulty in, agreeing on a uniform set of rules. In 1904, the evidence case law that had developed to that time was consolidated into a monumental treatise by Professor John Henry Wigmore. Professor Wigmore's work in evidence has remained the dominant authority on common law evidence to this day.

In 1939, the American Law Institute (ALI) started work on the Model Code of Evidence with the assistance of Professor Edmund M. Morgan of Harvard Law School, who served as the

Reporter for the project. During the drafting process two camps emerged. Wigmore favored a detailed and lengthy evidence code. Others preferred a more condensed set of rules. Professor Morgan urged adoption of a middle ground, a position the Institute adopted. The Code, published in 1942, however, was not simply a codification of existing evidence law; it included many radical changes. Consequently, these reforms were not immediately accepted. Although no jurisdiction adopted the ALI's Model Code, it would eventually become part of later codifications.

In 1949, a drafting committee of the National Conference of Commissioners on Uniform State Laws started work on yet another evidence code which simply restated existing evidence law in an effort to promote uniformity. In 1953, the Conference unanimously approved the code and several days later it was endorsed by the American Bar Association. Even so, the seventy-two Uniform Rules of Evidence as they were called, were adopted in only three states: Kansas, New Jersey, and Utah. California considered adoption of the rules but rejected them in favor of its own more detailed evidence code, which became effective in 1967. Despite the cool reception to the Uniform Rules, the work of the National Conference of Commissioners continues and the Uniform Rules, which are amended from time to time, may still serve as models for jurisdictions wishing to change their evidence rules.

The momentum for codification resulted in the United States Judicial Conference considering adoption of a uniform set of evidence rules for federal proceedings. In response, Chief Justice Earl Warren appointed a Special Committee on Evidence in 1961 to determine whether uniform rules of evidence for the federal courts was desirable and attainable. Within a year, the Committee reported that such a code should be drafted. *See* 30 F.R.D. 73. After struggling with potential obstacles such as the *Erie* doctrine and the extent of Supreme Court's authority to promulgate rules of evidence, the Committee concluded that the time was ripe for evidentiary codification and reform. The Committee recommended that the 1953 Uniform Rules of Evidence, *supra*, could serve as a starting point. In 1963, the Committee's report was submitted to the Judicial Conference's Standing Committee on Rules of Practice and Procedure. That Committee in turn recommended that an advisory committee be appointed by the Chief Justice to begin drafting the rules. Chief Justice Warren appointed Albert E. Jenner, Jr. as the chair and Professor Edward W. Cleary as the Reporter to the new committee.

The Advisory Committee circulated its first draft of the rules in 1969 and after making revisions forwarded the rules through the Judicial Conference to the Supreme Court. Following additional consideration and revisions—largely at the insistence of the Department of Justice and conservative members of Congress who questioned the rulemaking power of the Supreme Court and who viewed the Rules as too favorable to criminal defendants—the Supreme Court made a few changes and then transmitted them to Congress in 1972, in accordance with the Rules Enabling Act procedures.

The rules would remain under Congressional consideration for another three years. After much debate and rewriting, especially with regard to the rules governing privileges, the Federal Rules of Evidence passed both houses and became law when signed by President Ford on January 2, 1975. The Federal Rules of Evidence became effective on July 1, 1975.

Since 1975, the Federal Rules have stood the test of time and have remained essentially unchanged. In 1987, they were gender-neutralized. Following a hiatus of almost 20 years, Chief Justice Rehnquist revitalized the Advisory Committee on the Federal Rules of Evidence in 1993. Since then that Committee has considered, and recommended a number of amendments to the rules. Proposed amendments are processed though the Rules Enabling Act procedures. 28 U.S.C. §§

2071-2077. Under those procedures, the initial proposals for amendments come from the Judicial Conference's Advisory Committee and are published for public comment. The amendments are then forwarded to the Standing Committee on Rules of Practice and Procedure, through the Judicial Conference, to the Supreme Court. If the Supreme Court approves the amendments they are transmitted to Congress, which under the Rules Enabling Act, reserves the power to modify, reject or defer any amendments. Absent any changes by Congress, the amendments become effective on December 1st of the year they are sent by the Court to Congress.

On December 1, 2011, a completely restyled version of the Federal Rules of Evidence went into effect. The Committee Notes accompanying the changes note that the purpose of the complete revision to those Rules was intended to "reduce inconsistencies, ambiguities, and redundant, repetitive, and archaic words." See 2011 Advisory Committee Notes, Fed. R. Evid. 101. With only a few exceptions, the amendments made no substantive changes in the Rules.

Appendix A of this text includes the official text of the Federal Rules of Evidence—as of December 1, 2020. Appendix C provides a comparison chart between the Texas Rules of Evidence and the Federal Rules of Evidence.

§ 1-4(B). The Federal Rules of Evidence in the States.

The impact of codifying the Federal Rules of Evidence cannot be overstated. Not only did the rules represent the first major, successful effort to codify rules of evidence, they prompted similar efforts at codification in the States. Currently, thirty-four states and two other jurisdictions, the armed forces and Puerto Rico, have adopted some version of the Federal Rules. Notably absent from the list are California and New York which have maintained their pre-existing evidence codes and which ironically, served as points of reference for some of the federal rules. Texas finally adopted the rules in 1983 for civil cases and in 1985 for criminal cases. In 1998 the two sets of rules were merged into one unified code. In 2015, the Texas Rules were "restyled" to conform them to the Federal Rules of Evidence. Although the Rule numbering remained the same, the amendments changed a significant number of the Rules in their internal numbering.

§ 1-5. Reading and Applying Codified Rules of Evidence

While the codification of the law of evidence created a more uniform and consistent set of rules, it also limited to some extent the ability of a particular judge or appellate court to redefine the law of evidence—an option that had existed under the common law. Not surprisingly there has been debate over whether the rules should be read to mean what they say or whether the courts should view them as mere guidelines which may be read to reflect broader, unstated, policy considerations.

The Supreme Court itself has indicated that it will treat the Federal Rules of Evidence as though they were a statute and apply a "plain meaning" approach to the language of the rules. Thus, if a rule of evidence clearly and explicitly indicates that a particular piece of evidence is not admissible, the Court will apply the rule to that end. On the other hand, where a rule of evidence on its face gives the trial judge some discretion in ruling on a piece of evidence, the Court will recognize the broad discretion vested in trial judges to rule on such matters. Notwithstanding the Court's approach, commentators and courts may argue that the real guiding principle in applying a particular rule of evidence is the judge's sense of what is the right thing to do in a particular case.

That is, they will start with examining general public policy considerations and then move toward application, if at all, of the rule of evidence.

It is important to note that the drafters of the Federal Rules recognized that from time to time there might be unexpected gaps in the rules and to that end promulgated Federal Rule of Evidence 102, which recognizes the ability of a judge to fill such gaps. But at the same time, it is also important to note that Rule 102 is rarely relied on or cited to support a particular ruling. That is because in most evidentiary issues, a specific rule of evidence will govern and require a particular ruling.

§ 1-6. The Flow of a Typical Trial

As noted above, the rules of procedure and rules of evidence are often interrelated. It is therefore important to have some background knowledge of how a typical trial proceeds. A chart demonstrating the typical flow of a trial follows the discussion.

§ 1-6(A). Pretrial Motions and Objections

Before the trial begins, the proponent of an item of evidence may make a *motion in limine* or objection to obtain an advance ruling admitting evidence. Although motions in limine are not mentioned anywhere in the Federal Rules of Evidence, they are a vital part of trial practice because a pretrial ruling on the admissibility of evidence can affect the proponent's trial strategy in offering that evidence. It is important to note, however, that rulings on motions in limine are not necessarily final. If the judge grants the motion, it usually means that counsel must approach the bench and obtain a ruling before introducing the evidence.

The opponent of an item of evidence has two main pretrial options for attempting to exclude evidence. If law enforcement agents seized evidence in violation of constitutional provisions, e.g. the fourth amendment, the opponent of the evidence may file a *motion to suppress* before the case is even assigned to a trial judge. Such rulings are usually final and are sufficient to preserve error. If there are nonconstitutional or nonstatutory grounds for excluding the evidence, the opponent may resort to a *motion in limine*, noted above.

§ 1-6(B). Selection of the Jury; Bench Trials

At the beginning of a jury trial, the judge introduces the attorneys and parties to the prospective jurors and generally describes the substance of the case. The judge and attorneys then conduct the *voir dire* examination of the prospective jurors in order to establish whether they are qualified to sit as jurors. At the conclusion of the questioning, the attorneys exercise their *challenges*. There are two types of challenges: *challenges for cause* and *peremptory challenges*. The bases for a challenge for cause are usually specified by statute and consist of reasons, such as bias, that disqualify a prospective juror. On the other hand, a peremptory challenge gives the attorney a qualified right to strike the prospective juror. Ordinarily no reason is given for exercising a peremptory challenge. *Cf. Batson v. Kentucky*, 476 U.S. 79 (1986).

If the case is to be tried to the trial judge, i.e., the trial judge will serve as the finder of fact (or fact finder), the trial proceedings are usually referred to as a *bench trial*. In those cases, the judge will not only rule on the admissibility of evidence, but will also ultimately decide the facts in the case, e.g., that the criminal defendant is guilty or that the civil defendant is liable.

§ 1-6(C). Exclusion of Witnesses

Under Federal Rule of Evidence 615, a party may request the trial judge to exclude all of the witnesses from the courtroom, until they are called to testify. The purpose of the rule is to prevent witnesses from hearing each other's version of what took place. There are exceptions, however. The Rule states that the following individuals may remain: a party who is a natural person, an office or employee of a party, a person whose presence is essential to the presentation of the case, and finally, a person authorized by statute to be present. That last category will normally include victims of crimes. The Texas counterpart is Rule 614 and is usually triggered by one of the parties "invoking the Rule," a colloquial term for asking the judge to sequester the witnesses.

§ 1-6(D). Opening Statements

Following jury selection, the attorneys present their *opening statements*. The party with the burden of proof, i.e. the plaintiff or prosecutor, goes first. The defense attorney may present an *opening statement* directly after the plaintiff's or prosecutor's opening statement, or defer making an opening statement until the start of the defense's case-in-chief.

The purpose of the *opening statement* is to make known to the jury what the attorney intends to prove. It is a preview of the admissible evidence for the jurors. An *error* may be committed by the attorney if he or she alludes to any matter that will not be supported by admissible evidence. In effect, the attorney may not be argumentative or conclusory. To avoid objections, the attorney must know beforehand what evidence is likely to be admitted during the trial. *See* Disciplinary Rule 7-106(c)(1), ABA Code of Professional Responsibility (lawyer shall not state or allude to evidence which will not be supported by admissible evidence).

§ 1-6(E). Plaintiff's or Prosecutor's Case-in-Chief

The plaintiff and prosecutor have the first opportunity to present evidence to the jury because they have the ultimate *burden of proof* on most factual issues in the case. During the *case-in-chief* (sometimes referred to as the *merits* portion of the case), they have the opportunity to present any evidence *logically relevant* to any factual issue on which they have the *burden of proof*. In some jurisdictions, the scope is broader, including any evidence *logically relevant* to any factual issue in the case. In such jurisdictions, the plaintiff and prosecutor can anticipate defenses and offer rebuttal evidence.

In making their cases, the plaintiff and prosecutor may call witnesses for the defense as hostile or adverse witnesses and they may also attempt to obtain stipulations of fact or expected testimony. Or they request the court to take judicial notice of well-known facts. *See* Rule 201. Usually, evidence is presented one witness at a time, with one party presenting evidence before the opposing party presents counter evidence. Evidence is presented in the form of *direct examination* of witnesses (*cross examination* by the defense and *redirect questioning* are also included), *physical* and *documentary evidence*. At the conclusion of its case-in-chief, the prosecutor or plaintiff *rests*.

§ 1-6(F). Defense Motions for Instructed or Directed Verdict, or Finding of Not Guilty

When the plaintiff or prosecutor rests, the defense may make a motion to challenge the *legal sufficiency* of the evidence. The defense does so if he or she thinks that even if the jury believes all the evidence, the evidence lacks *sufficient cumulative probative value* to prove all the facts on which the plaintiff or prosecutor has the burden. To survive that motion, the plaintiff or prosecutor must show that he or she has presented a prima facie case. This motion may be called a *motion for a nonsuit, judgment of acquittal, finding of not guilty, or directed verdict*. If the judge grants the motion, the trial is terminated. If the judge overrules the defense motion, the trial continues.

In ruling on the defense motion, the judge must decide if the plaintiff or prosecutor has sustained the *burden of production*. There are three options possible. The evidence could have been so persuasive of a fact that if the jury believes the evidence, they must conclude the fact exists. Or the evidence could be sufficient enough that if the jurors believe it is true, they may conclude that the fact exists. If either of these inferences is created, the defense motion will be denied. On the other hand, if the evidence is not strong enough to support even a permissive inference, the judge will grant the motion and the trial comes to an end. For a discussion on presumptions and inferences and how they relate to burdens of production and proof, see Chapter 3, *infra*.

§ 1-6(G). Defense Case-in-Chief

The conventional sequence is that the defense case follows the plaintiff's or prosecutor's case. The rules governing the defense case are very similar to the rules governing the opening case in that the scope includes evidence *logically relevant* to any *fact in issue* in the case. Usually, the defense case-in-chief consists of *direct examination* of the witnesses with *cross examination* by the plaintiff or prosecutor, *redirect questioning* by the defense and the introduction of *physical* or *documentary* evidence. Also, as is true of the plaintiff's or prosecutor's case, the defendant may call adverse or hostile witnesses. At the completion of its case-in-chief, the defense *rests*.

§ 1-6(H). Plaintiff's Motion for Directed Verdict

At the close of the defense's case-in-chief, the plaintiff in a civil case may move that the trial judge grant a directed verdict in favor of the plaintiff. In effect, the motion alleges that the plaintiff's case is so strong that no rational juror could vote in favor of the defense. Granting of such motions is rare.

§ 1-6(I). Plaintiff's or Prosecutor's Rebuttal

After the defense's case-in-chief, the plaintiff or prosecutor may present *rebuttal* evidence, which is normally limited to refuting evidence presented during the defense case-in-chief. The judge may limit the plaintiff or prosecutor to testimony specifically aimed at rebutting a new matter or theory presented by the defense's case-in chief. But, the judge may, under unusual circumstances, broaden the scope to permit the plaintiff or prosecutor to introduce evidence mistakenly left out of the case-in-chief. The appellate court will only reverse the trial judge's ruling if there has been a clear abuse of discretion.

§ 1-6(J). Defense Surrebuttal

It is rare that a trial proceeds to defense surrebuttal. The standards applicable to the surrebuttal are very similar to those for the rebuttal. The defendant has an opportunity to present surrebuttal only when a new ground is covered during the rebuttal. Again, the judge has broad discretion in delineating the scope and appellate courts generally uphold the judge's decision to preclude surrebuttal.

§ 1-6(K). Witnesses Called by Judge

In federal cases, if the trial judge decides that he or she is not satisfied with the witnesses called by either party, the judge may call other witnesses. A witness may possess highly relevant knowledge but have such an unsavory background and could be easily impeached that neither party wants to call them as a witness. If the jury associates the witness with a party, they may transfer their suspicions to the party's case. Federal Rule 614 allows the court to call witnesses in order to disclose the truth and administer justice. In Texas, however, there is no similar rule because of the fear of judges commenting on the evidence. But the judge may point out gaps in the evidence.

§ 1-6(L). Witnesses Requested by Jury; Questioning by Jurors

Under Federal Rule of Evidence 614 the judge has the authority to call other witnesses, but the jury may only request that the judge do so. When the jurors make their request, the judge reviews it and decides whether the interests of justice necessitate the presentation of that person's testimony. Although the Federal Rules of Evidence do not specifically address the practice, Federal common law permits the jurors to present questions to the witnesses. At least one court, however, has cautioned that such questioning should be reserved for truly exceptional circumstances. *See, e.g., United States v. Ajmal*, 67 F.3d 12 (2d Cir. 1995). In Texas, the practice is absolutely forbidden for criminal cases by case law. *See Morrison v. State*, 845 S.W.2d 882 (Tex. Crim. App. 1992).

§ 1-6(M). Closing Argument or Summation

Although evidence law normally restricts the attorneys from mentioning inferences in the opening statement, in the closing argument or summation the attorneys are allowed to argue inferences from all the evidence. This is the time when the attorneys may draw conclusions from the evidence presented and attempt to persuade the jury of their reasonableness. Because the plaintiff or prosecutor has the burden of proof, he or she usually has the privilege of both opening and closing.

The attorneys may argue several forms of inferences during closing. An important type of inference is credibility. The attorneys will try to persuade the jury with the evidence that their witnesses should be believed and not the opposing party's and the attorneys may argue historical inferences from the circumstantial evidence. Also, the attorneys may argue that the jurors should apply the law to the facts of the case in a specific way. It is important to note that the inferences and conclusions argued during summation must be from the evidence formally admitted at trial. Both the disciplinary rules and the A.B.A. Model Rule of Professional Conduct preclude references to information outside the trial record. The order of jury instructions and closing statements may vary between Federal and Texas practice. In Texas practice, the closing arguments follow the judge's instructions to the jury, while under federal practice, the arguments usually precede the instructions.

§ 1-6(N). Judge's Instructions to the Jurors; The Charge

In the final jury instruction, or *charge*, the presiding judge explains the substantive law, mentions any pertinent evidentiary rules, and describes the voting procedures the jury must use. There are six different categories of evidentiary instructions.

§ 1-6(N)(1). Admissibility Instructions

In most instances the trial judge decides whether a certain item of evidence is admissible, and the jury simply decides how much weight to attach to the item. But, in a few cases, the jurors finally decide whether certain evidence should be considered. For example, the judge explains to the jury the test to be used to determine whether certain evidence is authentic and instructs the jury that the evidence may be used in deliberations only if the evidence is determined to be authentic. *See, e.g.*, Fed. R. Evid. 104(b).

§ 1-6(N)(2). Corroboration Instructions

Corroboration requirements are rare in the United States, but a few jurisdictions require them for the testimony of an infant complainant in child sex abuse prosecutions and for accomplice's testimony. In these jurisdictions, the final jury charge instructs the jury that they cannot convict the defendant on the testimony standing alone. The jurors must be satisfied that there is other credible evidence that connects the defendant with the commission of the offense.

§ 1-6(N)(3). Cautionary Instructions

Cautionary instructions direct the jury to be careful in evaluating the weight of particular testimony. Many jurisdictions use cautionary instructions about testimony from accomplices, eyewitnesses, and drug addicts.

§ 1-6(N)(4). Limiting Instructions

If an item of evidence is admissible for one purpose but inadmissible for another, that item may not have to be excluded. Federal Rule of Evidence 105 states, "When evidence which is admissible as to one party or for one purpose but not admissible as to another party or for another purpose is admitted, the court, upon request, shall restrict the evidence to its proper scope and instruct the jury accordingly." A limiting instruction directs the jury to differentiate between permissible and impermissible uses of the item of evidence. This type of an instruction can be very important, especially where a thin line separates permissible use and impermissible use of potentially prejudicial evidence. A common example of this sort of instruction arises where a criminal defendant's uncharged acts are admissible for a narrow permissible purpose, but not admissible to show that the defendant has a propensity to engage in such conduct. *See* Chapter Four.

§ 1-6(N)(5). Curative Instructions

Curative instructions direct the jury to disregard something they have already heard or seen. The evidence is inadmissible, but the jury has already been exposed to it so the judge will instruct them not to consider it in their deliberations. If the evidence is highly prejudicial and the judge concludes that the jury will be unable to disregard the statement, the judge may grant a mistrial. Typically, in order to preserve error, the opponent will not only move to strike inadmissible evidence but will also request the court to give an *instruction to disregard*.

§ 1-6(N)(6). Sufficiency Instructions

As part of their deliberations, the jurors are instructed to evaluate the factual sufficiency of the evidence. To guide their decision, the judge instructs them on the ultimate burden of proof on the facts. The judge's instruction concerns the allocation and the measure of the burden. In allocating the burden, the judge explains to the jury which party has the burden of proof on particular issues in the case. The judge must also inform the jury of the measure of the burden, e.g., proof beyond a reasonable doubt.

§ 1-6(O). Jury Deliberations

Following instructions and arguments, the jury retires to deliberate. During their deliberations the jury will normally be permitted to examine and handle any exhibits which have been formally admitted into evidence. If during their deliberations they have questions about what a particular witness said, they may request the court to read back portions of that testimony. Normally, what goes on during deliberations is privileged information and only under limited circumstances will a court even consider evidence of what transpired during those deliberations. *See* Fed. R. Evid. 606(b).

§ 1-6(P). The Verdict

When the jury reaches a decision, its verdict is announced in open court. The verdict does not make reference to what evidence the jury considered important or unimportant. And no reference is made to what weight, if any, the jurors attached to a particular witness's testimony. Thus, although great emphasis may have been placed on the court's evidentiary rulings during the trial itself, counsel may never really know what impact a particular piece of evidence might have had unless he or she interviews the jurors after the trial is over.

If counsel discovers that the jury may have considered inadmissible evidence or evidence from outside sources, counsel will have to overcome the hurdles stated in Federal Rule of Evidence 606(b), which generally prevents jurors from testifying about their deliberations.

§ 1-7. Flow Chart of a Typical Trial —Texas Cases

The following chart demonstrates graphically the flow of a typical state trial before a jury. Note that in a federal trial, the closing arguments normally precede the judge's final instructions (or charge) to the jury.

Pretrial Motions

Selection of Jury

Exclusion of Witnesses from Courtroom

Opening Statement by Plaintiff
or Prosecutor

                                Defense's Opening Statement

Plaintiff's or Prosecutor's
"Case-in-Chief"
        Direct Exam. of Witnesses
        (Cross-X by Defense and Redirect Q)
        Phys/Doc. Evidence, etc.

                                Defense Motion for Nonsuit or Directed
                                Verdict

                                  Defense "Case-in-Chief"
                                        Direct Exam. of Wit.
                                        (Cross-X by Plaintiff
                                        or Pros and Redirect Q)
                                        Phys/Doc. Evidence, etc.

Plaintiff's or Prosecutor's
Rebuttal

                                Defense Surrebuttal

Judge's Instructions

Plaintiff's or Prosecutor's
Closing Arguments

                                Defense Closing Arguments

Jury Deliberations

Verdict

§ 1-8. Role of the Participants

As an aid to understanding how the rules of evidence work, it is helpful to discuss briefly the respective roles of the trial participants. Each has assigned responsibilities with regard to evidentiary matters. Those roles are the focus of the following discussion.

§ 1-8(A). Role of the Proponent of Evidence

§ 1-8(A)(1). Pretrial Actions

The proponent of an item of evidence may make a motion *in limine* to obtain an advance ruling from the trial court on whether a piece of evidence is admissible. *See, e.g., Ohler v. United States*, 529 U.S. 753 (2000) (prosecution filed motions in limine to admit defendant's prior conviction). The proponent usually makes this motion in the judge's chambers before the trial begins. The advantage of pretrial motions for a proponent is the security it offers when proving up an item of evidence that requires a lengthy foundation. In many federal cases the judge will require counsel for both sides to identify in pretrial conferences whether they expect any evidentiary objections or issues which can be easily resolved before the trial starts.

In some instances, rules of evidence or procedure may require the proponent to provide notice to the opponent that certain evidence will be offered at trial. *See, e.g.,* Fed. R. Evid. 404(b)(notice regarding extrinsic acts of an accused).

If the opponent has filed either a motion *in limine* or a motion to suppress evidence which the proponent intends to offer, the proponent should be prepared to counter any arguments or objections to the evidence.

§ 1-8(A)(2). Conducting Direct & Redirect Examination

At trial the proponent of evidence may present his or her case through the direct examination of favorable witnesses. A court official administers the oath or affirmation under penalty of perjury, and the witness takes the stand. The direct examination of the witness takes the form, normally, of nonleading questions. The scope of the examination is typically limited to evidence or information which is relevant to the case or which lays the predicate or foundation for another piece of evidence. *See* Fed. R. Evid. 611. After the witness is cross-examined, the proponent may conduct redirect examination using nonleading questions about issues raised on cross-examination.

§ 1-8(A)(3). Laying the Foundation or Predicate for Evidence

At trial the burden is on the proponent to lay the foundation through use of a *sponsoring*, *predicate*, or *foundation* witness for introducing evidence. It is a "foundation" in the sense that there is usually a condition precedent to the admission of evidence. Depending on the type of evidence, laying the predicate requires different elements which can be found in the specific rules or case law. While there are several accepted methods for laying foundations, the following represents the most commonly accepted form.

A four-step procedure for "proving up" an item of evidence by "walking and talking" the exhibit into evidence is as follows:

Step One: **Have the item of evidence marked by reporter and show it to the opposing counsel and the witness**. This is normally accomplished by approaching the reporter and stating: "We request that this exhibit be marked as "State's/ Plaintiff's/ Defense Exhibit ____ for identification."

Once the exhibit is marked and recorded or logged by the court reporter, the proponent should determine how it has been designated. Thereafter, the proponent should refer to the exhibit by that marking, or "handle."

Some counsel premark their exhibits before trial. Before doing so, however, it is best to check with the court reporter and the judge to determine if they have any strong feelings or preferences for marking exhibits.

Next, the proponent should show the marked exhibit to the opposing counsel and announce for the record: "Let the record reflect that I am showing what has been marked by the Reporter as [the exhibit] to [the opponent]."

In some courts, the judge may also ask to see the exhibit before it is shown to the witness.

After opposing counsel has seen the exhibit, the proponent should approach the witness and show the marked exhibit to the witness: "I show you what has been marked as Plaintiff's/State's/Defense Exhibit ____ for identification." "Do you recognize it?" "Would you please tell the Court what it is?" "How is it that you recognize it as...?"

Step Two: **Lay the Foundation or Predicate**. It is at this step that the foundation or predicate is laid. That is, the proponent must insure that each element of the foundation is established through the testimony of the foundation witness. The proponent should do so with nonleading questions. This step is sometimes referred to as "proving up" the evidence.

Step Three:.   **Formally offer the item into evidence**: "Your Honor, we offer into evidence what has been marked as State's/Plaintiff's/Defense Exhibit ____ for Identification."

Step Four: **Show or read the exhibit to the jury**. This step is sometimes referred to as "publishing the exhibit."

§ 1-8(A)(4). Meeting the Opponent's Objections (Rule 103(a))

The proponent of the evidence should expect that specific and generic objections will be made by opposing counsel to an offer of evidence. Therefore, the proponent should be prepared to defend the admission of the item of evidence using the rules of evidence and applicable case law.

That may mean in a particular case that the proponent "brief" the issue and be prepared to present copies of cases, the rules of evidence, and other authority to the trial judge.

§ 1-8(A)(5). Make an "Offer of Proof"

If the judge agrees with the opponent and excludes the item of evidence, the proponent should make an *offer of proof* in order to preserve the issue for appeal. *See, e.g.,* Fed. R. Evid. 103(b). An offer of proof or bill of exceptions should make known to the court the substance of the evidence excluded. That may be accomplished, out of the presence of the jury, by simply stating for the record what the evidence would have shown or by asking the witness questions which establish the scope of the testimony. Offers of proof accomplish two things. First, they provide the trial judge an opportunity to reconsider his or her ruling and second, they inform the appellate court of the nature of the excluded evidence. If the proponent fails to make an offer of proof, any error is ordinarily waived.

§ 1-8(B). Role of the Opponent of Evidence

§ 1-8(B)(1). Pretrial Actions

During pretrial stages the opponent may file motions in limine or motions to suppress evidence. While rulings on motions to suppress are normally considered final, rulings on motions in limine may not be. In those jurisdictions where motions in limine are not final rulings, the opponent will have to object again at trial when the evidence is offered in order to preserve error.

§ 1-8(B)(2). Taking a Witness on Voir Dire

At trial the opponent may challenge the witness's competency or basis of personal knowledge by taking the witness on voir dire. That term is used in this context to describe the process of the opponent effectively interrupting the proponent's direct questioning of the witness by posing questions which go directly to the witness's ability to testify. It is most commonly used with regard to expert witnesses.

§ 1-8(B)(3). Make Specific and Timely Objections

At trial the opponent should be prepared to offer specific and timely objection each time a piece of objectionable evidence is offered. Failure to do so will normally amount to a waiver. In order to be timely, counsel must object as soon as it is apparent that an objection is in order. That normally means that the opponent must object after a question is asked but before the answer is given or as soon as an objectionable piece of physical or documentary evidence is offered.

The objection must also be specific in that the judge and the proponent should be put on notice of the defect. Sometimes citing a rule of evidence or case alone is not enough. Generally, the opponent should object every time the evidence in question is offered or referred to. But some judges allow running, or continuing, objections. Running objections must be specific and cannot be counted on to "run" throughout the trial. The proponent's formally tendering or offering an exhibit into evidence signals to the opponent to make any foundational objections he or she may have to the evidence.

§ 1-8(B)(4). Motion to Strike

If the proponent asks a proper question but obtains an improper answer to inadmissible evidence, the opponent should promptly move to strike the response and request that the judge instruct the jury to disregard the answer. Failure to do so will normally amount to a waiver of the issue.

§ 1-8(B)(5). Request Limiting Instruction in Jury Trial

If the item of evidence is admitted which is admissible for one purpose, but not for another, the opponent should request a limiting instruction. *See* Fed. R. Evid. 105. A limiting instruction explains to the jury the permissible and impermissible uses of the item of evidence.

§ 1-8(B)(6). Cross-Examine Proponent's Witnesses

If the proponent calls a witness the opponent may cross-examine that witness, normally through use of leading questions. The idea is to lead the witness to give answers which support the opponent's viewpoint without being argumentative. The scope of the cross-examination varies. Under the Federal Rules, cross-examination is limited to issues raised during direct examination. That approach is the majority, American, rule. But under the Texas rules, the scope of cross-examination is wide open and may cover any issue relevant to the case. That approach represents the minority, English, rule. After cross-examination, the proponent may conduct redirect examination and then the opponent may conduct re-cross examination, asking questions concerning issues raised in redirect only.

§ 1-8(C). Role of the Judge

§ 1-8(C)(1). Rule on Pretrial Motions

The trial judge has discretion whether to entertain motions *in limine*. The advantage of ruling on a pretrial motion is it reduces the risk of a mistrial by limiting what the jury hears. When the judge grants a motion in limine, it usually does not amount to an actual or final ruling on the admissibility of the evidence. Instead, it is an order directing the proponent to approach the bench and obtain a ruling on the evidence before actually offering it during trial. The judge may also rule on other pretrial objections or motions to suppress evidence.

§ 1-8(C)(2). Decide Qualification of Witness

The trial court decides questions concerning the qualification of a witness to testify in two situations. First, it is up to the judge to make a determination about the competency of a witness based on moral capacity and mental capacity to observe, recall and narrate. *See* Fed. R. Evid. 601.

Second, the judge decides whether a witness qualifies as an expert under Rule 702. *See* Fed. R. Evid. 104(a).

§ 1-8(C)(3). Decide Whether a Privilege Exists

Some types of information are excluded because the exclusion promotes an extrinsic social policy and not because the information is unreliable. Protection of the attorney-client relationship, for example, is one of these policies. Where a party argues that evidence is privileged, and therefore excludable, the trial judge determines whether the information qualifies as privileged.

§ 1-8(C)(4). Finally Determines Admissibility of Evidence

Federal Rule of Evidence 104(a) provides that, subject to Rule 104(b), the court is responsible for finally determining the admissibility of evidence. Relevance, character evidence, and hearsay are examples of issues on which the judge will have a final say when deciding the admissibility of the evidence.

§ 1-8(C)(5). Determinations on Relevant Conditions of Fact

Under Federal Rule of Evidence 104(b), the judge acts as a preliminary screener ensuring that the proponent has introduced "evidence sufficient to support a [rational] finding" of the existence of the fact. The preliminary fact of a document's authenticity or a witness's personal knowledge are examples of Rule 104(b) conditional relevance questions. When that issue arises, the judge asks whether the proponent has offered enough evidence to convince a rational juror by a preponderance of the evidence that the offered piece of evidence is what it is purported to be. *See also* Chapter Nine, *infra.*

§ 1-8(C)(6). Take Judicial Notice

The formal introduction of evidence is not the only way of establishing a fact at trial. As noted in Chapter Two, *infra*, judicial notice is another way; the judge notes the existence of a fact and instructs the jury that the fact exists. *See* Fed. R. Evid. 201. Many counsel and judges favor the use of judicial notice as it speeds up the trial process by dispensing with formal proof of the fact. As noted in Chapter 2, *infra*, the effect of taking judicial notice is slightly different for civil and criminal cases.

§ 1-8(D). Role of the Jury

The jury's role vis a vis evidence issues focuses on three key points. First, while the trial judge decides questions of law, the jury decides the facts of the case. That is, under appropriate instructions from the judge, the jury decides whether the party bearing the ultimate burden of persuasion in the case, i.e. the prosecutor or the plaintiff, has produced sufficient evidence to prove the alleged offense or alleged cause of action.

Second, in reaching its decision the jury decides what weight, if any, to give to the admitted evidence. That includes deciding the credibility of the witnesses. *See, e.g.,* Fed. R. Evid. Rule 104(e). While the court determines the qualification of a witness to testify, the jury ultimately decides which witnesses to believe and how much weight, if any to give to their testimony.

Third, the jury finally determines relevant conditions of fact which determine whether a piece of evidence is authentic or whether a witness had personal knowledge. *See* Rules 901 and 602. Jurors resolve only the types of factual issues falling under Rule 104(b). With these kinds of facts, the judge decides initially only whether the evidence is legally sufficient to support a finding that the fact exists. If it is, the evidence is conditionally admitted and the jury actually makes the finding. The items of evidence governed by this procedure are sometimes termed "conditionally relevant," i.e., they are logically relevant only on the condition that they are genuine.

§ 1-9. Rules of Completeness

In some instances, one of the parties may introduce only a portion of a document, or a portion of a recording, or introduce evidence concerning one of several transactions. The reason for doing that may rest in the fact that other portions of the writing or other acts are not relevant to the case. And in some instances, counsel may believe that the remaining, unintroduced portions, are inadmissible. The common law recognized that the opponent could introduce the remainder of the document, for example, if it was necessary to insure that the jury received a fair picture of the contents. Federal Rule of Evidence 106, entitled "Remainder of Related Writings or Recorded Statements," is a codification of that common law rule. But the rule also provides that the adverse party may require the proponent of the evidence to introduce the remainder of the writing — at that time. In the alternative, counsel could offer the remainder of the writing later in the trial.

Texas Rule 106 mirrors the Federal Rule. Texas Rule 107, entitled "Rule of Optional Completeness," provides a rule of completeness for evidence of acts, conversations, writings, and recordings. Unlike Rule 106, there is no provision in Rule 107 for forcing the proponent to introduce the remainder of the information. There is not Federal Rule counterpart for Texas Rule 107. A chart comparing the Texas Rules 106 and 107 is at § 1-10(D).

§ 1-10. Charts

The following charts demonstrate: First, the order of examination of a single witness (showing direct, cross-examination, etc.); second, the role of the parties in offering a single item of evidence; third, the respective roles of the judge and jury; and fourth, a chart comparing the rules of completeness.

The charts are designed to help you visualize the narrative material in the preceding sections.

Note that the charts include references to both the Federal Rules of Evidence and the Texas Rules of Evidence.

§ 1-10(A). Chart: The Order of Examination of a Witness

The following chart demonstrates the typical flow in the examination of a single witness.

ORDER OF EXAMINATION OF WITNESS

Direct Examination
(Fed. R. 611)
(Tex. R. 611)

Form:

      Normally Nonleading
      Questions

Scope:

      Relevant
      Admissible Evidence
      Lay Foundations

Cross-Examination
(Fed. R. 611(b))
(Tex. R. 611(b))

Form:

      Normally Leading
      Questions
Scope

      Texas—Wide Open
      Federal—Limited
      Lay Foundations

Redirect Examination

Form

      Normally Nonleading
      Questions

Scope

      Limited To Issues
      raised on Cross-X

Recross-Examination

Form

      Normally Leading
      Questions
Scope

      Limited to Issues Raised
      on Re-direct-X

§ 1-10(B). Chart: Role of Parties: Single Item of Evidence

```
┌──────────────────────────────────────────────────┐
│          ROLE OF PARTIES: SINGLE ITEM OF EVIDENCE  │
│            (Testimonial, Documentary, Physical)    │
└──────────────────────────────────────────────────┘
```

```
┌────────────────────────────────┐
│          Proponent             │
│ Pretrial:                      │
│    Motion in Limine            │
│                                │
│ Trial:                         │
│    Lay Found./Predicate        │
│    (See 602, 901, 902)         │
│    "Prove Up" Evidence         │
└────────────────────────────────┘
```

```
                    ┌────────────────────────────────┐
                    │          Opponent              │
                    │ Pretrial:                      │
                    │    Motion in Limine            │
                    │    Motion to Suppress          │
                    │                                │
                    │ Trial                          │
                    │    Voir Dire of Witness        │
                    │    Objection or Waiver         │
                    │        Timely                  │
                    │        Specific                │
                    │        "Running"               │
                    │        "In context" Exception  │
                    │        Motions to Strike        │
                    │        Obtain Ruling on        │
                    │            Objection           │
                    │    Curative Admissibility      │
                    └────────────────────────────────┘
```

```
         ┌──────────────────────────────┐
         │      RULING BY COURT         │
         │         Rule 104             │
         └──────────────────────────────┘
```

Evidence Admitted

```
                    ┌──────────────────────────────────┐
                    │ Request Limiting Instruction     │
                    │ (Rule 105)                       │
                    └──────────────────────────────────┘
```

OR

Evidence Excluded

```
┌──────────────────────────────┐
│ Make Offer of Proof          │
│ (Rule 103)                   │
│    Timing                    │
│    Form                      │
│    Content                   │
└──────────────────────────────┘
```

§ 1-10(C). Chart: Role of Judge and Jury

ROLE OF JUDGE AND JURY Who Decides?	
Trial Judge	**Jury**
Decides Questions of Law	**Decides Questions of Fact**
Decides Qualification of Witness **(Rule 104(a))** — **Competency (Rule 601)** — **Expert Witness (Rule 702)**	**Decides Credibility of Witness** **(Rule 104(e))**
Decides Whether Privilege Exists **(Rule 104(a))**	
Finally Determines Admissibility of Evidence **(Rule 104(a))** **E.g.: Relevancy, Character Evidence,** **Hearsay; Scientific Evidence**	
Preliminary Determination on Relevant **Conditions of Fact** **(Rule 104(b))** — **Personal Knowledge (Rule 602)** — **Authenticity of Evidence** **(Rule 901, 902)** — **Whether Rule 404(b) Act Occurred**	**Finally Determines Relevant Conditions of Fact** **(Rule 104(b))** — **Personal Knowledge (Rule 602)** — **Authenticity of Evidence** **(Rule 901, 902)** — **Whether Rule 404(b) Act Occurred**
Takes Judicial Notice **(Article II)**	

§ 1-10(D). Chart: Comparison of Texas Rules 106 and 107

	Rule 106	Rule 107
Purpose of Rule?	Rule of "timing"— (Acceleration for Introducing "Rest of the Story")	Rule of "admissibility"— Generally adopts Common Law Rule of Optional Completeness (No federal rule counterpart)
Applies to What Evidence?	Any "related" writing or recording, including depositions that have been *introduced* by opposing party.	Virtually any type of evidence that has been *introduced* by opposing party.
Procedural Issues?	Under Texas Rule 106, opponent can *interrupt* opposing party and introduce related evidence that "ought in fairness be considered contemporaneously…" (Subject to Rule 611). (Criminal cases indicate that evidence must be on "same subject") Under Federal Rule 106, counsel can force *opposing party* to introduce remainder of related writing, etc.	Under Rule 107, opponent must show that offered evidence is "necessary to make it fully understood" or "to explain" the admitted evidence.
Trumps Other Rules of Evidence, E.g. hearsay?	Yes. Rule generally permits counsel to introduce rebuttal evidence through door opened by opposing counsel. But court not required to admit offered evidence	Yes. Same as for Rule 106.

§ 1-11. Questions, Notes & Problems

a. Considering the reasons for evidence law, what other possible reasons might there be for imposing limits on what evidence may be admitted in a trial? Is it possible that rules of evidence, no matter how well intentioned, might keep the jury from hearing critical evidence?

b. Who should decide what evidence the jury hears in a case? The judge? The jury itself? Counsel? Who is in the best position to decide?

c. Should the jury have the right to decide what evidence it will hear? Is that practical? If that were the system, what, if any, rules would govern the procedure for considering such evidence?

d. Draft a line of foundation questions and "stage directions" to walk and talk an exhibit into evidence. Assume that your foundation witness is a Ms. Jones who will authenticate a map she found in her kitchen. The case is a civil cause of action and you are the plaintiff. Use only nonleading questions.

e. How should the rules of evidence be read and applied? Are they mere "guidelines" for the judge? Are they statutory rules which act as limits on a judge's discretion to admit or exclude evidence? Do you agree with the view expressed by the Supreme Court of the United States that it will read and apply the Federal Rules of Evidence as it would any other federal statute?

f. During trial, the plaintiff introduces the first page of a four page memo outlining a demand for compliance with the contract. The defendant discovers that important information is on page three of the same memo. May the defendant request the judge to order the plaintiff to introduce the remainder of the memo? Even if the material on the third page is otherwise inadmissible hearsay?

CHAPTER TWO

JUDICIAL NOTICE & STIPULATIONS

§ 2-1. Introduction

As a substitute (and sometimes a shortcut) for formally introducing evidence about the case, a proponent may ask the trial judge to judicially notice certain facts or attempt to obtain a stipulation of facts from the opponent. This chapter briefly introduces those topics.

§ 2-2. Judicial Notice

§ 2-2(A). In General

A commonly invoked technique of presenting one's case at trial is to ask the court to take judicial notice of facts which are not subject to dispute. It is important to note, however, that as simple as the rule sounds, there may be questions about (1) what types of facts may, or should, be noticed by the court and (2) whether the fact is really beyond dispute.

As to the first question, courts and commentators typically divide judicially noticeable facts into two subcategories: (1) Adjudicative Facts; and (2) Legislative Facts. The law of evidence also recognizes the ability of the court to take judicial notice of law.

The Federal Rules of Evidence contain a single rule on the subject of judicial notice: Rule 201 addresses the taking of judicial notice of what are called "adjudicative facts." Article II of the Texas Rules of Evidence, on the other hand, includes four rules on taking judicial notice: Rule 201 (adjudicative facts); Rule 202 (Determination of Law of Other States); Rule 203 (Determination of Laws of Foreign Countries); and Rule 204 (Determination of ordinances, etc.).

The following material briefly addresses the types of facts or information which may be judicially noticed by the court.

§ 2-2(B). Judicial Notice of Adjudicative Facts

Adjudicative facts are considered to be the facts actually involved in the litigation, i.e., those which would normally be considered and decided by the jury. For example, the time that the sun set on a particular date could be a factual issue to be addressed in a personal injury case. Adjudicative facts have been defined as follows:

> "When a court or an agency finds facts concerning the immediate parties—who did what, where, when, how, and with what motive or intent—the court or agency is performing an adjudicative function, and the facts are conveniently called adjudicative facts..."

> "Stated in other terms, the adjudicative facts are those to which the law is applied in the process of adjudication. They are the facts that normally go to the jury in a jury case. They relate to the parties, their activities, their properties, their

businesses." Advisory Committee Note, Fed. R. Evid. 201, *citing* Davis, 2 ADMINISTRATIVE LAW TREATISE (1958).

If the fact is adjudicative in nature, then counsel must consult, and the judge must apply, Rule of Evidence 201. That rule, in both Texas and Federal versions, addresses the type of facts which may be judicially noticed, timing, notice to the parties, and effect of judicial notice. If a judge in a civil case takes judicial notice of an adjudicative fact, the jury is instructed to accept the fact as having been established; the jury is not free to disregard the fact. *See* Rule 201(g). On the other hand, in a criminal case, the jury is instructed that they may, but need not, find the fact as being established. Thus counsel in a criminal case may dispute a fact judicially noticed.

Not all adjudicative facts, however, are subject to judicial notice. As required by the rules of evidence and the case law, the facts must be verifiably certain, or beyond dispute.

§ 2-2(C). Judicial Notice of Legislative Facts

While judicial notice of adjudicative facts is closely regulated by the Rules of Evidence, no similar limitations are present when the court judicially notices "legislative facts." Legislative facts are defined as those which relate to lawmaking and policy decisions. These facts, which go beyond the facts of the case at bar, are virtually limitless, depending on how far the trial court is willing to go in interpreting a particular statute, regulation, or common law. For example, in a drug case, the court may judicially notice that a particular compound or substance is a controlled substance within the definition of state or federal law. *See, e.g., United States v. Gould*, 536 F.2d. 216 (8th Cir. 1976)(court took judicial notice of legislative fact that substance was derivative of cocoa leaves and hence on Schedule II; court instructed that jury was bound to accept that as conclusive fact). If the trial court determines that the fact to be noticed is legislative, and not adjudicative, Rule 201 does not apply. That is, there are no timing and notice requirements, and no real limit on the scope of what may be noticed.

§ 2-2(D). Judicial Notice of Law

As noted above, the Federal Rules of Evidence contain no rules governing the court's ability to take judicial notice of law. The Texas Rules of Evidence, however, contain three rules on the subject. *See* Tex. R. Evid. 202-204. Those rules contain specific procedural requirements which require the party requesting judicial notice to provide information on the law to be noticed which will assist the court.

§ 2-3. Stipulations

§ 2-3(A). In General

Another short-cut to formally presenting evidence at trial is to obtain a stipulation with the opposing party. Virtually any evidence may be stipulated to by the parties. And it is easy to see how doing so may expedite the trial and reduce the need for laying foundations for evidence which will probably come in anyway. If counsel offers to stipulate in the jurors' presence, the jury may be left with the favorable impression that counsel is generally agreeable and anxious to move on with the trial. There are three types of stipulations: stipulations to facts; stipulations to evidentiary foundations; and stipulations of expected testimony.

While the exact form and content of a stipulation may vary, it is important to note that in some jurisdictions court rules may require the stipulation to be made in writing, signed by the parties, and entered into the record as an exhibit. In other jurisdictions, the rules may permit one of the parties to the stipulation to simply orally dictate its contents into the record. Before accepting the stipulation, a trial judge will normally question the parties as to whether they are both agreeing to the contents of the stipulation.

§ 2-3(B). Stipulations of Fact

In a stipulation of fact the parties agree that a certain fact exists, or existed. For example, the parties might stipulate the fact that the substance tested at the laboratory was the defendant's blood and that it contained traces of certain drugs. If a stipulation is entered, the parties are not free to contradict it. And in some instances, the court may consider the stipulation to be an admission. Although the parties may not attempt to rebut what they have stipulated to, they may nonetheless offer supporting or explanatory evidence on the fact stipulated to.

§ 2-3(C). Stipulations to Foundations for Evidence

To facilitate the introduction of evidence, a party may stipulate, for example, to the authenticity of a particular piece of evidence. Doing so does not necessarily waive, however, any other objections to the evidence.

§ 2-3(D). Stipulations of Expected Testimony

In a stipulation of expected testimony the parties agree that if a particular person were present in court they would offer specified testimony. Unlike the stipulation of fact, however, the parties do not by entering into that sort of stipulation, necessarily concede that the testimony is truthful. Thus, they are free to contract the stipulation with rebuttal evidence.

The following case is an example of the use that may be made of stipulations of expected testimony.

AUSTIN v. AUSTIN
603 S.W.2d 204 (Tex. 1980)

McGEE, Justice.

This is the second appeal from a suit for divorce filed in 1975 by Mildred Austin. At the time of the trial Mrs. Austin was seriously ill and was unable to attend. Following a trial to the court, the judge announced in open court the manner in which the property was to be divided. Mrs. Austin died before a written decree was signed. Mr. Austin filed a plea in abatement and the trial court dismissed the divorce suit. On appeal by Mrs. Austin's legal representatives, the court of civil appeals reversed the dismissal order, holding that the divorce judgment had been rendered before

Mrs. Austin died, and the divorce action did not abate upon her death. The cause was remanded with instructions to the trial court to render a written judgment either granting or denying the divorce...

In response to this mandate, the trial judge ordered a hearing, granted the divorce, and divided the property. Mr. Austin appealed. The court of civil appeals reversed, the majority holding that there was no evidence of grounds for divorce. A dissenting opinion was written in which it was urged that the divorce judgment was supported by evidence. We agree with the dissenting opinion, and accordingly the judgment of the court of civil appeals is reversed.

The ground of divorce alleged by Mrs. Austin was insupportability as provided in § 3.01 of the Texas Family Code.

"Section 3.01. Insupportability

"On the petition of either party to a marriage, a divorce may be decreed without regard to fault if the marriage has become insupportable because of discord or conflict of personalities that destroys the legitimate ends of the marriage relationship and prevents any reasonable expectation of reconciliation."

Tex. Family Code Ann. § 3.01 (Vernon 1975). The evidence offered for Mrs. Austin to establish insupportability was presented in open court at trial by her attorney. Because of the seriousness of Mrs. Austin's illness, rather than require her appearance as a witness, Mrs. Austin's attorney offered to state what her testimony would be if she appeared to testify. According to Mrs. Austin's attorney, both parties had agreed upon certain statements that would be made by Mrs. Austin were she to testify. The manner in which the evidence offered in Mrs. Austin's behalf is set out in the statement of facts as follows:

"MR. BELT: Your Honor, one of the items that we have got some stipulations, that I think that we need to discuss. We have agreed that were the Petitioner, Mildred Austin, here that she would testify certain things. Her testimony would have been, and Counsel for the Respondent has agreed, that her name is as stated in the Petition, Mildred E. Austin; that she was married to the Respondent, Victor Leon Austin, on or about June 15th, 1958; that she separated from Victor Leon Austin on or about October 15th, 1975; that she had lived in Burnet County for ninety days preceding the filing of the divorce; that she was a domiciliary of the State of Texas for six months prior to the filing of the divorce; no children were born of the marriage or adopted or expected of the marriage; and that the marriage has become insupportable due to discord and conflict of personality; that there is no hope of reconciliation. Had she been here she would have testified to that, and we appreciate the Respondent's attorney agreeing to that stipulation.
"THE COURT: Well, I would just like to swear the Respondent and have him affirm that and state that those things are true that you want to stipulate. He heard the stipulation.
"MR. RUSSELL: I think Your Honor, too, more likely you want to call him.
"MR. BELT: My next step was to put him on the stand.

* * * * *

"MR. RUSSELL: I do want to state in respect to it, we may have a discrepancy in the date of the marriage. I am sure he'll bring it out in the testimony, but I think we overlooked that.

"MR. BELT: I would like to call Leon Austin to the stand.

* * * * *

"Questions by Mr. Belt:

"Q   Mr. Austin, please state your name to the Court.

"A   Victor Leon Austin.

"Q   And are you Respondent in this cause of action for divorce filed by Mildred E. Austin?

"A   Yes, sir.

"Q   It is stipulated, as you heard me introduce to the Court, that you were married to Mrs. Austin and I stated a date of on or about June of 1958. Is that date correct or incorrect?

"A   That's wrong.

"Q   What date were you all married?

"A   June, 1959.

"Q   June, 1959?

"A   Uh-huh.

"Q   Do you know that she did live in Burnet County for ninety days prior to filing this divorce?

"A   Oh, yeah.

"Q   And certain had been a domiciliary of the State of Texas for the last six months?

"A   Yes.

"Q   You agree that your marriage has become unsupportable due to discord and conflict of personalities?

"A   According to her testimony, yes, sir.

"Q   Is there any hope of reconciliation?

"A   It's up to her.

"Q   As far as you know, is there any hope?

"A   Not as I can see, unless she changed her mind.

"Q   No children were born?

"A   No.

"Q   You have not adopted any?

"A   No.

"Q   There is none expected?

"A   No."

This portion of the proceedings was reintroduced at a hearing held after the first appeal of the suit, directing the trial court to render a written decree granting or denying the divorce. On the basis of this evidence, the trial court granted the divorce.

Rule 11 of the Texas Rules of Civil Procedure provides that agreements between the parties to a suit or their attorneys are enforceable if made in open court and entered of record. Pursuant to Rule 11, to avoid delay and expense, counsel may stipulate concerning evidence material to the suit. To be distinguished from situations in which the parties agree on the truth of specific facts, are situations in which the parties agree on the admissibility of evidence. Thus, the parties may agree upon the statements an absent witness would make were that witness present to testify. They may also agree that the absent witness's statements may be introduced as evidence. In these situations the truth of the absent witness's statements is not necessarily admitted; the statements may be controverted with opposing evidence. The probative effect of the absent witness's testimony, as with other controverted evidence, is for the trier of fact. This is an application of the rule that the agreement between the parties will not be given greater effect than intended. A stipulation will not be construed as an admission of a fact intended to be controverted. *United States Fire Insurance Co. v. Carter*, 468 S.W.2d 151, 154 (Tex.Civ.App. Dallas 1971), writ ref'd n. r. e. per curiam, 473 S.W.2d 2 (Tex. 1971).

The manner in which Mrs. Austin's testimony was offered complied with Rule 11. The stipulation was discussed in open court and appears in the statement of facts, which is signed by both counsel and is part of the official record. It is not contended that Mrs. Austin's attorney was not authorized to stipulate her testimony. The agreement of the parties is clear and unambiguous. Mrs. Austin's attorney stated, "We have agreed that were the Petitioner, Mildred Austin, here that she would testify to certain things. Her testimony would have been, and Counsel for the Respondent has agreed . . . that the marriage has become insupportable due to discord and conflict of personality. . . ." No objection was made to the offer of evidence in this manner. When called to the stand to verify the stipulation, Mr. Austin corrected the stipulation only with respect to the marriage date. He acknowledged that "according to (Mrs. Austin's) testimony" the marriage had become insupportable. Apparently satisfied with the validity of the stipulation, the trial court made no indication that it was unacceptable. We hold that Mrs. Austin's testimony that the marriage had become insupportable was validly stipulated. Thus, her testimony was probative evidence of insupportability and the trial court was entitled to find in favor of Mrs. Austin in her suit for divorce.

Mr. Austin argues that the offered testimony should have no effect because his own testimony relating to the existence of grounds for divorce was equivocal. Although Mr. Austin did not agree when asked if the marriage was insupportable, he conceded that Mrs. Austin would say it was. His reluctance to agree with the truth of Mrs. Austin's testimony does not detract from the validity of the stipulation. The stipulation was that Mrs. Austin would testify in a certain manner, not that her testimony was true. Mrs. Austin's testimony having been stipulated as evidence, its probative value was for the trier of fact. On the basis of that evidence, the trial judge found that Mrs. Austin had proved a statutory ground for divorce and entered judgment accordingly.

For the reasons stated above, the judgment of the court of civil appeals, which reversed the judgment of the trial court and rendered judgment denying the divorce, is reversed.

§ 2-4. Questions & Notes

a. Determining whether a fact is "adjudicative" or "legislative" is sometimes a close call. What test, if any, would you devise for determining that issue? Is there a good argument that all facts, whether legislative or adjudicative, should be covered by the procedural requirements of Rule 201.

b. Rule 201 of the Federal and Texas Rules of Evidence indicates that to be noticed, a fact must "that is not subject to reasonable dispute because it is (1) generally known within the trial court's territorial jurisdiction or (2) can be accurately and readily determined from sources whose accuracy cannot reasonably be questioned." What does that mean? Should opposing counsel be permitted to present rebutting evidence that a source is not accurate? What about those areas of science which are constantly and rapidly changing? What options does the trial judge have if the parties start arguing about whether a particular fact is beyond dispute?

c.   Are the parties required to enter into stipulations? Assume that a prosecutor wants to introduce autopsy photographs of the victim and the defense offers to stipulate to the cause of death, thus rendering the photos irrelevant. Is the prosecutor required to stipulate? Why would the prosecutor not want to take advantage of an obvious short-cut to proving the case? What would be an appropriate negative response by counsel to an offer by the other counsel to stipulate? For example, you are laying the predicate for one of your stellar experts and opposing counsel offers to stipulate to the fact that your expert is qualified. What might you say to decline that offer and proceed with your foundation?

d.   For sample foundations on both judicial notice and stipulations, see Schlueter & Imwinkelried, TEXAS EVIDENTIARY FOUNDATIONS Chapter 12 (6th ed. 2020).

CHAPTER THREE

PRESUMPTIONS, INFERENCES
& BURDENS OF PROOF

§ 3-1. Introduction

The topic of presumptions in civil cases is covered in Article III of the Federal Rules of Evidence. Rule 301 covers the topic of presumptions generally, and how they work in federal civil cases. And Rule 302 indicates that in federal civil cases where state law supplies the rule regarding an element of a claim or defense, the state's law of presumptions will apply. Thus, in federal diversity actions, state law will provide the rules regarding presumptions in that case.

The Texas drafters declined to adopt any rules of evidence governing presumptions. Instead, they left the topic for case law development.

While presumptions are really not evidence, they do relate to the topic. And it is important for students to have some knowledge about how they relate to evidence offered at trial and the effect they can have on the burdens of persuasion and production of evidence.

§ 3-2. Burdens of Persuasion (Proof)

The substantive law assigns the burdens of persuasion which must be carried by the parties at trial. In a civil case, the burden of persuasion rests upon the shoulders of the plaintiff, who must persuade the jurors. Normally, that burden requires the plaintiff to prove the elements of the cause of action by a preponderance of the evidence. In a criminal case, the burden rests upon the prosecution to prove beyond a reasonable doubt that the defendant committed the charged crime. In some instances, the law may assign burdens of persuasion to the defense. For example, in a criminal case, in some jurisdictions, the burden of establishing an affirmative defense in a criminal case may rest on the defendant. Normally, the assigned burdens of persuasion do not shift during the trial. The exception may arise where the substantive law recognizes a presumption which may shift the burden of persuasion. For example, in some jurisdictions, the burden of showing contributory negligence rests upon the defendant.

It is important to note that while the parties focus on the admissibility of evidence, ultimately the fact finder will have to decide whether the sum total of the admitted evidence is sufficient to sustain the burden of persuasion. An illustration of how this might work is demonstrated in a tactic sometimes used by prosecutors in closing argument. They make the analogy to a picture of the defendant which is in the form of a puzzle. As they go through each piece of admitted evidence, they piece together the picture of the defendant. Even though some pieces may be missing, it is clear that it is the defendant's picture in the puzzle. The prosecutors will argue that taken together the pieces of the puzzle demonstrate that the evidence is sufficient to sustain the prosecution's burden of proof.

§ 3-3. Burdens of Producing Evidence

In addition to burdens of persuasion, the substantive law imposes certain burdens of producing evidence on the parties. Unlike burdens of persuasion, burdens of production of evidence may shift during a trial from one side to another. For example, in a civil trial, the burden of producing evidence initially rests on the plaintiff. The burden requires the plaintiff to introduce sufficient evidence to convince the trial judge that there is enough evidence to support the necessary findings of fact, i.e., what is commonly referred to as a prima facie case. If the plaintiff fails to meet that burden, the plaintiff risks a ruling by the judge withdrawing the case from the jury and ruling for the defendant.

Assuming that a prima facie case is established and the trial judge denies the defense motion for a directed verdict, the defense must decide whether to produce contradicting evidence. If the plaintiff's case is strong, the defense runs the risk of non-production. That is, if the defense rests without submitting any evidence, the jury may conclude by a preponderance of the evidence that the plaintiff has proved his or her case. Thus, in those cases, the practical effect is that the burden of production of evidence has shifted to the defense, even though the ultimate burden of persuasion still rests on the plaintiff.

The foregoing rules are similar in criminal cases. That is, if the prosecutor fails to present sufficient evidence to show that a rational trier of fact could conclude beyond a reasonable doubt that the defendant committed the crime, the judge may summarily rule against the prosecution. *See* 2 MCCORMICK ON EVIDENCE, § 338, at p. 654-56 (7th ed. 2013) (discussing constitutional burden of production of evidence in criminal cases to avoid directed verdict against prosecution); *Madden v. State*, 799 S.W.2d 683 (Tex. Crim. App. 1990) (challenge to judge's ruling on instructed verdict is challenge to sufficiency of evidence and that requires court to determine if rational trier of fact could have found essential elements of crime beyond reasonable doubt, considering evidence in light most favorable to the prosecution).

§ 3-4. Presumptions

§ 3-4(A). In General

Presumptions are not evidence. Although it is often difficult to pin down one specific definition of presumptions, it is generally agreed that they are procedural devices which permit a presumed fact to be assumed from the existence of another, or basic fact. If a presumed fact is not rebutted by other evidence, it has the effect of creating prima facie evidence of the fact assumed. Thus, the plaintiff's reliance on an unrebutted presumption during its case-in-chief may assist it in overcoming a defense motion for an instructed verdict.

§ 3-4(B). Shifting Burdens of Production and Persuasion

Most presumptions only shift the burden of production of evidence. That is, if evidence of a basic fact is admitted, a presumption may arise and effectively shifts to the opponent the burden of presenting some rebuttal evidence. As noted, *infra*, the practical effect is that a failure to produce rebutting evidence may result in an instructed verdict on that point.

Some presumptions, however, actually result in shifting the burden of persuasion to the opponent which means that the opponent has the burden of disproving the presumed fact. Such presumptions are normally limited to civil cases. Any attempt to shift the burden of persuasion, through a mandatory presumption, to a criminal defendant will be unconstitutional. Permissible presumptions in criminal cases are constitutional, however. *See* D. Schlueter & J. Schlueter, TEXAS RULES OF EVIDENCE MANUAL, § 301.01[10] (11th ed. 2020).

§ 3-4(C). Effects of Presumptions

There are generally two theories on the effect of presumptions. The first is referred to as the "bursting bubble" or "vanishing presumption." This theory, which was advocated by Professors Thayer and Wigmore, is the theory followed in Federal Rule of Evidence 301 and by Texas case law. Under this theory, once the opponent has presented any evidence to rebut the presumed fact, the presumption bursts, or vanishes, and the jury hears no reference to the fact that the presumption even arose in the case.

A second theory, and minority view, was advocated by Professors Morgan and McCormick. Under that theory, once the basic fact is proved (and the presumption arises), the opponent bears the burden of persuading the fact finder that the presumed fact is not true. The opponent's burden of rebutting the presumption is thus greater under the second theory.

An example of how "bursting bubble" presumptions work can be demonstrated through the following example. Assume that an issue in the civil case is whether the defendant received timely notice. At trial the plaintiff offers evidence that written notice was properly addressed, stamped, and deposited in the mail. That evidence (basic fact) gives rise to the well-known rebuttable presumption that the notice was delivered to the defendant (presumed fact). The defendant does not challenge that evidence but at the close of the plaintiff's case moves for an instructed verdict on the ground, inter alia, that the plaintiff has failed to prove that the notice was actually delivered. The judge should reject that argument because the presumption creates a prima facie case that the letter was delivered. In effect, the presumption shifted the burden of production, but not the burden of proof (which remains on the plaintiff) to the defendant to rebut that evidence.

Now assume that during its case-in-chief, the defendant presents evidence through testimony of the person in charge of the mailroom that it never received the plaintiff's notice. That defense evidence bursts the "bubble," the presumption vanishes, and the jury will have to resolve the factual dispute. But in making that assessment, the jury will not hear any instruction on the presumption. It will simply be apprised that the burden of proof rests on the plaintiff to show that the notice was received. Note that if the defendant offers no rebuttal evidence whatsoever about the delivery of the notice, the jury does not even consider the issue because the unrebutted presumption permits the judge to decide as a matter of law that the notice was received.

§ 3-5. An Example: Criminal Case

Assume that in a criminal case, the defendant is charged with theft by avoiding payment of services. The evidence showed that the defendant, Timmy Ransalot, rented a hotel room in the Regency Hotel for several days and without paying, left very early one morning through a rear entrance. His exit was captured by a security camera. Ransalot testified that he did not intend to leave without paying and that he simply forgot to pay his bill. The hotel manager testified that final payment of the hotel bill is paid as soon as the guest checks out and leaves the room key at the desk. Under Texas law, for example, the State's evidence regarding the circumstances of his departure without paying would raise a rebuttable presumption that the defendant intended to do so. *See* Tex. Penal Code § 31.04(b). The judge would give the following instructions in accordance with Tex. Penal Code § 2.05:

> "Ladies and gentlemen of the jury, you are instructed that intent to avoid payment, as referred to in my earlier instructions, is presumed if the actor absconded, or left, without paying for the service in circumstances where payment is ordinarily made immediately upon rendering of service, as in hotels, restaurants, and comparable establishments. That presumption, however, is rebuttable.

You are further instructed that:

> (a)   the facts giving rise to the presumption must be proved beyond a reasonable doubt;
>
> (b)   if such facts are proved beyond a reasonable doubt, you may find that this element of the offense sought to be presumed (that is, the intent to avoid payment) exists, but you are not bound to so find;
>
> (c)   even though you may find the existence of this element, the State must prove beyond a reasonable doubt each of the other elements of the offense charged; and
>
> (d)   that if you have a reasonable doubt as to the existence of a fact or facts giving rise to the presumption, the presumption fails, and you shall not consider the presumption for any purpose.

> Thus, in this case, before you may presume that the defendant intended to avoid payment to the Regency Hotel, as alleged, you must first find from the evidence beyond a reasonable doubt that the defendant, Mr. Ransalot, absconded without paying his hotel bill in circumstances where payment is ordinarily made immediately upon rendering of the service. If you have a reasonable doubt as to such matter, then the presumption fails and you must not consider such presumption for any purpose.

> Further, even if you find from the evidence beyond a reasonable doubt that the defendant absconded without paying his hotel bill in question in circumstances where payment is ordinarily made immediately upon rendering of services still, while you may presume that he intended to avoid payment for the services, as alleged, you are not bound to do so.

> Even if you find from the evidence beyond a reasonable doubt that at the time and place, and on the occasion, in question the defendant, Mr. Ransalot, had the intent to avoid payment for the service, as alleged, you are instructed that the State must prove each of the other elements of the offense charged in the indictment beyond a reasonable doubt."

CHAPTER FOUR

RELEVANCY AND ITS LIMITS

§ 4-1. In General

Article IV of the Federal Rules of Evidence contains fifteen rules focusing on the subject of "relevancy." Relevancy is *the* threshold issue—the first evidentiary hurdle encountered when determining the admissibility of any piece of evidence, whether it be in the form of testimony, a written document, or the alleged murder weapon. Relevancy is a universal concept and it applies to every piece of evidence sought to be admitted at trial.

Irrelevant evidence is inadmissible evidence. *See* Fed. R. Evid 402. When a piece of evidence is found by the court to be irrelevant (a Rule 104(a) decision), all evidentiary analysis stops. Only when a piece of evidence is relevant need the opponent determine the piece's compliance with the other evidentiary rules, such as the rule against admitting hearsay, and other specific rules in Article IV which exclude otherwise relevant evidence.

§ 4-2. The Concept of Relevancy

§ 4-2(A). Relevancy Defined — Materiality Distinguished

Federal Rule of Evidence 401 defines relevant evidence. Evidence is relevant when it has *any* tendency to make the existence of *any material* fact more or less probable. Relevancy is a relatively easy hurdle to cross. Rule 401 only requires any tendency to prove a material fact. The tendency need not be strong, unwavering, or absolute. A material fact may, but need not be the case's ultimate issue. Generally, a case's material facts will fall into one of three categories: the plaintiff's or prosecutor's claims (as determined by the substantive law) the defendant's defenses (as determined by substantive law), and the credibility of both parties' witnesses.

Often confused with the concept of relevancy, is the issue of *materiality*. At the common law, those two concepts were distinguished: *Materiality* meant that the offered evidence had legal significance to the case at bar. *Relevancy*, on the other hand, focused on whether the offered piece of evidence had probative value, i.e. whether logically the offered evidence tended to prove or disprove a particular point. For example, assume that the defense offers expert testimony that the accused is sane. Although the testimony may have probative value—in tending to prove that the accused was of sound mind—it would be immaterial to the case if the accused's mental state was not in issue in the case. Now, under Federal Rule 401, the two concepts have been merged into one definition and a simple relevancy objection should suffice to cover what under the common law would have been a materiality objection.

The key to determining relevancy is knowing the function of the offered evidence. Or put more simply: WHY is the evidence being offered? If the evidence is being offered to prove a material fact and has any tendency to prove that fact, the evidence is relevant under Rule 401.

§ 4-2(B). Relevant Evidence is Generally Admissible

Federal Rule 402 mandates that all irrelevant evidence is absolutely inadmissible and that all relevant evidence is generally (but not always) admissible. Relevant evidence can still be excluded on statutory grounds, constitutional grounds or reasons codified in the other rules of evidence. The bulk of Article IV enumerates the exceptions to the admissibility of otherwise relevant evidence. This is sometime referred to as the doctrine of legal irrelevance, that is, the authority of the court to exclude otherwise relevant evidence. Even though the evidence complies with 401, the law deems the evidence inadmissible for various policy reasons.

§ 4-2(C). General Grounds for Excluding Relevant Evidence

Federal Rule of Evidence 403 provides for the exclusion of relevant evidence where the probative value of the evidence is outweighed by one or more identified dangers: danger of unfair prejudice, confusing the issues, misleading the jury, undue delay, the needless presentation of cumulative evidence, or waste of time.

How strong a logical connection a piece of evidence has toward proving a material issue determines the evidence's probative value. For example, in a bank robbery prosecution, testimony from an eyewitness that she saw the defendant driving away from the scene of the crime would carry more probative value than other evidence showing that the defendant lived near the bank, and thus only indirectly links the defendant with the event. Although both pieces of evidence would probably pass muster under Rule 401, the former piece would carry greater weight.

The opponent who raises a "403" objection has the burden of proving that an identified prejudicial danger substantially outweighs the probative value of the evidence. The judge will make this determination under Rule 104(a). The 403 objection is an important one because it potentially applies to every piece of evidence offered, and also may serve as an opponent's last chance to exclude a piece of evidence which otherwise complies with the evidence rules.

§ 4-2(D). Specific Rules of Exclusion

Article IV contains a number of rules which specifically exclude certain types of evidence, even if they are otherwise relevant under the definition of Rule 401. The following discussion briefly introduces those rules.

§ 4-2(D)(1).Character Evidence

The topic of character evidence is the subject of Federal Rules 404, 405 and Rules 412-415. The rules generally exclude evidence of a person's character. Although a person's character may serve as a valid predictor on how that person would act on a particular occasion, the rules generally exclude such evidence, subject to a number of exceptions. The topic of character evidence is broad and is discussed in more detail, *infra*.

§ 4-2(D)(2). Evidence of Habit

While the rules of evidence restrict the use of character evidence, Rule 406 expressly authorizes admission of habit (or routine) evidence to prove that a person or business acted in conformity with the habit or routine on the occasion in question. Habit evidence is admissible regardless of whether the habit has been corroborated or established through the use of eyewitnesses. Like character evidence, habit evidence is probative of propensity and habit may be established through the use of opinion testimony, reputation testimony, or specific instances of conduct.

§ 4-2(D)(3). Subsequent Remedial Measures

Federal Rule of Evidence 407 generally excludes evidence of subsequent remedial measures, or a manufacturer's recall to prove negligence or culpable conduct. For example in a slip and fall case, the plaintiff generally cannot offer evidence that right after the injury the defendant placed nonskid flooring in the store. As with all the legal irrelevance rules, the evidence is excluded only if it is offered to prove the material issue codified in the rule. And it only excludes those measures or steps which were taken after the injury or damage occurred. Thus, remedial measures taken, for example, after a product was manufactured, but before the plaintiff was actually injured, are not excluded under the Rule. If there is another independent logically relevant reason to admit evidence of a remedial measure, it will not be excluded under Rule 407. Rule 407 provides a non-exclusive list of other relevant purposes the evidence may be admitted to prove such as the issues of ownership or control.

§ 4-2(D)(4). Compromise and Offers to Compromise

Federal Rule 408 prevents the admission of statements or conduct made during settlement negotiations to prove either liability or the amount of a claim. This rule applies only when there is an actual offer or an actual acceptance given in return for a concession. Under Rule 408 compromise evidence may be admissible, however, to prove something besides liability, such as the bias or prejudice of a witness.

§ 4-2(D)(5). Payment of Medical Expenses

Rule 409 forbids the admissibility of an offer to pay (or the actual payment of) an injured person's medical expenses to prove the payer's liability for the injury. The rule does not contain a list of independent purposes which the payment may be offered to prove.

§ 4-2(D)(6). Pleas, Plea Discussions, and Related Statements

Rule 410 generally excludes evidence of certain withdrawn pleas or plea negotiations. The Texas versions vary from the federal model. Texas Rule 410 also makes *nolo contendere* pleas inadmissible in civil cases, whereas it only prohibits the admissibility of *withdrawn nolo contendere* pleas in criminal cases. Both the Texas and the federal rules codify a rule of optional completeness similar to that codified in Rule 106. Where one party has introduced evidence relating to a plea discussion, the other party may out of fairness introduce other statements which it feels ought to be contemporaneously considered with the previously admitted statement. The rule does not contain a list of independent purposes.

The federal rule (but not the Texas rule) contains a "perjury" exception that permits use of a Rule 410 statement in a criminal case where the defendant is charged with perjury or false statement—if the defendant made the statement under oath, and on the record in the presence of counsel.

The following chart demonstrates the key differences in the Federal and Texas versions of Rule 410.

Comparison Between Texas Rule 410 (in Civil and Criminal Cases) and Federal Rule 410

	Texas Civil Case Rule 410	Texas Criminal Case; Rule 410	Federal Rule 410
Guilty Plea	Admissible	Admissible	Admissible
Withdrawn Guilty Plea	Inadmissible	Inadmissible	Inadmissible
Nolo Contendere Plea	Inadmissible	Admissible	Inadmissible
Withdrawn Nolo Contendere Plea	Inadmissible	Inadmissible	Admissible
Plea Questions	Inadmissible	Inadmissible	Inadmissible
Plea Bargaining	Inadmissible	Inadmissible	Inadmissible

Although Federal Rule of Evidence 410 explicitly calls for the exclusion of any statements made during plea bargaining sessions between the prosecution and a criminal defendant, is it possible for the parties to waive that rule of exclusion? That issue was addressed by the Supreme Court in *United States v. Mezzanatto*

UNITED STATES v. MEZZANATTO
513 U.S. 196 (1995)

Justice THOMAS delivered the opinion of the Court.

Federal Rule of Evidence 410 and Federal Rule of Criminal Procedure 11(e)(6) provide that statements made in the course of plea discussions between a criminal defendant and a prosecutor are inadmissible against the defendant. The court below held that these exclusionary provisions may not be waived by the defendant. We granted certiorari to resolve a conflict among the Courts of Appeals, and we now reverse.

I

On August 1, 1991, San Diego Narcotics Task Force agents arrested Gordon Shuster after discovering a methamphetamine laboratory at his residence in Rainbow, California. Shuster agreed to cooperate with the agents, and a few hours after his arrest he placed a call to respondent's pager. When respondent returned the call, Shuster told him that a friend wanted to purchase a pound of methamphetamine for $13,000. Shuster arranged to meet respondent later that day.

At their meeting, Shuster introduced an undercover officer as his "friend." The officer asked respondent if he had "brought the stuff with him," and respondent told the officer it was in his car. Respondent was arrested and charged with possession of methamphetamine with intent to distribute.

On October 17, 1991, respondent and his attorney asked to meet with the prosecutor to discuss the possibility of cooperating with the Government. At the beginning of the meeting, the prosecutor informed respondent that he had no obligation to talk, but that if he wanted to cooperate he would have to be completely truthful. As a condition to proceeding with the discussion, the prosecutor indicated that respondent would have to agree that any statements he made during the meeting could be used to impeach any contradictory testimony he might give at trial if the case proceeded that far. Respondent conferred with his counsel and agreed to proceed under the prosecutor's terms.

Respondent then admitted knowing that the package he had attempted to sell to the undercover police officer contained methamphetamine, but insisted that he had dealt only in "ounce" quantities of methamphetamine prior to his arrest. Initially, respondent also claimed that he was acting merely as a broker for Shuster and did not know that Shuster was manufacturing methamphetamine at his residence, but he later conceded that he knew about Shuster's laboratory. Respondent attempted to minimize his role in Shuster's operation by claiming that he had not visited Shuster's residence for at least a week before his arrest. At this point, the Government confronted respondent with surveillance evidence showing that his car was on Shuster's property the day before the arrest, and terminated the meeting on the basis of respondent's failure to provide completely truthful information.

Respondent eventually was tried on the methamphetamine charge and took the stand in his own defense. He maintained that he was not involved in methamphetamine trafficking and that he had thought Shuster used his home laboratory to manufacture plastic explosives for the CIA. He also denied knowing that the package he delivered to the undercover officer contained methamphetamine. Over defense counsel's objection, the prosecutor cross-examined respondent about the inconsistent statements he had made during the October 17 meeting. Respondent denied having made certain statements, and the prosecutor called one of the agents who had attended the meeting to recount the prior statements. The jury found respondent guilty, and the District Court sentenced him to 170 months in prison.

A panel of the Ninth Circuit reversed., We granted certiorari because the Ninth Circuit's decision conflicts with the Seventh Circuit's decision in *United States v. Dortch*, 5 F.3d 1056, 1067-1068 (1993).

II

Federal Rule of Evidence 410 and Federal Rule of Criminal Procedure 11(e)(6) (Rules or plea-statement Rules) are substantively identical. Rule 410 provides: "Except as otherwise provided in this rule, evidence of the following is not, in any civil or criminal proceeding, admissible against the defendant who ... was a participant in the plea discussions:... (4) any statement made in the course of plea discussions with an attorney for the prosecuting authority which do not result in a plea of guilty...."

The provisions of those rules are presumptively waivable, though an express waiver clause may suggest that Congress intended to occupy the field and to preclude waiver under other, unstated circumstances.

The presumption of waivability has found specific application in the context of evidentiary rules. Absent some "overriding procedural consideration that prevents enforcement of the contract," courts have held that agreements to waive evidentiary rules are generally enforceable even over a party's subsequent objections. Courts have "liberally enforced" agreements to waive various exclusionary rules of evidence. Thus, at the time of the adoption of the Federal Rules of Evidence, agreements as to the admissibility of documentary evidence were routinely enforced and held to preclude subsequent objections as to authenticity. And although hearsay is inadmissible except under certain specific exceptions, we have held that agreements to waive hearsay objections are enforceable.

Indeed, evidentiary stipulations are a valuable and integral part of everyday trial practice. Prior to trial, parties often agree in writing to the admission of otherwise objectionable evidence, either in exchange for stipulations from opposing counsel or for other strategic purposes. Both the Federal Rules of Civil Procedure and the Federal Rules of Criminal Procedure appear to contemplate that the parties will enter into evidentiary agreements during a pretrial conference. During the course of trial, parties frequently decide to waive evidentiary objections, and such tactics are routinely honored by trial judges. .

III

Because the plea-statement Rules were enacted against a background presumption that legal rights generally, and evidentiary provisions specifically, are subject to waiver by voluntary agreement of the parties, we will not interpret Congress' silence as an implicit rejection of waivability. Respondent bears the responsibility of identifying some affirmative basis for concluding that the plea-statement Rules depart from the presumption of waivability.

Respondent offers three potential bases for concluding that the Rules should be placed beyond the control of the parties. We find none of them persuasive.

A

Respondent first suggests that the plea-statement Rules establish a "guarantee [to] fair procedure" that cannot be waived. We agree with respondent's basic premise: there may be some evidentiary provisions that are so fundamental to the reliability of the fact-finding process that they may never be waived without irreparably "discredit[ing] the federal courts." But enforcement of agreements like respondent's plainly will not have that effect. The admission of plea statements for impeachment purposes enhances the truth-seeking function of trials and will result in more accurate verdicts. Under any view of the evidence, the defendant has made a false statement, either to the prosecutor during the plea discussion or to the jury at trial; making the jury aware of the inconsistency will tend to increase the reliability of the verdict without risking institutional harm to the federal courts.

B

Respondent also contends that waiver is fundamentally inconsistent with the Rules' goal of encouraging voluntary settlement. *See* Advisory Committee Notes on Fed. Rule Evid. 410 (purpose of Rule is "promotion of disposition of criminal cases by compromise"). Because the prospect of waiver may make defendants "think twice" before entering into any plea negotiation, respondent suggests that enforcement of waiver agreements acts "as a brake, not as a facilitator, to the plea-bargain process."

We need not decide whether and under what circumstances substantial "public policy" interests may permit the inference that Congress intended to override the presumption of waivability, for in this case there is no basis for concluding that waiver will interfere with the Rules' goal of encouraging plea bargaining. The court below focused entirely on the defendant's incentives and completely ignored the other essential party to the transaction: the prosecutor. Thus, although the availability of waiver may discourage some defendants from negotiating, it is also true that prosecutors may be unwilling to proceed without it.

Prosecutors may be especially reluctant to negotiate without a waiver agreement during the early stages of a criminal investigation, when prosecutors are searching for leads and suspects may be willing to offer information in exchange for some form of immunity or leniency in sentencing. In this "cooperation" context, prosecutors face "painfully delicate" choices as to "whether to proceed and prosecute those suspects against whom the already produced evidence makes a case or whether to extend leniency or full immunity to some suspects in order to procure testimony against other, more dangerous suspects against whom existing evidence is flimsy or nonexistent." Because prosecutors have limited resources and must be able to answer "sensitive questions about the credibility of the testimony" they receive before entering into any sort of cooperation agreement, prosecutors may condition cooperation discussions on an agreement that the testimony provided may be used for impeachment purposes. If prosecutors were precluded from securing such agreements, they might well decline to enter into cooperation discussions in the first place and might never take this potential first step toward a plea bargain.

Indeed, as a logical matter, it simply makes no sense to conclude that mutual settlement will be encouraged by precluding negotiation over an issue that may be particularly important to one of the parties to the transaction. A sounder way to encourage settlement is to permit the interested parties to enter into knowing and voluntary negotiations without any arbitrary limits on their bargaining chips.

In sum, there is no reason to believe that allowing negotiation as to waiver of the plea-statement Rules will bring plea bargaining to a grinding halt; it may well have the opposite effect. Respondent's unfounded policy argument thus provides no basis for concluding that Congress intended to prevent criminal defendants from offering to waive the plea- statement Rules during plea negotiation.

C

Finally, respondent contends that waiver agreements should be forbidden because they invite prosecutorial overreaching and abuse. Respondent asserts that there is a "gross disparity" in the relative bargaining power of the parties to a plea agreement and suggests that a waiver agreement is "inherently unfair and coercive." Because the prosecutor retains the discretion to "reward defendants for their substantial assistance" under the Sentencing Guidelines, respondent argues that defendants face an " 'incredible dilemma' " when they are asked to accept waiver as the price of entering plea discussions.

The dilemma flagged by respondent is indistinguishable from any of a number of difficult choices that criminal defendants face every day. The plea bargaining process necessarily exerts pressure on defendants to plead guilty and to abandon a series of fundamental rights, but we have repeatedly held that the government "may encourage a guilty plea by offering substantial benefits in return for the plea.

The mere potential for abuse of prosecutorial bargaining power is an insufficient basis for foreclosing negotiation altogether. "Rather, tradition and experience justify our belief that the great majority of prosecutors will be faithful to their duty." Thus, although some waiver agreements "may not be the product of an informed and voluntary decision," this possibility "does not justify invalidating all such agreements." Instead, the appropriate response to respondent's predictions of abuse is to permit case-by-case inquiries into whether waiver agreements are the product of fraud or coercion. We hold that absent some affirmative indication that the agreement was entered into unknowingly or involuntarily, an agreement to waive the exclusionary provisions of the plea-statement Rules is valid and enforceable.

IV

Respondent conferred with his lawyer after the prosecutor proposed waiver as a condition of proceeding with the plea discussion, and he has never complained that he entered into the waiver agreement at issue unknowingly or involuntarily. The Ninth Circuit's decision was based on its per se rejection of waiver of the plea-statement Rules. Accordingly, the judgment of the Court of Appeals is reversed.

Although the Court's opinion focused specifically on the ability of the parties to waive the provisions of Rule 410, note that the Court also stated that other rules of evidence, which might otherwise call for the exclusion of evidence, may be the subject of an agreement or waiver, a topic covered in Chapter One.

§ 4-2(D)(7). Liability Insurance

Under Federal Rule 411, whether a party has liability insurance is not admissible to prove either negligence or wrongful acts. The rule contains a non-exclusive list of purposes for which evidence of insurance may be offered. For example, evidence of insurance is admissible to prove agency, ownership, or control.

§ 4-2(D)(8). Sexual Offense Cases

In addition to the general character evidence rules, Rules 404 and 405, Federal Rule of Evidence 412 specifically addresses the admissibility of a sexual misconduct victim's character. According to Rule 412(a) evidence offered to show that the victim engaged in other sexual behavior or evidence offered to prove the victim's sexual predisposition is not admissible, in criminal or civil cases. Rule 412(b), however, does recognize limited exceptions to the general rule of exclusion. Note that this rule does not address the admissibility of character evidence of the alleged perpetrator's character. That issue is addressed in Rule 404(b) and new Rules 413-415.

In 1995, Congress added three rules to the Federal Rules of Evidence—Rules 413, 414, and 415. Rule 413 makes affirmatively admissible in a criminal case, evidence of an accused's prior sexual assaults in those cases where the accused has been charged with sexual assault. Similarly, under Rule 414, a criminal defendant's prior acts of child molestation are affirmatively admissible where the defendant is charged with molesting a child. Rule 415, which applies to civil cases, incorporates the provisions of Rules 413 and 414. All three rules include notice provisions. Because these three rules seem to cut so deeply into the general principle of not convicting someone for their prior acts, they have been the subject of considerable debate. *See, e.g.*, Imwinkelried, *A Small Contribution to the Debate Over the Proposed Legislation Abolishing the Character Evidence Prohibition in Sex Offense Prosecutions*, 44 SYRACUSE L. REV. 1125 (1995).

§ 4-3. Character Evidence — In General

As noted, *supra*, a number of rules in Article IV specifically address the issue of character evidence. In order to understand and apply those rules, it is important to first, know the general rules and exceptions stated in Rule 404, 412-415, and how to prove character in Rule 405. It is critical to see how the various character evidence rules fit together.

Character evidence is evidence which shows that a person is predisposed to act in a certain way. Typical character traits would include a person's honesty, law-abidingness, carelessness, or peaceableness, or the opposite of those traits, e.g., dishonesty. Stated legally, character evidence establishes a person's propensity to do a certain act. We expect good people (people of good character) to do good things, and we assume bad people (people of bad character) will do bad things. We rely daily on such assessments in deciding who to trust, who to count on, or who to avoid. We make those decisions on what we have heard about a particular person, i.e., their reputation, or based upon our personal opinion of that person's character, which is in turn based upon our prior contacts with that person. We may even take into consideration their specific prior acts. For example, if someone is always late in repaying a loan, we take that into account in deciding whether to lend money to the person or in simply counting on the fact that the repaid loan will be late in coming.

While a person's character may be clearly relevant to numerous issues at trial, the Rules of Evidence heavily regulate the ability of a party to use character evidence. Under the doctrine of *legal irrelevance*, character evidence may only be used under certain circumstances. Because the issues in most cases focus on whether a person did or did not do a particular act on the occasion in question, the person's propensity to engage in certain conduct raises real concerns about whether the jury may properly limit its focus to the alleged occasion, and not what the person had a propensity to do. This is particularly problematic in criminal cases. The rules reflect the general rule that a person accused of criminal activity should not be found guilty simply because they have a demonstrated propensity to do that sort of act.

Thus, Rule 404(a) states the general rule of exclusion—where a person's character is being used circumstantially to show that the alleged act was committed.

§ 4-3(A). When Is Character Evidence Admissible?

§ 4-3(A)(1). Circumstantial Use

Rule 404 prohibits the use of character evidence when it is offered circumstantially to prove that an individual acted in conformity with his or her character. This prevents the jury from making findings of guilt or liability based upon a person's character. For example, in a civil case the jury generally cannot conclude: "X is a careless person. Because X is a careless person he must have driven negligently and caused the accident." And in a criminal case, the jury may not conclude: "D has robbed banks before and because D is a robber, he must have robbed the bank as alleged in this case." A difficulty in understanding and applying character evidence is that it is often counter-intuitive. That is, any reasonable person would take another's propensity for carelessness into account in everyday decisions.

Federal Rule 404, however, includes specific exceptions to this general rule of exclusion. Under Federal Rule 404(a)(2)(A), the defendant in a federal criminal case may introduce evidence of a pertinent trait of character to prove that he or she is not the kind of person who would commit the alleged crime. In some jurisdictions, this is referred to as the "Mercy Rule." Once the defendant opens the door to character evidence, the prosecution may respond in kind. Under Rule 404(a)(2)(B), (C), character evidence regarding a victim in a criminal case may be admitted and under Rule 404(a)(3) either side may present character evidence about a witness in the case. That rule directs the reader to Rules 607, 608 and 609, which all deal with a witness's credibility.

The Texas Rules of Evidence contain similar exceptions to the general rule that character evidence is not admissible to prove that a person acted in conformity with their character.

§ 4-3(A)(2). Character in Issue — Direct Use

Rule 404 does not address the admissibility of character evidence when a person's character is an essential element of a claim or defense. When character is such an element, it is said that "character is in issue." This sort of use is very rare in criminal cases and is usually only recognized in those cases where the defendant has asserted that he was entrapped and the applicable substantive law regarding that defense permits the defense to introduce evidence of the defendant's subjective intent, i.e., he did not have the propensity to engage in the alleged conduct and was improperly induced by government agents to do so. The issue might arise in criminal cases where an insanity defense is urged. In civil cases, character may be an essential element in libel or slander cases, child custody cases, and negligent entrustment cases.

Thus, in contrast to not being permitted to make circumstantial use of character evidence, where character is in issue, the jury may conclude: "P is a violent and nasty person. Because P is a violent and nasty person, D's newspaper article saying that P is a violent and nasty person is true and D is not guilty of libel."

If character is in issue in the case, the proponent may prove character by reputation or opinion testimony or through evidence of specific instances of conduct.

§ 4-3(B). How Character May Be Proved

As recognized in Federal Rule of Evidence 405, there are three forms of character evidence: (1) opinion testimony, (2) reputation testimony, and (3) specific instances of conduct (SICs).

Opinion testimony is presented through the testimony of a witness who has formed a personal opinion of another person's character. This opinion must be based on the witness's personal knowledge of X and X's particular character trait that the witness will testify about.

Reputation testimony is testimony relating to another person's reputation in a particular community, whether it be in professional or work-related circles or social relationships. The proponent of the reputation testimony must show that the reputation witness has personal knowledge of X's reputation, i.e. what the witness has heard about X. Thus, a reputation witness may have personal knowledge of X's reputation without having ever met X. Additionally, the reputation must relate to some issue in the case. For example, X's reputation for being soft-spoken will have no relevance in X's trial for mail fraud, but may have relevance if X were being tried for inciting a riot.

Specific instances of conduct (SICs) are particular acts done by an individual. SICs allow the jury to form an inference regarding the character of an individual: that X once assaulted his wife allows the jury to infer that X is a violent individual.

Where character evidence is admissible under Rule 404, the form the character evidence may take is determined by Rule 405. Under Rule 405, reputation and opinion character evidence are almost always admissible. In comparison in sexual assault prosecutions, reputation or opinion evidence of the *victim's* past sexual behavior is not admissible under Rule 412.

Specific rules, however, govern the use of SICS. Again, each of these rules regulating the use of SICs assumes the SIC will be used only in the circumstances authorized under Rule 404 or other rules of evidence.

§ 4-4. Ten Character Evidence Rules — Texas and Federal

The following "ten rules" provide a summary of the key points in Texas and Federal Rules of Evidence 404 and 405.

RULE 1. If character is itself in issue as an essential element of a claim or defense, the proponent may use opinion testimony, reputation testimony, and SICs (Specific Instances of Conduct) to prove character. Rule 405(b). This is rarely encountered. Although the limitations of Rule 404 are not applicable, Rule 402 is applicable.

RULE 2. As a general rule, character evidence is not admissible to prove circumstantially a person's conduct on a particular occasion. Rule 404(a)(1). The Federal Rules are different. *See* Fed. R. Evid. 413-415.

RULE 3. Exceptions to Rule 2 do exist but the proponent is: (i) limited to presenting character evidence in the form of opinion or reputation testimony (Rule

405(a)); and (ii) the character evidence must relate to a "pertinent" character trait. Rule 404(a).

RULE 4.   Although a person's SICs may be admissible for other reasons, see, e.g., Rule 404(b) and bias rules, they are not admissible to prove the person's propensity on a particular occasion. They may be inquired into during cross-examination of a character witness in the form of "have you heard" or "did you know" questions. Rule 405(a). *Cf.* 608(b).

RULE 5.   In a Texas civil case, character evidence may be introduced by a person accused of conduct involving moral turpitude to show that he or she did not commit the act. Rule 404(a)(2)(B).

    i..   The person accused must first open the door by presenting favorable character evidence.

    ii.   The other side may respond with unfavorable character evidence.

    iii.   This provision does not exist in the Federal Rules.

RULE 6.   In a Texas criminal case, the accused may introduce evidence of character, or a pertinent character trait, to show that he or she did not commit the offense. Rule 404(a)(2)(A). This is sometimes referred to as the "good character" defense.

    i.   The accused must first open the door by presenting favorable character evidence.

    ii.   The prosecution may respond with unfavorable character evidence.

    iii.   The Federal rule is similar. However, if the defense attacks the character of a victim, noted below, the prosecution may respond by attacking the character of the defendant — even if the defense did not first open the door by presenting good character evidence about the defendant.

RULE 7.   Character evidence may be used in both criminal and civil cases to impeach or rehabilitate a witness. Rules 404(a)(4). The Federal Rule is the same.

RULE 8.   In a Texas civil case, character evidence regarding a victim of assaultive conduct may be introduced on the issue of self-defense to show that the victim had a violent character. That may be rebutted with evidence of peaceable character. Rule 404(a)(3)(C). There is no Federal Rules counterpart.

RULE 9.   In a Texas criminal case, character evidence of a victim is admissible, subject to Rule 412. In a homicide case, character evidence of peaceableness is admissible to rebut evidence that the victim was the first aggressor. The Federal Rule is similar.

RULE 10.   In a Texas criminal case, character evidence of the defendant is admissible on sentencing. There is no Federal Rules counterpart.

§ 4-5. Character Evidence Regarding Victims — Texas and Federal

The following material summarizes the key points of law concerning admissibility of a victim's character.

§ 4-5(A). The Civil Case:

1.   In a civil case, the plaintiff/victim alleges that the defendant assaulted him.

2.   The defendant responds that his actions were in self-defense and presents character evidence (reputation/opinion) that the plaintiff/victim has a character for violence. Rule 404(a)(3)(C). This evidence would be used, under Rule 404, to show that the plaintiff/victim had a propensity for violence/nonpeaceable behavior, in an attempt to show that the victim started the fight. The same evidence (including evidence of SICs) might be admissible to show that the defendant acted reasonably because he had heard of the plaintiff's propensities.

3.   If the defendant opens the door, the plaintiff/victim may respond with character evidence that he has a peaceful character.

4.   The defendant is *not* permitted to introduce evidence about his own character of peacefulness because Rule 404(a)(2)(B) is limited to acts involving moral turpitude in civil cases.

5.   There is no comparable Federal Rule governing a "victim's character" in civil cases.

§ 4-5(B). The Criminal Case:

1.   In a non-homicide criminal case, the accused is permitted to "open the door" and introduce character evidence (reputation/opinion) of a "pertinent" character trait of the victim. The prosecution is permitted to respond to that evidence. Rule 404(a)(3)(A). This rule is subject to the limitations of Rule 412. As in civil cases, this evidence would be used under Rule 404, to show the victim's propensity. But it might also be independently admissible to show that the defendant's actions were in response to what he had heard about the victim's propensities.

2.   In a homicide case, the prosecution is free to offer evidence of the peaceable character of the victim to rebut evidence that the victim was the "first aggressor." Note that the prosecution need not wait for the defendant to present character evidence on the homicide victim. Rule 404(a)(3)(B).

3.   The defendant in a criminal case may also present favorable character evidence about himself. Rule 404(a)(2)(A).

4.   The Federal Rule is similar, except that if the accused in a criminal case offers adverse character evidence about the victim, the prosecution may respond by presenting unfavorable character evidence about the accused.

§ 4-6. Specific Instances of Conduct (SIC's)

Intuitively, we measure a person by what they do, how they act. Dishonest people tend to act dishonestly. Untruthful people tend to be untruthful. Ironically, because a person's prior conduct can be so powerful in the courtroom, the rules of evidence generally forbid a proponent from introducing a person's SICs. This is especially true when the SICs may be offered to show the person's character. The following rules summarize the topic of SICs vis a vis character and also note possible ways of introducing SICs without running afoul of the general rules of exclusion.

§ 4-6(A). Using SICs to Show Character

Although "character evidence" may be admissible under Rule 404(a), Rule 405(a) specifically limits counsel to using only "reputation" or "opinion" evidence to show good or bad character traits.

1.   SIC's are generally not admissible to show a person's character (propensities). Rule 404(b). *Cf.* Art. 38.37, C.C.P. (child victims); Fed. R. Evid. 413-415 (sexual offenses).

2.   Where character is an essential element of a claim or a defense, SIC's are admissible. Rule 405(b). This Rule is rarely encountered.

3.   Impeachment of Character Witnesses:

a.   A character witness, like any other witness, may not be impeached in Texas through questioning about his or her personal SIC's which have not resulted in a conviction. Rule 608(b). *Cf.* Fed. R. Evid. 608(b).

b.   A character witness may be asked "have you heard" and "did you know" questions about the target (or principal) witness's SIC's. Rule 405(a). But the cross-examiner is stuck with the answer.

§ 4-6(B). Noncharacter Use of SICs (To Show Something Other Than Propensity)

A person's SIC's may be admitted for some reason other than to show that the person has the propensity to act in a certain way:

1.   Impeachment/Rehabilitation of a Witness:

   a.   The general rule is that a witness may not be impeached by showing that the witness has engaged in "bad" SIC's, e.g., lying on a job application. (Texas Rule 608(b)). Nor may a witness be rehabilitated through introduction of "good" SIC's.

   b.   A witness may, however, be impeached with a SIC which has resulted in a conviction (Rule 609).

   c.   In Federal cases, a witness may be impeached with his personal SIC's. (Fed. Rule 608(b).

   d.   A witness may be impeached through SIC's which show a witness's bias. (Texas Rule 613(b); there is no Federal Rule of Evidence explicitly covering this topic).

   e.   Blanket denial of any wrongdoing may be rebutted with SIC's.

2.   The SIC may be admitted under Rule 404(b) for one or more non-character purposes (MIMIC).

3.   Under Federal Rules of Evidence 413-415, the defendant's prior similar crimes (SIC's) in sexual assault and child molestation cases are admissible on any matter relevant to the case, including propensity.

4.   In Texas, notwithstanding Rules 404 and 405, evidence of a defendant's SIC's against a child victim "shall be admitted" for its bearing on relevant matters, including the state of mind of the defendant and the child and the previous and subsequent relationship between the defendant and the child. Art. 38.37, Tx. Code of Crim. Pro.

5.   Under both Federal and Texas Rules of Evidence 406, SIC's may be used to prove a person or organization's "habit."

§ 4-6(C). Proving the Extrinsic Act (SIC) — The Burden of Proof

Assuming that evidence of an extrinsic act, i.e., uncharged or extraneous act, is admissible, how much evidence must the proponent present to show the court that the act was actually committed by the person? That issue was addressed by the Supreme Court in *Huddleston v. United States.*

The same issue was later addressed by the Texas Court of Criminal Appeals in *Harrell v. State.* Both cases follow.

HUDDLESTON v. UNITED STATES
485 U.S. 681 (1988)

[During a federal criminal trial on charges of possession of 500 stolen video tapes, the trial judge admitted evidence that the defendant had engaged in similar, uncharged, sales of allegedly stolen televisions and appliances. He was convicted and unsuccessfully appealed to the Court of Appeals. The Supreme Court granted certiorari.]

Chief Justice REHNQUIST

Federal Rule of Evidence 404(b) provides: "Other crimes, wrongs, or acts—Evidence of other crimes, wrongs, or acts is not admissible to prove the character of a person in order to show action in conformity therewith. It may, however, be admissible for other purposes, such as proof of motive, opportunity, intent, preparation, plan, knowledge, identity, or absence of mistake or accident." This case presents the question whether the district court must itself make a preliminary finding that the Government has proved the "other act" by a preponderance of the evidence before it submits the evidence to the jury. We hold that it need not do so.

Petitioner, Guy Rufus Huddleston, was charged with one count of selling stolen goods in interstate commerce, 18 U.S.C. § 2315, and one count of possessing stolen property in interstate commerce, 18 U.S.C. § 659. The two counts related to two portions of a shipment of stolen Memorex videocassette tapes that petitioner was alleged to have possessed and sold, knowing that they were stolen.

[The evidence at trial showed that the petitioner had sold 500 stolen videocassette tapes to various purchasers, who believed the sales were lawful]

There was no dispute that the tapes which petitioner sold were stolen; the only material issue at trial was whether petitioner knew they were stolen. The District Court allowed the Government to introduce evidence of "similar acts" under Rule 404(b), concluding that such evidence had "clear relevance as to [petitioner's knowledge]".. The first piece of similar act evidence offered by the Government was the testimony of Paul Toney, a record store owner. He testified that in February 1985, petitioner offered to sell new 12" black and white televisions for $28 apiece. According to Toney, petitioner indicated that he could obtain several thousand of these televisions. Petitioner and Toney eventually traveled to the Magic Rent-to-Own, where Toney purchased 20 of the televisions. Several days later, Toney purchased 18 more televisions.

The second piece of similar act evidence was the testimony of Robert Nelson, an undercover FBI agent posing as a buyer for an appliance store. Nelson testified that in May 1985, petitioner offered to sell him a large quantity of Amana appliances—28 refrigerators, 2 ranges, and 40 icemakers. Nelson agreed to pay $8,000 for the appliances. Petitioner was arrested shortly after he arrived at the parking lot where he and Nelson had agreed to transfer the appliances. A truck containing the appliances was stopped a short distance from the parking lot, and Leroy Wesby, who was driving the truck, was also arrested. It was determined that the appliances had a value of approximately $20,000 and were part of a shipment that had been stolen.

Petitioner testified that the Memorex tapes, the televisions, and the appliances had all been provided by Leroy Wesby, who had represented that all of the merchandise was obtained legitimately. Petitioner stated that he had sold 6,500 Memorex tapes for Wesby on a commission basis. Petitioner maintained that all of the sales for Wesby had been on a commission basis and that he had no knowledge that any of the goods were stolen.

In closing, the prosecution explained that petitioner was not on trial for his dealings with the appliances or the televisions. The District Court instructed the jury that the similar acts evidence was to be used only to establish petitioner's knowledge, and not to prove his character. The jury convicted petitioner on the possession count only.

* * * * *

We granted certiorari to resolve a conflict among the Courts of Appeals as to whether the trial court must make a preliminary finding before "similar act" and other Rule 404(b) evidence is submitted to the jury. We conclude that such evidence should be admitted if there is sufficient evidence to support a finding by the jury that the defendant committed the similar act.

Federal Rule of Evidence 404(b)—which applies in both civil and criminal cases—generally prohibits the introduction of evidence of extrinsic acts that might adversely reflect on the actor's character, unless that evidence bears upon a relevant issue in the case such as motive, opportunity, or knowledge. Extrinsic acts evidence may be critical to the establishment of the truth as to a disputed issue, especially when that issue involves the actor's state of mind and the only means of ascertaining that mental state is by drawing inferences from conduct. The actor in the instant case was a criminal defendant, and the act in question was "similar" to the one with which he was charged. Our use of these terms is not meant to suggest that our analysis is limited to such circumstances.

Before this Court, petitioner argues that the District Court erred in admitting Toney's testimony as to petitioner's sale of the televisions. The threshold inquiry a court must make before admitting similar acts evidence under Rule 404(b) is whether that evidence is probative of a material issue other than character. The Government's theory of relevance was that the televisions were stolen, and proof that petitioner had engaged in a series of sales of stolen merchandise from the same suspicious source would be strong evidence that he was aware that each of these items, including the Memorex tapes, was stolen. As such, the sale of the televisions was a "similar act" only if the televisions were stolen. Petitioner acknowledges that this evidence was admitted for the proper purpose of showing his knowledge that the Memorex tapes were stolen. He asserts, however, that the evidence should not have been admitted because the Government failed to prove to the District Court that the televisions were in fact stolen.

Petitioner argues from the premise that evidence of similar acts has a grave potential for causing improper prejudice. For instance, the jury may choose to punish the defendant for the similar rather than the charged act, or the jury may infer that the defendant is an evil person inclined to violate the law. Because of this danger, petitioner maintains, the jury ought not to be exposed to similar act evidence until the trial court has heard the evidence and made a determination under Federal Rule of Evidence 104(a) that the defendant committed the similar act. Rule 104(a) provides that "[p]reliminary questions concerning the qualification of a person to be a witness, the existence of a privilege, or the admissibility of evidence shall be determined by the court, subject to the provisions of subdivision (b)." According to petitioner, the trial court must make this preliminary finding by at least a preponderance of the evidence.

We reject petitioner's position, for it is inconsistent with the structure of the Rules of Evidence and with the plain language of Rule 404(b). Article IV of the Rules of Evidence deals with the relevancy of evidence. Rules 401 and 402 establish the broad principle that relevant evidence— evidence that makes the existence of any fact at issue more or less probable—is admissible unless the Rules provide otherwise. Rule 403 allows the trial judge to exclude relevant evidence if, among other things, "its probative value is substantially outweighed by the danger of unfair prejudice." Rules 404 through 412 address specific types of evidence that have generated problems. Generally, these latter Rules do not flatly prohibit the introduction of such evidence but instead limit the purpose for which it may be introduced. Rule 404(b), for example, protects against the introduction of extrinsic act evidence when that evidence is offered solely to prove character. The text contains no intimation, however, that any preliminary showing is necessary before such evidence may be introduced for a proper purpose. If offered for such a proper purpose, the evidence is subject only to general strictures limiting admissibility such as Rules 402 and 403.

Petitioner's reading of Rule 404(b) as mandating a preliminary finding by the trial court that the act in question occurred not only superimposes a level of judicial oversight that is nowhere apparent from the language of that provision, but it is simply inconsistent with the legislative history behind Rule 404(b). The Advisory Committee specifically declined to offer any "mechanical solution" to the admission of evidence under 404(b). Rather, the Committee indicated that the trial court should assess such evidence under the usual rules for admissibility: "The determination must be made whether the danger of undue prejudice outweighs the probative value of the evidence in view of the availability of other means of proof and other factors appropriate for making decisions of this kind under Rule 403." *See also* S.Rep. No. 93-1277, p. 25 (1974) ("[I]t is anticipated that with respect to permissible uses for such evidence, the trial judge may exclude it only on the basis of those considerations set forth in Rule 403, i.e. prejudice, confusion or waste of time").

Petitioner's suggestion that a preliminary finding is necessary to protect the defendant from the potential for unfair prejudice is also belied by the Reports of the House of Representatives and the Senate. The House made clear that the version of Rule 404(b) which became law was intended to "plac[e] greater emphasis on admissibility than did the final Court version." The Senate echoed this theme: "[T]he use of the discretionary word 'may' with respect to the admissibility of evidence of crimes, wrongs, or other acts is not intended to confer any arbitrary discretion on the trial judge." Thus, Congress was not nearly so concerned with the potential prejudicial effect of Rule 404(b) evidence as it was with ensuring that restrictions would not be placed on the admission of such evidence.

We conclude that a preliminary finding by the court that the Government has proved the act by a preponderance of the evidence is not called for under Rule 104(a). This is not to say, however, that the Government may parade past the jury a litany of potentially prejudicial similar acts that have been established or connected to the defendant only by unsubstantiated innuendo. Evidence is admissible under Rule 404(b) only if it is relevant. "Relevancy is not an inherent characteristic of any item of evidence but exists only as a relation between an item of evidence and a matter properly provable in the case." In the Rule 404(b) context, similar act evidence is relevant only if the jury can reasonably conclude that the act occurred and that the defendant was the actor. See *United States v. Beechum*, 582 F.2d 898, 912-913 (CA5 1978) (en banc). In the instant case, the evidence that petitioner was selling the televisions was relevant under the Government's theory only if the jury could reasonably find that the televisions were stolen.

Such questions of relevance conditioned on a fact are dealt with under Federal Rule of Evidence 104(b). *See also* E. Imwinkelried, Uncharged Misconduct Evidence § 2.06 (1984). Rule 104(b) provides: "When the relevancy of evidence depends upon the fulfillment of a condition of fact, the court shall admit it upon, or subject to, the introduction of evidence sufficient to support a finding of the fulfillment of the condition." In determining whether the Government has introduced sufficient evidence to meet Rule 104(b), the trial court neither weighs credibility nor makes a finding that the Government has proved the conditional fact by a preponderance of the evidence. The court simply examines all the evidence in the case and decides whether the jury could reasonably find the conditional fact—here, that the televisions were stolen—by a preponderance of the evidence. The trial court has traditionally exercised the broadest sort of discretion in controlling the order of proof at trial, and we see nothing in the Rules of Evidence that would change this practice. Often the trial court may decide to allow the proponent to introduce evidence concerning a similar act, and at a later point in the trial assess whether sufficient evidence has been offered to permit the jury to make the requisite finding. If the proponent has failed to meet this minimal standard of proof, the trial court must instruct the jury to disregard the evidence.

We emphasize that in assessing the sufficiency of the evidence under Rule 104(b), the trial court must consider all evidence presented to the jury. [I]ndividual pieces of evidence, insufficient in themselves to prove a point, may in cumulation prove it. The sum of an evidentiary presentation may well be greater than its constituent parts." *Bourjaily v. United States*, 483 U.S. 171, 179-180 (1987). In assessing whether the evidence was sufficient to support a finding that the televisions were stolen, the court here was required to consider not only the direct evidence on that point—the low price of the televisions, the large quantity offered for sale, and petitioner's inability to produce a bill of sale—but also the evidence concerning petitioner's involvement in the sales of other stolen merchandise obtained from Wesby, such as the Memorex tapes and the Amana appliances. Given this evidence, the jury reasonably could have concluded that the televisions were stolen, and the trial court therefore properly allowed the evidence to go to the jury.

We share petitioner's concern that unduly prejudicial evidence might be introduced under Rule 404(b). . .. We think, however, that the protection against such unfair prejudice emanates not from a requirement of a preliminary finding by the trial court, but rather from four other sources: first, from the requirement of Rule 404(b) that the evidence be offered for a proper purpose; second, from the relevancy requirement of Rule 402—as enforced through Rule 104(b); third, from the assessment the trial court must make under Rule 403 to determine whether the probative value of the similar acts evidence is substantially outweighed by its potential for unfair prejudice....and fourth, from Federal Rule of Evidence 105, which provides that the trial court shall, upon request, instruct the jury that the similar acts evidence is to be considered only for the proper purpose for which it was admitted...

Affirmed.

While the Supreme Court's opinion in *Huddleston* answered the question of what burden of proof would apply in federal courts, it was not until six years later, in *Harrell v. State*, that the Texas Court of Criminal Appeals finally addressed the issue head on.

HARRELL v. STATE
884 S.W.2d 154 (Tex. Crim. App. 1994)
(en banc)

MALONEY, Judge.

A jury convicted appellant of engaging in organized criminal activity and sentenced him to fifteen years in prison. Initially, the Twelfth Court of Appeals reversed the conviction. This Court reversed and remanded. On remand, the Court of Appeals affirmed. We granted appellant's petition for discretionary review to determine, for purposes of admissibility, the standard of proof applicable to the State in proving the defendant committed an extraneous offense. We will reverse the judgment of the Court of Appeals.

At the guilt/innocence phase of trial, the State introduced State's exhibit number 76, a ledger depicting drug transactions during February and March of an unspecified year. Although it is unclear, the ledger reflected that someone named Wesley made four four-ounce purchases during

March for $27,100. A Texas Ranger testified that the year was 1986 because "the prices of the cocaine at that time were the same as what they would have been in '86." The instant offense was alleged to have occurred in September 1986. Although some of the first names in the ledger, like appellant's, are the same as some indicted for this offense, most of the names are not.

Appellant objected to the admission of State's exhibit number 76 under TEX.R.CRIM.EVID. 401, 403, and 404(a) & (b). He claimed it was an extraneous offense which the State had the burden of proving beyond a reasonable doubt, and that the State had not met that burden because no connection was shown between appellant and the ledger entries other than the name "Wesley." The trial court overruled the objection, stating that the relationship of the parties before the conspiracy was "germane" to whether a conspiracy existed.

* * * * *

Appellant contends the Court of Appeals erred in applying a preponderance of the evidence standard because evidence of an extraneous offense is only admissible if the State "clearly prove[s]" or makes a "clear showing" that the defendant committed such offense. The State contends that since the enactment of the Texas Rules of Criminal Evidence, the trial court should admit evidence of an extraneous offense if there is sufficient evidence from which the jury could find the defendant committed the extraneous offense. *See* TEX.R.CRIM.EVID. 104(b). The State urges us to follow the United States Supreme Court's interpretation of rule 104(b) of the Federal Rules of Evidence that evidence of an extraneous offense is admissible if the jury could reasonably conclude by a preponderance of the evidence that the defendant committed such offense. *See Huddleston*; FED.R.EVID. 104(b). A review of our case law is helpful in resolving this issue. . .

This Court has long required that juries be instructed not to consider extraneous offense evidence unless they believed beyond a reasonable doubt that the defendant committed such offense.

In many cases where the issue was, as here, the standard of admissibility for extraneous offenses, this Court relied in part upon jury instruction cases requiring that juries be instructed not to consider extraneous offense evidence unless they believed beyond a reasonable doubt that the defendant committed such offense. Thus, with respect to the State's burden of proof in proving a defendant committed an extraneous offense, this Court has perceived a connection between the standard of admissibility and the jury instruction.

However, while this Court has remained consistent in requiring that the trial court instruct the jury not to consider extraneous offense evidence unless it believes beyond a reasonable doubt that the defendant committed such offense, we have not been as consistent in our holdings regarding the standard of admissibility of extraneous offenses. Almost fifteen years ago, in an attempt to resolve the inconsistencies of our previous holdings, we held that extraneous offense evidence was inadmissible unless:

> [there [was] a clear showing that: 1) the evidence of the extraneous offense is material, i.e., going to an element of the offense charged in the indictment or information, 2) the accused participated in the extraneous transaction being offered into evidence, and 3) the relevancy to a material issue outweighs its inflammatory or prejudicial potential. [citations omitted].

McCann v. State, 606 S.W.2d 897, 901 (Tex. Crim. App. 1980). Since *McCann*, we have required that the State clearly prove or make a clear showing that the defendant committed the extraneous offense sought to be offered against him. This standard of admissibility of extraneous offense evidence is known as the "clear" proof standard. We have never clarified what is meant by "clear" proof, perhaps because most "clear" proof cases involve either no proof or overwhelming proof that the defendant committed the extraneous offense. Presumably, the standard of admissibility and the jury instruction were intended to mirror one another. Thus, given that the standard for jury consideration of extraneous offenses is well-settled as proof beyond a reasonable doubt, we hold that the standard of admissibility for extraneous offense evidence is also proof beyond a reasonable doubt.

II

The State contends that the Texas Rules of Criminal Evidence, effective September 1, 1986, now govern the connection that must be shown between the defendant and an extraneous offense. Relying upon *Huddleston* and Federal Rule of Evidence 104(b), the State argues that evidence of an extraneous offense is admissible if the jury could reasonably find by a preponderance of the evidence that the defendant committed the extraneous offense. In *Huddleston*, the petitioner contended that the trial court must make a preliminary factual finding by a preponderance of the evidence under federal rule 104(a) that the defendant committed the extraneous act. The Supreme Court noted that federal rule 404(b) does not indicate that "any preliminary showing is necessary before [extrinsic act] evidence may be introduced for a proper purpose." Consequently, the trial court does not make a "preliminary finding" under federal rule 104(a) that the Government has proved the extrinsic act.

While we do not agree with all of *Huddleston*'s conclusions, we do agree with some of its analysis. We first point out that while the trial court might not be compelled to make a "preliminary finding" as to the proof of the extrinsic evidence under rule 104(a), under rule 104(b) the trial court must nevertheless make an initial determination as to the relevancy of the evidence, dependent "upon the fulfillment of a condition of fact."

In *Huddleston*, the conditional fact was whether the televisions were stolen. In the instant case, the conditional fact is whether appellant committed the extraneous offenses depicted in State's Exhibit 76. If appellant committed the extraneous offense, the evidence is relevant and admissible, provided it is not too prejudicial and is offered for a proper purpose. *See* TEX.R.CRIM.EVID. 401, 403, & 404(b). However, if appellant did not commit the extraneous offenses, the evidence is irrelevant and therefore inadmissible. TEX.R.CRIM.EVID. 402.

Neither the federal nor Texas rules of evidence specify what quantum of proof governs admissibility when the relevancy of the evidence is contingent upon the fulfillment of a conditional fact under rule 104(b). *Huddleston* concluded that the trial court must determine that the jury could reasonably conclude by a preponderance of the evidence the conditional fact. We decline to follow *Huddleston* to this extent. As discussed in Part I of this opinion, we are convinced that the proper quantum of proof in establishing that the defendant committed the extraneous offense is beyond a reasonable doubt. We therefore hold that in deciding whether to admit extraneous offense evidence in the guilt/innocence phase of trial, the trial court must, under rule 104(b), make an initial determination at the proffer of the evidence, that a jury could reasonably find beyond a reasonable doubt that the defendant committed the extraneous offense. In making that determination, the "strength of the evidence establishing the similar act is one of the factors the [trial]court may consider when conducting the Rule 403 balancing."

In the instant case, in order for the evidence to have been sufficient for the trial court to admit it, it had to determine that a jury could find beyond a reasonable doubt that appellant committed the extraneous offenses depicted in State's exhibit number 76. Otherwise, that portion of the exhibit depicting extraneous offenses was inadmissible. Indeed, the trial court instructed the jury not to consider evidence of extraneous offenses unless it believed beyond a reasonable doubt that appellant committed them and then the jury could only consider them on the issue of intent. The Court of Appeals, therefore, erred in holding that State's exhibit number 76 was admissible because the jury could find by a preponderance of the evidence that the defendant committed the extraneous offenses depicted in the ledger.

§ 4-7. Character Evidence Chart

The following chart demonstrates the general relationship between character evidence and credibility evidence, topics which sometimes overlap. The chart also indicates the relationship between the three methods of introducing character evidence (reputation, opinion, and SICs) and when those methods may be used.

CHARACTER EVIDENCE RELATIONSHIP TO CREDIBILITY EVIDENCE

Methods of Proving Character

Admissible to Show--

Reputation Evidence (Rule 405(a))

Direct Evidence of Character: (Character in Issue) Rule 405(b)

CHARACTER EVIDENCE

Opinion Evidence (Rule 405(a))

Circumstantial Evidence of Propensity to Show Conduct (Rule 404(a))

Circumstantial. Evidence of Propensity to Show Untruthfulness or Truthfulness (Rule 404(a)(4), 608(a))

Specific Acts (Rules 404(b), 405, 608, 609

Prior Conviction (Rule 609)

Nonpropensity Evidence E.g., 404(b)

Bias (Rule 613)

Prior Inconsistent Statements (Rule 613)

CREDIBILITY EVIDENCE

Specific Contradiction

§ 4-8. Questions and Notes

a.   Assume that the defendant is charged with shooting his wife with his deer rifle, through the window of their home in the country, late one night. She survived the shooting. There were no eyewitnesses to the shooting. The investigation indicates that the shooter shot the rifle from a distance of 100 yards. Which of the following pieces of evidence is logically relevant to the case? Assuming that the pieces of evidence are logically relevant, are they necessarily admissible? Explain.

1.   The fact that the defendant told a witness, upon hearing that his wife had been shot that he felt bad that she had been shot.

2.   The fact that the defendant was told the day before the shooting that he had stage-four cancer.

3.   The fact that the defendant was seen one week before the shooting, pricing deer rifles at Bass Pro Shop.

4.   The fact that police have been repeatedly called to the defendant's home on domestic violence reports involving his wife.

5.   The fact that the defendant was having an affair with a woman and his wife found out about it the day of the shooting and she told him she wanted a divorce.

6.   The fact that there was a full moon on the night of the shooting.

7.   The fact that the defendant learned two weeks before the shooting that his wife was having an affair and planning to divorce him.

8.   The fact that the defendant took out a very large life insurance policy in his wife's name the day of the shooting.

9.   The fact that the defendant was seen driving at a high speed out of his driveway an hour before his wife was shot.

10. The fact that the defendant has a long history of aggressive acts involving guns.

b.   Assume that you are the trial judge in a child abuse case and that the prosecution wishes to introduce eight very graphic pictures of the injuries to the child victim, i.e., burns, scars, bruises, lacerations. Are those photos relevant to the case? On what theory? Assume that the defense also objects on the basis of Rule 403. What factors, if any, would you consider in deciding whether to admit the photos, in whole, or in part? Does it make a difference what the pictures show?

§ 4-9. Problems

a.   In a Texas criminal case, *State v. Massie,* the accused, Johnny Massie, is on trial on charges of assaulting a woman, Melinda Juarez, at a grocery store parking lot. Massie hit the victim with a six pack of beer after they got into a verbal altercation in the parking lot over a parking space. The accused takes the stand in his own defense and testifies that although he hit the victim with the six pack, he did not intend to injure her and the fact that the six pack came into contact with the victim's back, was an accident. On cross-examination, the prosecutor questions Massie about whether it was true that four years earlier he was arrested on charges of assault in Houston, Texas and that just one year earlier she had been arrested for aggravated assault in Santa Fe, New Mexico. And that in the first instance he had thrown an umbrella at the victim and in the New Mexico incident, he had thrown plastic unopened Mountain Dew bottle at the victim's head. The accused denies that he was involved in those two incidents.

After the defense rests, and in rebuttal, the prosecution calls a woman to the stand to testify that she was assaulted in Houston, Texas, by the accused who threw an umbrella at her when she became angry at her. The prosecution also introduces an authenticated copy of a police report from Santa Fe, New Mexico, which shows that the accused was arrested on charges of assault, when he threw a soft-drink bottle at the victim.

Assume that the case is being tried in a Texas court and that you are the judge. Without regard to whether an objection should have been made, is the prosecutor's introduction of evidence of the two prior incidents of assault permissible? Explain your answer.

Would your answer be the same under the Federal Rules of Evidence?

b. Assume the facts in the preceding problem, *State v. Massie*, and also assume that you are working for the defense counsel who is representing the defendant. Your firm has received notice under Texas Rule of Evidence 404(b)(2), of the prosecution's intent to introduce the defendant's past acts during the case. The lead defense counsel has asked you to prepare a written pretrial motion *in limine* on behalf of the defendant, to exclude any mention or introduction of the defendant's prior acts by the prosecution during the trial. Your motion should include a brief legal argument (two or three paragraphs, including Texas case law) supporting the motion. It must be typewritten, double-spaced. You must also include an order for the judge to sign granting or denying your motion and a certificate of service.

c. Assume the facts in the preceding problem, *State v. Massie*, and assume that the judge in the Texas case admits the evidence of the prior acts of the defendant on the ground that it was relevant to rebut the defendant's testimony that his actions were not accidental. Draft an instruction to be read to the jury which discusses the prosecution's burden of proof on the issue and properly limits the jury's consideration of the evidence. Your instruction, which must be typewritten, must be no more than one page in length, double-spaced.

d. Assume the facts in the preceding question, *State v. Massie*. You are working for the defense firm and the lead counsel has asked you to tell her whether its possible to introduce defense evidence that the victim, Melinda Juarez, has a police record of prior assaults on other persons and that she has a very short temper. The lead counsel tells you that she has three character witnesses willing to testify that Ms. Juarez has a propensity to start fights. What advice can you give the lead counsel? What Rules of Evidence would apply? Would your answer be the same if this was a federal criminal case?

e. Assume that you are representing the defendant in a Texas civil case, *Gomez v. Atomic Auto*. Emily Gomez has alleged that your client, Atomic Auto Repairs, Inc., was negligent in repairing the breaks on her truck and as a result she could not stop her car at an intersection and sustained personal injuries. During discovery you produced evidence showing that Atom Auto had liability insurance in the amount of $ 525,000.00. Draft a motion *in limine* blocking the plaintiff from mentioning or introducing evidence of that liability insurance policy. Your motion must include a brief legal argument (two or three paragraphs, including Texas case law) supporting the motion and an order that can be signed by the trial judge. The motion must be typewritten, double-spaced, and must an order for the judge to sign and also include notice of service on the plaintiff.

f.   Assume that you are representing Phillip Baird in *Walters v. Baird*, a civil lawsuit in Texas. The plaintiff, Cynthia Walters, a next door neighbor of Baird, alleges that due to an overgrown bush next to Baird's driveway that she was not able to see on-coming traffic and was broadsided by a large truck when she backed into the street. She intends to introduce evidence that despite her pleas with Baird to cut down the bush, he did not do so until two days after the accident. She wants to argue that by cutting down the bush, Baird has admitted that it posed a danger. Draft a motion in limine to present to the judge in the case, Judge Jones, asking the judge to block any mention of your client's post-accident remedial measures. Your motion should include a brief legal argument (two or three paragraphs, including Texas case law) supporting the motion. It must be typewritten, double-spaced. You must also include an order for the judge to sign granting or denying your motion and a certificate of service.

g.   Assume that the defendant in *State v. Johnson* is charged with assault on Johnny Cantu and that you are representing the defendant, Dan Johnson. The two got into a fight for a parking space outside a Bass Pro Shop. Defense counsel has decided to present a "good character" defense under Texas Rule 404(a)(1)(A). The defense theory is that Cantu actually started the fight and that Johnson has a peaceful character.

One of the defense's character witnesses is David Roberts. He has known the defendant for three years. They have worked together at the Bass Pro Shop, located in San Antonio. They see each other professionally at least seven or eight times a week. Roberts visits with Johnson socially, and with his family, at company events. They attend the same men's Bible Study at a local Methodist church. Roberts considers himself a good friend of Johnson and is prepared to offer opinion testimony that Johnson is a nonviolent person and believes that God has called him, Johnson, to life of nonviolence.

The prosecution has evidence that on January 2, 2016, while working for Dominos, in Weatherford, Texas, Johnson got into a fight with a co-worker over an office prank where the co-worker added hot sauce to Johnson's pizza. No charges were ever filed. In addition, Johnson was given an oral reprimand in July 2016, for confronting his manager at Dominos and was ordered to enroll in an anger management program, offered by the company. Several weeks later, Johnson dropped out of the program, resigned his position, moved his family to San Antonio, and got his current job at Bass Pro Shop .

The prosecution learned this information while speaking off the record, on the telephone, with Johnson's former co-workers. They consider him a dangerous person with a very short temper. But the prosecution has no documentary evidence to support the information and those co-workers are not willing to testify at the trial.

Students should be prepared to play the role of defense counsel, prosecutor, judge, or court-reporter.

CHAPTER FIVE

PRIVILEGES

§ 5-1. Introduction to Privileges

Unlike the hearsay and best evidence rules, which are intended to exclude unreliable evidence, evidentiary privileges may prevent disclosure of otherwise relevant and reliable information. Thus, they are generally disfavored. *See Branzburg v. Hayes*, 408 U.S. 665 (1972) (public has right to evidence unless it is protected by constitutional, common law or statutory privilege). Privileges exist because public policy deems that certain relationships should be protected or furthered; that interest will be accomplished if confidential communications in those relationships are protected.

Two types of privileges exist: testimonial privileges and confidential communications privileges. Testimonial privileges prevent certain individuals from being called as witnesses. *See e.g.* Texas Rule of Evidence 504(b). Communications privileges, on the other hand, prevent the disclosure of certain specified confidential communications. *See e.g.* Texas Rule of Evidence 503(b). *Cf.* Texas Rule of Evidence 508 (identity of informant, but not communication, is privileged).

An important distinction exists between the laws governing privileges in Texas and the laws governing privileges in federal courts. In Texas, as codified in Texas Rule of Evidence 501, the law of privileges encompasses constitutional privileges (such as the Fifth Amendment's right against self-incrimination), statutory privileges (such as the attorney work product provision found in Texas Rule of Civil Procedure 192), and the privileges found in the Rules of Evidence. Texas courts are exclusively limited to these sources when interpreting the law of privileges. The courts cannot look to common law to broaden or limit the law of privileges.

Federal Rule of Evidence 501 also recognizes constitutional and statutory privileges. But the Federal Rules contain no specific privilege rules. Instead, Federal Rule 501 mandates that the law of privileges be governed by the common law, as interpreted and applied in the federal courts. Accordingly, Federal Courts thus have the power to expand and limit privileges as their reason or experience dictates. An exception to this, of course, exists with federal diversity cases ("*Erie*" problems) where state law (such as the Texas Rules of Evidence) would govern.

Privilege issues often arise during pretrial discovery where one party has requested the other side to produce documents or provide testimony in a deposition which involves privileged information. For example, in a typical personal injury action, the defendant will normally seek any and all communications or information which is relevant to the plaintiff's past and present medical condition. That information will almost always involve confidential communications between the patient and the doctor.

§ 5-2. Testimonial Privileges

The common law recognized a testimonial privilege for spouses. A criminal defendant could prevent his or her spouse from testifying for the prosecution. Over the years, however, that privilege has generally disappeared, as noted by the Supreme Court in *Trammel v. United States*.

TRAMMEL v. UNITED STATES
445 U.S. 40 (1980)

[Otis Trammel was convicted before the United States District Court of importation of heroin and conspiracy to import heroin. The Court of Appeals affirmed, 583 F.2d 1166 and on a writ of certiorari to the Court of Appeals, the Supreme Court, Mr. Chief Justice Burger, addressed the questions of whether the accused had a privilege to block his wife from testifying against him.]

Mr. Chief Justice BURGER

We granted certiorari to consider whether an accused may invoke the privilege against adverse spousal testimony so as to exclude the voluntary testimony of his wife... This calls for a re-examination of *Hawkins v. United States*, 358 U.S. 74 (1958).

I

On March 10, 1976, petitioner Otis Trammel was indicted with two others, Edwin Lee Roberts and Joseph Freeman, for importing heroin into the United States from Thailand and the Philippine Islands and for conspiracy to import heroin... The indictment also named six unindicted co-conspirators, including petitioner's wife Elizabeth Ann Trammel.

According to the indictment, petitioner and his wife flew from the Philippines to California in August 1975, carrying with them a quantity of heroin. Freeman and Roberts assisted them in its distribution. Elizabeth Trammel then traveled to Thailand where she purchased another supply of the drug. On November 3, 1975, with four ounces of heroin on her person, she boarded a plane for the United States. During a routine customs search in Hawaii, she was searched, the heroin was discovered, and she was arrested. After discussions with Drug Enforcement Administration agents, she agreed to cooperate with the Government.

Prior to trial on this indictment, petitioner moved to sever his case from that of Roberts and Freeman. He advised the court that the Government intended to call his wife as an adverse witness and asserted his claim to a privilege to prevent her from testifying against him. At a hearing on the motion, Mrs. Trammel was called as a Government witness under a grant of use immunity. She testified that she and petitioner were married in May 1975 and that they remained married. She explained that her cooperation with the Government was based on assurances that she would be given lenient treatment. She then described, in considerable detail, her role and that of her husband in the heroin distribution conspiracy.

After hearing this testimony, the District Court ruled that Mrs. Trammel could testify in support of the Government's case to any act she observed during the marriage and to any communication "made in the presence of a third person"; however, confidential communications between petitioner and his wife were held to be privileged and inadmissible. The motion to sever was denied.

At trial, Elizabeth Trammel testified within the limits of the court's pretrial ruling; her testimony, as the Government concedes, constituted virtually its entire case against petitioner. He was found guilty on both the substantive and conspiracy charges...

In the Court of Appeals petitioner's only claim of error was that the admission of the adverse testimony of his wife, over his objection, contravened this Court's teaching in *Hawkins v. United States, supra*, and therefore constituted reversible error. The Court of Appeals rejected this contention. It concluded that *Hawkins* did not prohibit "the voluntary testimony of a spouse who appears as an unindicted co-conspirator under grant of immunity from the Government in return for her testimony."

II

The privilege claimed by petitioner has ancient roots. Writing in 1628, Lord Coke observed that "it hath beene resolved by the Justices that a wife cannot be produced either against or for her husband." This spousal disqualification sprang from two canons of medieval jurisprudence: first, the rule that an accused was not permitted to testify in his own behalf because of his interest in the proceeding; second, the concept that husband and wife were one, and that since the woman had no recognized separate legal existence, the husband was that one. From those two now long-abandoned doctrines, it followed that what was inadmissible from the lips of the defendant-husband was also inadmissible from his wife.

Despite its medieval origins, this rule of spousal disqualification remained intact in most common-law jurisdictions well into the 19th century. Indeed, it was not until 1933, in *Funk v. United States*, 290 U.S. 371, that this Court abolished the testimonial disqualification in the federal courts, so as to permit the spouse of a defendant to testify in the defendant's behalf. *Funk*, however, left undisturbed the rule that either spouse could prevent the other from giving adverse testimony. The rule thus evolved into one of privilege rather than one of absolute disqualification.

The modern justification for this privilege against adverse spousal testimony is its perceived role in fostering the harmony and sanctity of the marriage relationship. Notwithstanding this benign purpose, the rule was sharply criticized. Professor Wigmore termed it "the merest anachronism in legal theory and an indefensible obstruction to truth in practice." The Committee on Improvements in the Law of Evidence of the American Bar Association called for its abolition. In its place, Wigmore and others suggested a privilege protecting only private marital communications, modeled on the privilege between priest and penitent, attorney and client, and physician and patient.

In *Hawkins v. United States*, 358 U.S. 74 (1958), this Court considered the continued vitality of the privilege against adverse spousal testimony in the federal courts. There the District Court had permitted petitioner's wife, over his objection, to testify against him. With one questioning concurring opinion, the Court held the wife's testimony inadmissible; it took note of the critical comments that the common-law rule had engendered, but chose not to abandon it. Also rejected was the Government's suggestion that the Court modify the privilege by vesting it in the witness-spouse, with freedom to testify or not independent of the defendant's control. The Court viewed this proposed modification as antithetical to the widespread belief, evidenced in the rules then in effect in a majority of the States and in England, "that the law should not force or encourage testimony which might alienate husband and wife, or further inflame existing domestic differences."

Hawkins, then, left the federal privilege for adverse spousal testimony where it found it, continuing "a rule which bars the testimony of one spouse against the other unless both consent." However, in so doing, the Court made clear that its decision was not meant to "foreclose whatever changes in the rule may eventually be dictated by 'reason and experience.' "

A

The Federal Rules of Evidence acknowledge the authority of the federal courts to continue the evolutionary development of testimonial privileges in federal criminal trials "governed by the principles of the common law as they may be interpreted . . . in the light of reason and experience." Fed. Rule Evid. 501. The general mandate of Rule 501 was substituted by the Congress for a set of privilege rules drafted by the Judicial Conference Advisory Committee on Rules of Evidence and approved by the Judicial Conference of the United States and by this Court. That proposal defined nine specific privileges, including a husband-wife privilege which would have codified the *Hawkins* rule and eliminated the privilege for confidential marital communications. See proposed Fed. Rule Evid. 505. In rejecting the proposed Rules and enacting Rule 501, Congress manifested an affirmative intention not to freeze the law of privilege. Its purpose rather was to "provide the courts with the flexibility to develop rules of privilege on a case-by-case basis," and to leave the door open to change.

Although Rule 501 confirms the authority of the federal courts to reconsider the continued validity of the *Hawkins* rule, the long history of the privilege suggests that it ought not to be casually cast aside. That the privilege is one affecting marriage, home, and family relationships—already subject to much erosion in our day—also counsels caution. At the same time, we cannot escape the reality that the law on occasion adheres to doctrinal concepts long after the reasons which gave them birth have disappeared and after experience suggest the need for change.

B

Since 1958, when *Hawkins* was decided, support for the privilege against adverse spousal testimony has been eroded further. Thirty-one jurisdictions, including Alaska and Hawaii, then allowed an accused a privilege to prevent adverse spousal testimony. The number has now declined to 24. In 1974, the National Conference on Uniform State Laws revised its Uniform Rules of Evidence, but again rejected the *Hawkins* rule in favor of a limited privilege for confidential communications. *See* Uniform Rules of Evidence, Rule 504. That proposed rule has been enacted in Arkansas, North Dakota, and Oklahoma—each of which in 1958 permitted an accused to exclude adverse spousal testimony. The trend in state law toward divesting the accused of the privilege to bar adverse spousal testimony has special relevance because the laws of marriage and domestic relations are concerns traditionally reserved to the states. *See Sosna v. Iowa*, 419 U.S. 393, 404 (1975). Scholarly criticism of the *Hawkins* rule has also continued unabated.

C

Testimonial exclusionary rules and privileges contravene the fundamental principle that " 'the public . . . has a right to every man's evidence.' " *United States v. Bryan*, 339 U.S. 323, 331 (1950). As such, they must be strictly construed and accepted "only to the very limited extent that permitting a refusal to testify or excluding relevant evidence has a public good transcending the normally predominant principle of utilizing all rational means for ascertaining truth." *Elkins v. United States*, 364 U.S. 206, 234 (1960) (Frankfurter, J., dissenting). Here we must decide whether the privilege against adverse spousal testimony promotes sufficiently important interests to outweigh the need for probative evidence in the administration of criminal justice.

It is essential to remember that the *Hawkins* privilege is not needed to protect information privately disclosed between husband and wife in the confidence of the marital relationship—once described by this Court as "the best solace of human existence." *Stein v. Bowman*, 13 Pet., at 223. Those confidences are privileged under the independent rule protecting confidential marital communications. *Blau v. United States*, 340 U.S. 332 (1951). The *Hawkins* privilege is invoked, not to exclude private marital communications, but rather to exclude evidence of criminal acts and of communications made in the presence of third persons.

No other testimonial privilege sweeps so broadly. The privileges between priest and penitent, attorney and client, and physician and patient limit protection to private communications. These privileges are rooted in the imperative need for confidence and trust. The priest-penitent privilege recognizes the human need to disclose to a spiritual counselor, in total and absolute confidence, what are believed to be flawed acts or thoughts and to receive priestly consolation and guidance in return. The lawyer-client privilege rests on the need for the advocate and counselor to know all that relates to the client's reasons for seeking representation if the professional mission is to be carried out. Similarly, the physician must know all that a patient can articulate in order to identify and to treat disease; barriers to full disclosure would impair diagnosis and treatment.

The *Hawkins* rule stands in marked contrast to these three privileges. Its protection is not limited to confidential communications; rather it permits an accused to exclude all adverse spousal testimony. As Jeremy Bentham observed more than a century and a half ago, such a privilege goes far beyond making "every man's house his castle," and permits a person to convert his house into "a den of thieves." It "secures, to every man, one safe and unquestionable and every ready accomplice for every imaginable crime."

The ancient foundations for so sweeping a privilege have long since disappeared. Nowhere in the common-law world—indeed in any modern society—is a woman regarded as chattel or demeaned by denial of a separate legal identity and the dignity associated with recognition as a whole human being. Chip by chip, over the years those archaic notions have been cast aside so that "[n]o longer is the female destined solely for the home and the rearing of the family, and only the male for the marketplace and the world of ideas." *Stanton v. Stanton*, 421 U.S. 7, 14-15 (1975).

The contemporary justification for affording an accused such a privilege is also unpersuasive. When one spouse is willing to testify against the other in a criminal proceeding—whatever the motivation—their relationship is almost certainly in disrepair; there is probably little in the way of marital harmony for the privilege to preserve. In these circumstances, a rule of evidence that permits an accused to prevent adverse spousal testimony seems far more likely to frustrate justice than to foster family peace. Indeed, there is reason to believe that vesting the privilege in the accused could actually undermine the marital relationship. For example, in a case such as this the Government is unlikely to offer a wife immunity and lenient treatment if it knows that her husband can prevent her from giving adverse testimony. If the Government is dissuaded from making such an offer, the privilege can have the untoward effect of permitting one spouse to escape justice at the expense of the other. It hardly seems conducive to the preservation of the marital relation to place a wife in jeopardy solely by virtue of her husband's control over her testimony.

IV

Our consideration of the foundations for the privilege and its history satisfy us that "reason and experience" no longer justify so sweeping a rule as that found acceptable by the Court in *Hawkins*. Accordingly, we conclude that the existing rule should be modified so that the witness-spouse alone has a privilege to refuse to testify adversely; the witness may be neither compelled to testify nor foreclosed from testifying. This modification—vesting the privilege in the witness-spouse—furthers the important public interest in marital harmony without unduly burdening legitimate law enforcement needs.

Here, petitioner's spouse chose to testify against him. That she did so after a grant of immunity and assurances of lenient treatment does not render her testimony involuntary. *Cf. Bordenkircher v. Hayes*, 434 U.S. 357(1978).

---

§ 5-3. Communications Privileges

Generally, most evidentiary privileges are "communications privileges." That is, the law indicates that certain confidential communications are protected and may not be disclosed without the consent of one or more persons. As noted, supra, in the federal courts, Federal Rule of Evidence 501 governs whether a certain communications privilege should be recognized. As stated in that Rule, the courts are guided by the federal "common law." The following case, *Jaffee v. Redmond*, provides insight into what factors may be applied by a federal court in deciding whether to adopt a new communications privilege.

JAFFEE v. REDMOND
518 U.S. 1 (1996)

[The survivors of a man whom police officer shot and killed sued the officer and the village that had employed him, alleging that the officer violated the deceased's constitutional rights by using excessive force. The United States District Court entered judgment for plaintiffs and the defendants appealed. The Court of Appeals for the Seventh Circuit, 51 F.3d 1346, reversed and remanded. Certiorari was granted on the issue of whether confidential communications between the officer and his psychotherapist were protected from compelled disclosure.]

Justice STEVENS delivered the opinion of the Court.

After a traumatic incident in which she shot and killed a man, a police officer received extensive counseling from a licensed clinical social worker. The question we address is whether statements the officer made to her therapist during the counseling sessions are protected from compelled disclosure in a federal civil action brought by the family of the deceased. Stated otherwise, the question is whether it is appropriate for federal courts to recognize a "psychotherapist privilege" under Rule 501 of the Federal Rules of Evidence.

I

Petitioner is the administrator of the estate of Ricky Allen. Respondents are Mary Lu Redmond, a former police officer, and the Village of Hoffman Estates, Illinois, her employer during the time that she served on the police force. Petitioner commenced this action against respondents after Redmond shot and killed Allen while on patrol duty.

* * * * *

Petitioner filed suit in Federal District Court alleging that Redmond had violated Allen's constitutional rights by using excessive force during the encounter at the apartment complex....

During pretrial discovery petitioner learned that after the shooting Redmond had participated in about 50 counseling sessions with Karen Beyer, a clinical social worker licensed by the State of Illinois and employed at that time by the Village of Hoffman Estates. Petitioner sought access to Beyer's notes concerning the sessions for use in cross-examining Redmond. Respondents vigorously resisted the discovery. They asserted that the contents of the conversations between Beyer and Redmond were protected against involuntary disclosure by a psychotherapist-patient privilege. The district judge rejected this argument. Neither Beyer nor Redmond, however, complied with his order to disclose the contents of Beyer's notes. At depositions and on the witness stand both either refused to answer certain questions or professed an inability to recall details of their conversations.

The Court of Appeals for the Seventh Circuit reversed and remanded for a new trial. Addressing the issue for the first time, the court concluded that "reason and experience," the touchstones for acceptance of a privilege under Rule 501 of the Federal Rules of Evidence, compelled recognition of a psychotherapist-patient privilege.

* * * * *

The United States courts of appeals do not uniformly agree that the federal courts should recognize a psychotherapist privilege under Rule 501. [Citations Omitted] Because of the conflict among the courts of appeals and the importance of the question, we granted certiorari…. We affirm.

II

Rule 501 of the Federal Rules of Evidence authorizes federal courts to define new privileges by interpreting "common law principles ... in the light of reason and experience." The authors of the Rule borrowed this phrase from our opinion in *Wolfle v. United States*, 291 U.S. 7, 12 (1934), which in turn referred to the oft-repeated observation that "the common law is not immutable but flexible, and by its own principles adapts itself to varying conditions." Funk v. United States, 290 U.S. 371, 383 (1933). The Senate Report accompanying the 1975 adoption of the Rules indicates that Rule 501 "should be understood as reflecting the view that the recognition of a privilege based on a confidential relationship ... should be determined on a case-by-case basis." The Rule thus did not freeze the law governing the privileges of witnesses in federal trials at a particular point in our history, but rather directed federal courts to "continue the evolutionary development of testimonial privileges."

The common-law principles underlying the recognition of testimonial privileges can be stated simply.'" For more than three centuries it has now been recognized as a fundamental maxim that the public ... has a right to every man's evidence. When we come to examine the various claims of exemption, we start with the primary assumption that there is a general duty to give what testimony one is capable of giving, and that any exemptions which may exist are distinctly exceptional, being so many derogations from a positive general rule."' Exceptions from the general rule disfavoring testimonial privileges may be justified, however, by a " 'public good transcending the normally predominant principle of utilizing all rational means for ascertaining the truth.' "

Guided by these principles, the question we address today is whether a privilege protecting confidential communications between a psychotherapist and her patient "promotes sufficiently important interests to outweigh the need for probative evidence...." 445 U.S., at 51. Both "reason and experience" persuade us that it does.

III

Like the spousal and attorney-client privileges, the psychotherapist-patient privilege is "rooted in the imperative need for confidence and trust." Treatment by a physician for physical ailments can often proceed successfully on the basis of a physical examination, objective information supplied by the patient, and the results of diagnostic tests. Effective psychotherapy, by contrast, depends upon an atmosphere of confidence and trust in which the patient is willing to make a frank and complete disclosure of facts, emotions, memories, and fears. Because of the sensitive nature of the problems for which individuals consult psychotherapists, disclosure of confidential communications made during counseling sessions may cause embarrassment or disgrace. For this reason, the mere possibility of disclosure may impede development of the confidential relationship necessary for successful treatment. Where there may be exceptions to this general rule ..., there is wide agreement that confidentiality is a sine qua non for successful psychiatric treatment." By protecting confidential communications between a psychotherapist and her patient from involuntary disclosure, the proposed privilege thus serves important private interests.

Our cases make clear that an asserted privilege must also "serve public ends." Thus, the purpose of the attorney-client privilege is to "encourage full and frank communication between attorneys and their clients and thereby promote broader public interests in the observance of law and administration of justice." And the spousal privilege, as modified in *Trammel*, is justified because it "furthers the important public interest in marital harmony," The psychotherapist privilege serves the public interest by facilitating the provision of appropriate treatment for individuals suffering the effects of a mental or emotional problem. The mental health of our citizenry, no less than its physical health, is a public good of transcendent importance.

In contrast to the significant public and private interests supporting recognition of the privilege, the likely evidentiary benefit that would result from the denial of the privilege is modest. If the privilege were rejected, confidential conversations between psychotherapists and their patients would surely be chilled, particularly when it is obvious that the circumstances that give rise to the need for treatment will probably result in litigation. Without a privilege, much of the desirable evidence to which litigants such as petitioner seek access—for example, admissions against interest by a party—is unlikely to come into being. This unspoken "evidence" will therefore serve no greater truth-seeking function than if it had been spoken and privileged.

That it is appropriate for the federal courts to recognize a psychotherapist privilege under Rule 501 is confirmed by the fact that all 50 States and the District of Columbia have enacted into law some form of psychotherapist privilege. We have previously observed that the policy decisions of the States bear on the question whether federal courts should recognize a new privilege or amend the coverage of an existing one. Because state legislatures are fully aware of the need to protect the integrity of the fact finding functions of their courts, the existence of a consensus among the States indicates that "reason and experience" support recognition of the privilege. In addition, given the importance of the patient's understanding that her communications with her therapist will not be publicly disclosed, any State's promise of confidentiality would have little value if the patient were aware that the privilege would not be honored in a federal court. Denial of the federal privilege therefore would frustrate the purposes of the state legislation that was enacted to foster these confidential communications.

It is of no consequence that recognition of the privilege in the vast majority of States is the product of legislative action rather than judicial decision.

The uniform judgment of the States is reinforced by the fact that a psychotherapist privilege was among the nine specific privileges recommended by the Advisory Committee in its proposed privilege rules.

Because we agree with the judgment of the state legislatures and the Advisory Committee that a psychotherapist-patient privilege will serve a "public good transcending the normally predominant principle of utilizing all rational means for ascertaining truth," we hold that confidential communications between a licensed psychotherapist and her patients in the course of diagnosis or treatment are protected from compelled disclosure under Rule 501 of the Federal Rules of Evidence.

IV

All agree that a psychotherapist privilege covers confidential communications made to licensed psychiatrists and psychologists. We have no hesitation in concluding in this case that the federal privilege should also extend to confidential communications made to licensed social workers in the course of psychotherapy. The reasons for recognizing a privilege for treatment by psychiatrists and psychologists apply with equal force to treatment by a clinical social worker such as Karen Beyer. Today, social workers provide a significant amount of mental health treatment. Their clients often include the poor and those of modest means who could not afford the assistance of a psychiatrist or psychologist, but whose counseling sessions serve the same public goals. Perhaps in recognition of these circumstances, the vast majority of States explicitly extend a testimonial privilege to licensed social workers. We therefore agree with the Court of Appeals that "drawing a distinction between the counseling provided by costly psychotherapists and the counseling provided by more readily accessible social workers serves no discernible public purpose."

Because this is the first case in which we have recognized a psychotherapist privilege, it is neither necessary nor feasible to delineate its full contours in a way that would "govern all conceivable future questions in this area."

V

The conversations between Officer Redmond and Karen Beyer and the notes taken during their counseling sessions are protected from compelled disclosure under Rule 501 of the Federal Rules of Evidence. The judgment of the Court of Appeals is affirmed.

---

§ 5-3(A). In General: Common Elements of Confidential Communications Privileges

Working with communications privileges requires understanding: 1) to what types of proceedings do privileges apply; 2) who holds the privilege; 3) who may claim the privilege; 4) what is the nature of the privilege; 5) what type of information is privileged from disclosure; 6) the effect, if any, of claiming the privilege; 7) whether an exception to the privilege exists; and 8) whether a waiver of the privilege has occurred.

§ 5-3(B). The Proceedings — When Do Privileges Apply?

Privileges apply to civil, criminal, and administrative proceedings. This remains true, regardless of whether the Rules of Evidence govern the proceeding.

§ 5-3(C). Who is the Holder of the Privilege?

Normally, the privilege rule specifies who holds the particular privilege. For communications privileges, the holder normally is the communicating party (i.e. the speaker). A holder may be, but is not always, a party to the litigation.

§ 5-3(D). Who May Claim the Privilege?

The holder of the privilege may always claim a privilege to prevent disclosure of the information sought. In addition to the holder, subsequent holders (i.e. guardians or executors) and the holder's agents (individuals authorized by the holder to invoke the privilege for him/her in the holder's absence or otherwise) may also prevent disclosure by claiming a privilege. Certain rules presume an agent's authority to invoke a privilege on behalf of the holder. *See e.g.* Texas Rule of Evidence 509(c). The person claiming the privilege has the burden of proving (using extrinsic evidence if necessary), that a privilege claimed does in fact exist. Whether the person claiming the privilege meets his or her burden of proof is a decision for the trial judge under Rule of Evidence 104(a).

§ 5-3(E). What is The Nature of the Privilege?

If a communications privilege exists, the holder may (1) refuse personally to disclose the privileged information, (2) prevent a third party from making an unauthorized disclosure of the privileged information, and (3) prevent, with some exceptions, an adverse comment on the invocation of the privilege.

§ 5-3(F) What Information is Privileged?

Communications privileges only prevent the disclosure of *confidential* communications. And confidentiality only attaches to those communications where the speaker intends to maintain secrecy. That intent normally is evidenced by physical privacy (the speaker discloses in a private room with only the hearer present, as opposed to disclosure in a restaurant) and the intent to maintain secrecy in the future.

In addition to being confidential, the information must directly relate to the confidential relationship specified in the applicable rule of evidence. For example, in order for a client's communication to the attorney to fall within the scope of the lawyer/client privilege (Texas Rule of Evidence 503), the client must be speaking to the lawyer *as a lawyer* and not as a best friend. If the intent to keep the communication confidential exists, the communication to the lawyer, as well as the lawyer's response to the client, will be privileged information. The communication may be oral, written, or non-verbal (with communicative intent). No privilege, however, will attach to pre-existing documents created independent of the confidential relationship. For example, a person cannot give a three-year-old incriminating letter to a recently hired attorney in an attempt to claim that it is a confidential communication between a client and an attorney. *Cf.* Tex. R. Evid. 503(b)(2)("[a] client has a privilege to prevent the lawyer...from disclosing any other fact which came to the knowledge of the lawyer...by reason of the attorney-client relationship.")

In addressing the question about the nature of the communications between an attorney and a client, the Supreme Court of Texas concluded in the case of *In re Silver*, 540 S.W.3d 530 (Tex. 2018), that communications between a person seeking a patent and that person's patent agent could be protected under Texas Rule of Evidence 503, the attorney-client privilege.

IN RE SILVER
540 S.W.3d 530 (Tex. 2018)

[A purported inventor brought a breach of contract action against a patent purchaser. The trial court granted purchaser's motion to compel the production of e-mails between the inventor and his non-attorney patent agent. Inventor sought mandamus relief. The Dallas Court of Appeals, denied relief. Inventor petitioned the Texas Supreme Court for mandamus relief. The case addresses the issue of whether non-attorney patent agents are covered by the attorney-client privilege]

Justice Devine delivered the opinion of the court.

In this petition for mandamus relief, relator Andrew Silver asks us to vacate the trial court's order compelling the production of e-mails between Silver and his non-attorney patent agent. The court of appeals, in a divided decision, denied Silver's mandamus petition. The court concluded that the communications between Silver and his patent agent were not protected from discovery because Texas law does not provide that patent agents are lawyers for purposes of Texas's lawyer-client privilege. Because we agree that a client's communications with his registered patent agent, made to facilitate the agent's provision of authorized legal services to the client, are privileged under Rule 503, we conditionally grant mandamus relief. *See* TEX. R. EVID. 503.

I

The United States Patent and Trademark Office (USPTO), an administrative body created by Congress, is responsible for granting and issuing patents. The USPTO has authority to regulate the persons who represent patent applicants. Among those the USPTO allows to provide such representation are, of course, patent attorneys. These are individuals who are in good standing with the bar of the highest court in any state and meet all the requirements for registration before the USPTO, which includes an examination. Practice before the USPTO is not limited to attorneys, however. Applicants also have the option of hiring a patent agent—someone who is not an attorney, but has properly registered with the USPTO. Patent agents must pass the same exam as patent attorneys. For purposes of prosecuting patents for clients before the USPTO, patent attorneys and patent agents can provide all the same services.

The underlying litigation concerns the Ziosk, a stand-alone tablet designed to allow customers at restaurants to order food and pay their check without having to interact with a waiter or waitress. The Ziosk is sold by Tabletop Media, LLC, which has partnered with chains such as Abuelo's, Chili's, and Red Robin to place the device in their restaurants.

Andrew Silver claims he invented the technology that became the Ziosk and sold the patent to Tabletop. Silver brought a breach-of-contract action against Tabletop, alleging it failed to pay him for his patent. Tabletop answered, generally denying Silver's allegations.

During discovery in the underlying contract action, Tabletop sought production of emails between Silver and Raffi Gostanian, the patent agent who represented Silver before the USPTO. Silver refused to produce the emails, claiming them to be covered by the lawyer-client privilege. Although Gostanian is a registered patent agent, he is not a licensed attorney.

Tabletop moved to compel production, which the trial court granted. Silver then sought mandamus relief in the court of appeals to compel the trial court to withdraw the production order, asserting again the communications were privileged. The court of appeals denied relief.

II

Rule 503(b)(1) states the basic elements of the lawyer-client privilege. Under the rule, a client is privileged from disclosing, and may prevent others from disclosing, communications made in confidence for the purpose of obtaining legal services. TEX. R. EVID. 503(b)(1). The rule also protects communications by the lawyer to the client. Rule 503(b)(1)(A)-(E).

At issue here is who may qualify as a lawyer for purposes of the privilege. The rule helpfully defines the term "lawyer" as "a person authorized, or who the client reasonably believes is authorized, to practice law in any state or nation." Rule 503(a)(3). Here, Silver does not contend he reasonably believed Gostanian to be a lawyer or that Gostanian was authorized to provide any legal services outside of the patent application and prosecution. Therefore, the sole issue is whether Gostanian was authorized to practice law when he provided patent-agent services to Silver. The parties disagree, however, about whether the phrase "authorized to practice law" is broad enough to include a registered patent agent.

Silver argues the rule's plain language includes a patent agent, such as Gostanian, within the definition of a "lawyer." He points to federal law that allows patent agents to provide the same services as patent attorneys before the USPTO upon passing the patent bar. Because the federal government allows patent agents to provide legal services to their clients, Silver concludes that patent agents are authorized to practice law within the rule's meaning. Finally, Silver submits the federal courts have already determined that a registered patent agent is a person authorized to practice law in the United States—albeit in a limited setting—and that these decisions should control the interpretation of the privilege under our own state rule. *See Sperry v. State of Florida ex rel. Florida Bar*, 373 U.S. 379 (1963); *In re Queen's Univ. at Kingston*, 820 F.3d 1287 (Fed. Cir. 2016).

In *Queen's University*, the Federal Circuit Court of Appeals extended the attorney-client privilege to communications with patent agents, recognizing as a matter of federal common law "a patent-agent privilege extending to communications with non-attorney patent agents when those agents are acting within the agent's authorized practice of law before the Patent Office." The Federal Circuit read the Supreme Court's decision in *Sperry* as confirmation that "patent agents are not simply engaging in law-like activity, they are engaging in the practice of law itself," thereby justifying the recognition of a privilege similar to that of the traditional attorney-client privilege.

In *Sperry*, the State of Florida sought to enjoin a registered patent agent from representing Florida clients before the USPTO because the agent was not a member of the Florida bar. The Florida Supreme Court concluded that Sperry's actions constituted the unauthorized practice of law, which the State could prohibit. The United States Supreme Court disagreed. Because Congress allowed the Commissioner of Patents to regulate who was authorized to appear before the USPTO, however, the Court held the Supremacy Clause prohibited Florida from "deny[ing] to those failing to meet its own qualifications the right to perform the functions within the scope of federal authority." Thus, the Supreme Court did not disagree that the work performed by a registered patent agent constitutes the practice of law under Florida law.

Both cases may be viewed as persuasive authority that the work of a registered patent agent is the practice of law, although neither speaks directly to the meaning of the phrase under Texas law. Therefore, contrary to Silver's contention, neither case controls our determination of Rule 503's meaning.

Our rules of evidence, like all rules promulgated by this Court, have "the same force and effect as statutes" and, as such, are interpreted in the same manner under state law. Thus, when determining a rule's meaning we typically rely on the ordinary meaning of the words used, unless the text or relevant definitions indicate a different meaning.. When determining the ordinary meaning of a word, we frequently consult dictionaries. We also examine any words at issue in context to give effect to the entire adopted text.. With these principles in mind, we turn to Rule 503's language to determine whether a registered patent agent is a "lawyer" for purposes of the lawyer-client privilege.

As previously noted, the rule defines "lawyer" as "a person authorized ... to practice law in any state or nation." TEX. R. EVID. 503(a)(3). The definition states two requirements for a person to qualify as a lawyer. First, the person must be engaged in a particular activity—the "practice [of] law." Second, the person must be "authorized" to perform the activity in a state or nation. Thus, understanding what it means to be a "lawyer" for purposes of the rule requires determining (1) what it means to "practice law" and (2) how one is "authorized" to do so.

A

Although Rule 503 does not define what the practice of law entails, a non-exclusive definition of the phrase is provided in the State Bar Act under its unauthorized-practice-of-law subchapter. *See* TEX. GOV'T CODE § 81.101. There, the "practice of law" is defined as:

> the preparation of a pleading or other document incident to an action or special proceeding or the management of the action or proceeding on behalf of a client before a judge in court as well as a service rendered out of court, including the giving of advice or the rendering of any service requiring the use of legal skill or knowledge, such as preparing a will, contract, or other instrument, the legal effect of which under the facts and conclusions involved must be carefully determined.

The definition is neither exclusive nor intended to deprive the courts from "determin[ing] whether other services and acts not enumerated may constitute the practice of law." In their respective contexts, however, what it means to be a lawyer under the State Bar Act and under Rule 503 are not necessarily coextensive. For example, a "lawyer" under Rule 503 includes a person whom the client "reasonably believes is authorized to practice law" even though the person does not have a license. TEX. R. EVID. 503(a)(3). By contrast, reasonable belief plays no part in determining whether a person is a lawyer under the State Bar Act. Moreover, the State Bar Act's definition applies to the act only.

Because the rule defines "lawyer" but does not otherwise explain what it means to practice law or be authorized to do so, we must rely on the ordinary meaning of the these terms. "Practice" means to exercise or pursue an employment or profession. WEBSTER'S THIRD NEW INTERNATIONAL DICTIONARY, 1780 (3d ed. 2002). "Law" means the legal profession. *Id.* at 1279. Therefore, "the practice of law" is to pursue the legal profession. Similarly, Black's Law Dictionary defines the entire phrase "practice of law" as "the work of a lawyer." *Practice of Law*, BLACK'S LAW DICTIONARY (10th ed. 2014). Black's goes on to state that the "practice of law" encompasses:

> [A] broad range of services such as conducting cases in court, preparing papers necessary to bring about various transactions from conveying land to effecting corporate mergers, preparing legal opinions on various points of law, drafting wills and other estate-planning documents, and advising clients on legal questions. The term also includes activities that comparatively few lawyers engage in but that require legal expertise, such as drafting legislation and court rules.

These types of activities are exactly what the USPTO says that patent agents can perform. It expressly states that the ability to practice before the office includes "preparing ... any patent application," which is a paper necessary to bring about a transaction—and a highly involved one at that. A patent agent's work also includes "representing a client" in various matters before the Patent and Trademark Office, which is the equivalent of conducting a case in court in the administrative context. Finally, practice before the Patent and Trademark Office entails giving advice to clients, including "the advisability of relying upon alternative forms of protection which may be available under state law." Patent agents participate in many activities that make up the practice of law.

Simply performing tasks or functions from this list, however, is not sufficient. Implicit in the definition in both Black's and Webster's, and in line with common understanding of what it means to practice law, is that the practitioner is providing these services directly to the client. Similarly, the definition of "practice of law" in the State Bar Act states that some of the listed activities are performed "on behalf of a client." TEX. GOV'T CODE § 81.101.

As applied here, if a patent agent stays within the sphere of patent law, the agent can provide services directly to the client. The patent agent has no need of a supervising or intermediary attorney because the agent can provide all the same services. In fact, the Intellectual Property Owners Association states in its amicus brief that non-attorney patent agents working without attorney involvement or supervision make up roughly 13% of the practitioners who appear before the Patent and Trademark Office. Patent agents are not just working in the legal field; they are independently providing professional legal services to a client.

Registered patent agents perform the same services and are subject to the same rules and requirements as patent attorneys in the application and prosecution of patents before the USPTO. Concluding that the work is something other than the practice of law when performed by a registered patent agent would be anomalous. Therefore, we hold that, within the scope of their practice before the USPTO, patent agents practice law.

B

The second part of Rule 503's definition of "lawyer" is that the individual practicing law must be authorized to do so by a state or nation. TEX. R. EVID. 503(a)(3). Tabletop submits that our

Rule 503 is modeled after the proposed Federal Rule of Evidence 503, and indeed the two rules are very similar. The proposed federal rule defines "lawyer" as "a person authorized, or reasonably believed by the client to be authorized, to practice law in any state or nation." Tabletop contends that the drafters of the federal rule intended the phrase "authorized to practice law" to mean that the person was licensed to practice law. To support this interpretation, Tabletop points to the Advisory Committee's Notes that state for purposes of the rule a "lawyer" is "a person *licensed* to practice in any state or nation." Because Silver's patent agent does not have a license to practice law, Tabletop concludes the agent is not "authorized" and thus not covered by Rule 503's privilege.

In the past, we have looked to federal case law for guidance in interpreting a Texas evidentiary rule when a similar federal rule exists. On at least one occasion, we have even looked to the Advisory Committee's Notes to the Federal Rules to aid in interpreting our own similar rule, as Tabletop suggests we do here. When persuasive, these federal sources are very helpful. But the federal commentary here is not helpful because the federal rule was never adopted and the sentence from the commentary on which Tabletop relies is taken out of context.

Because the similar federal rule was never adopted, no case law interpreting the proposed rule exists. The relevant federal case law—that does exist—does not support the commentary on which Tabletop relies or the notion that the rule used the term authorized to mean only licensed. Instead, the federal authorities recognize that a registered patent agent, who does not have a license to practice law, is nevertheless engaged in the authorized practice of law before the USPTO. Moreover, in context, the commentary indicates that the drafters did not intend to limit the privilege to communications with persons holding a law license. In its entirety, the note reads:

> A "lawyer" is a person licensed to practice law in any state or nation. There is no requirement that the licensing state or nation recognize the attorney-client privilege, thus avoiding excursions into conflict of laws questions. "Lawyer" also includes a person reasonably believed to be a lawyer. For similar provisions, see California Evidence Code § 950.

As previously noted, a "lawyer" under Texas Rule of Evidence 503 similarly includes a person whom the client "reasonably believes is authorized to practice law" even though the person does not have a license. TEX. R. EVID. 503(a)(3). A license is not a prerequisite to a person being classified as a "lawyer" under the rule.

Although the terms "authorized" and "licensed" are closely related, they do not mean the same thing. "Authorized" means "sanctioned by authority" or "approved." WEBSTER'S THIRD NEW INTERNATIONAL DICTIONARY, 147 (3d ed. 2002). On the other hand, "licensed" means "permitted or authorized by license." Similarly, Black's Law Dictionary defines "authorize" as "to give legal authority; to empower," and "license" as "a privilege granted by a state or city upon payment of a fee, the receipt of the privilege then being authorized to do some act or series of acts that would otherwise be impermissible." *Authorize*, BLACK'S LAW DICTIONARY (10th ed. 2014). These definitions indicate that authorized conveys a broader meaning than licensed and that being "licensed" is a subcategory of being "authorized." That is, licensure is a specific form of authorization.

The distinction was not lost on those responsible for drafting our rules. In other rules of privilege, the drafters chose to say licensed. *See, e.g.*, TEX. R. EVID. 509(a)(2) (stating that, for purposes of the physician-patient privilege, a "physician" is "a person *licensed* ... to practice medicine in any state or nation." Not only that, but in Rule 510, for purposes of the mental health information privilege, a "professional" is defined as a person either "*authorized* to practice medicine in any state or nation" or "*licensed* or certified by the State of Texas." TEX. R. EVID. 510(a)(1)(A), (B) (emphasis added). If the drafters intended for the lawyer-client privilege to apply only to licensed attorneys, they knew how to say that. When interpreting a statute or a rule, we presume that language has been chosen "with care and that every word or phrase was used with a purpose in mind."

As mentioned above, "authorized" means "sanctioned by authority" or "approved." WEBSTER'S THIRD NEW INTERNATIONAL DICTIONARY, 147 (3d ed. 2002). The Patent and Trademark Office has approved patent agents to practice before it. The Patent and Trademark Office, in turn, was given authority to do so by Congress. A registered patent agent's authority to represent clients before the USPTO therefore comes from the United States, which is one of the sovereigns identified in our rule. *See* TEX. R. EVID. 503(a)(3) (defining lawyer as a person authorized to practice law in any state or nation). And, because patent agents are authorized to practice law before the USPTO, they fall within Rule 503's definition of "lawyer," and, as such, their clients may invoke the lawyer-client privilege to protect communications that fall within the privilege's scope.

III

The trial court concluded, however, that a client's communications with a patent agent are privileged only to the extent that the patent agent is acting under an attorney's direction. But if a registered patent agent qualifies as a "lawyer" for purposes of Rule 503's protection, which we conclude he does in the prosecution of a patent, the agent's client may assert the lawyer-client privilege even though the patent agent's work is not under a licensed attorney's direction.

A client, however, can only refuse to disclose "confidential communications made to facilitate the rendition of professional legal services." TEX. R. EVID. 503(b)(1). This means that the communication must be "made by a client seeking legal advice from a lawyer in his capacity as such and the communication must relate to the purpose for which the advice is sought ...." The client's communications with a registered patent agent regarding matters outside the agent's authorized practice area might not be protected because these communications are not necessarily made to facilitate the rendition of professional legal services.

Because the privilege here could apply to some of the documents at issue, we conclude that the trial court abused its discretion by not conducting an *in camera* review.

* * * * *

Accordingly, we conditionally grant mandamus relief and direct the trial court to conduct an appropriate in camera review and vacate its order to the extent it compels production of Silver's privileged communications. We are certain that the trial court will comply. Our writ will issue only if it fails to do so.

§ 5-3(G). Effect of Claiming a Privilege?

Invoking a privilege will prevent compelled disclosure of privileged information. Not only will the holder not have to come forward with the information, but the holder can also preclude other individuals from disclosing the confidential communication. In judicial proceedings, this prevents the court from sanctioning nondisclosure with contempt proceedings. Additionally, as a general rule neither the court nor opposing counsel may comment on, or draw inferences from, the invocation of a privilege. For example, where a criminal defendant invokes his privilege (or right) against self-incrimination, the prosecution may not argue that the defendant's silence implies his guilt. *Cf.* Texas Rule of Evidence 513(c).

§ 5-3(H). Are There Exceptions to the Privileges?

Where an exception exists, privileged information must be disclosed. Normally, specific exceptions are included as a provision in the privilege rule. Usually exceptions exist because a countervailing social policy (such as preventing fraud or criminal activity) requires disclosure.

Although rare, exceptions may exist for interpretive reasons and out of fairness. In a will contest, for example, the attorney who drafted the will may break the attorney client privilege and clarify his deceased client's intent.

The party trying to pierce a privilege has the burden of proving that an exception does exist. The court will make the determination under Rule of Evidence 104(a).

§ 5-3(I). Has Waiver Occurred?

§ 5-3(I)(1). Voluntary Waiver

With one exception, once waiver has occurred, the communication permanently loses its privileged status and the holder may not prevent further disclosure. Waiver will occur where a holder voluntarily discloses the privileged communication either publicly or potentially through a more intimate disclosure (such as telling a group of friends).

There is a difference between involuntary and inadvertent disclosure. Involuntary disclosure exists where disclosure has been erroneously compelled. Inadvertent disclosure exists where the disclosure was voluntary but unintentional, i.e., not removing privileged documents from records turned over to opposing counsel during discovery. Where involuntary disclosure has occurred, Texas Rule 512 will reinstate the privilege to prevent further disclosure. Where inadvertent disclosure has occurred, waiver of the privilege may also occur. *Cf.,* Tex. R. Civ. P. 193.3(d) (provides that party does not waive privilege where material was not intentionally disclosed and party moves within 10 days to amend discovery response). Additionally, in Texas if a holder of the privilege calls a character witness whose personal knowledge includes relevant privileged information voluntary waiver will occur. *See* Texas Rule of Evidence 511.

The party claiming the waiver has the burden of proving that waiver has in fact occurred.

§ 5-3(I)(2). Consent

Where a holder fails to either assert the privilege, or object to questioning which asks for privileged information, the holder has consented to disclosure.

§ 5-3(I)(3). Waiver Through Offensive Use

When an affirmative act, such as filing a law suit, places privileged information directly in issue, the courts may conclude that the party filing the lawsuit has affirmatively waived the privilege. This concept is also called the offensive use doctrine, and it applies to all privileges—even those not codified in the rules of evidence.

The issue of offensive use of a privilege, and when it constitutes waiver in the context of the attorney client privilege, was addressed by the Texas Supreme Court in *Republic Insurance Co. v. Davis*.

REPUBLIC INSURANCE COMPANY v. DAVIS
856 S.W.2d 158 (Tex. 1993)

ENOCH, Justice.

This mandamus action calls for the resolution of [whether] the "offensive use" waiver, enunciated by this court in *Ginsberg v. Fifth Court of Appeals*, 686 S.W.2d 105 (Tex. 1985), applies to the attorney-client privilege? We conclude that the Ginsberg "offensive use" waiver, while potentially applicable to the attorney-client privilege, does not apply in this case. Because the trial court abused its discretion in ordering the production of documents protected by the attorney-client privilege, we conditionally grant the writ of mandamus.

I.

Republic Insurance Company ("Republic") reinsured certain policies issued by National County Mutual Fire Insurance Company ("National County"). One of those policies was issued to Culver Concrete ("Culver"). That policy provided $500,000 of primary coverage, with the first $50,000 being reinsured by Republic.

A Culver employee, Reginald Davis, was involved in an accident in 1985. The truck driven by Reginald Davis struck and killed Ezequiel Trevino. Trevino's representatives and survivors filed two suits, which were eventually consolidated, against Culver and Reginald Davis. Prior to the conclusion of the Trevino suit, National County was placed into receivership.

In 1988, National County was declared insolvent and placed into liquidation and receivership. As a part of National County's liquidation, a temporary and permanent injunction was issued prohibiting anyone with assets of National County from disposing of those assets. The reinsurance contract is an asset of National County, and Republic was enjoined from disposing of the proceeds of the contract to anyone except the receiver of National County.

The Trevino lawsuit against Culver and Reginald Davis ultimately resulted in a $19,000,000 judgment being entered against Culver and Reginald Davis. After the judgment was entered, the Trevino plaintiffs, Culver, Reginald Davis, and Canal Insurance Company all made demands on Republic for the insurance proceeds.

Republic filed a declaratory judgment action in Travis County. Republic acknowledged that it owed the reinsurance proceeds; however, it was faced with competing demands as it was enjoined from paying them to anyone but the Receiver. Republic offered to pay the reinsurance proceeds into the registry of the court pending resolution of the dispute.

The Trevino plaintiffs, Culver, and Reginald Davis filed counterclaims against Republic. The counterclaims allege claims under the Deceptive Trade Practices Act, the Insurance Code, and common law. The Trevino plaintiffs, Culver, and Reginald Davis contend that Republic is liable for the $19,000,000 judgment.

After the initiation of the counterclaims, the Trevino plaintiffs served Republic with a request for production of documents. Republic asserted objections to the request.

The discovery objections were heard before Judge Joe Dibrell who referred the dispute to a special master. The special master heard evidence and issued a report to the trial court on March 9, 1992. The special master determined that the party communication privilege was inapplicable because the communication had occurred in connection with another lawsuit.

II.

* * * * *

III.

The attorney-client privilege as embodied in TEX.R.CIV.EVID. 503(B) secures the free flow of information between attorney and client, and it assures that the communication will not later be disclosed. Although the aim of the modern discovery process is to yield full and complete information regarding the issues in dispute, courts also recognize the importance of the attorney-client privilege. Confidential communications promote effective legal services. This in turn promotes the broader societal interest of the effective administration of justice. Confidential communications, however, often result in the suppression of otherwise relevant evidence. Courts balance this conflict between the desire for openness and the need for confidentiality in attorney-client relations by restricting the scope of the attorney-client privilege. This case calls for us to determine whether a party's need for information can ever outweigh the benefits associated with the attorney-client privilege.

A.

The real parties in interest seek information that is protected by the attorney-client privilege. They contend that our decision in *Ginsberg* establishes a waiver by "offensive use" of the attorney-client privilege. We must determine whether there is a waiver by offensive use of the attorney-client privilege, and if there is, whether Relator waived its attorney-client privilege.

Ginsberg involved a trespass to try title suit. Ginsberg claimed that he owned a building by virtue of two deeds. One deed was from a Mr. Gaynier to Ginsberg conveying his interest in the building. After Mr. Gaynier died, Ginsberg had Mrs. Gaynier execute a deed ratifying the deed her husband signed.

Almost ten years later Mrs. Gaynier brought the trespass to try title action, claiming the first deed was forged and that she was fraudulently induced to sign the second deed. At deposition she testified that she could not remember signing the second deed and that she was unaware until 1981 that the ownership of the building had changed. She also revealed that she had seen a psychiatrist in 1972 and subsequent years. Ginsberg sought access to the medical records. The records contained information which virtually established Ginsberg's statute of limitations defense. The records revealed that Mrs. Gaynier told her psychiatrist in 1972 that the "building was sold while we were in Padre Island."

Mrs. Gaynier resisted disclosure of the records on the basis of the psychotherapist-patient privilege. This Court rejected her claim of privilege. In doing so, this court relied on the notion that "[a] plaintiff cannot use one hand to seek affirmative relief in court and with the other lower an iron curtain of silence against otherwise pertinent and proper questions which may have a bearing upon his right to maintain his action." The facts in *Ginsberg* mandated that Mrs. Gaynier either waive her psychotherapist privilege and pursue her claim for affirmative relief, or maintain her privilege and abandon her cause of action.

B.

Five courts of appeals have considered the issue of waiver by offensive use in the attorney-client context. Of those five, four hold that the offensive waiver applied to the attorney-client privilege; the fifth held that the offensive waiver was limited to the facts of *Ginsberg* and was not applicable to the attorney-client privilege.

* * * * *

We conclude the better position applies the *Ginsberg* offensive use waiver to the attorney-client privilege. The common law and now our rules of evidence acknowledge the benefit provided by the attorney-client privilege. In an instance in which the privilege is being used as a sword rather than a shield, the privilege may be waived. Privileges, however, represent society's desire to protect certain relationships, and an offensive use waiver of a privilege should not lightly be found. For that reason, the following factors should guide the trial court in determining whether a waiver has occurred.

First, before a waiver may be found the party asserting the privilege must seek affirmative relief. Second, the privileged information sought must be such that, if believed by the fact finder, in all probability it would be outcome determinative of the cause of action asserted. Mere relevance is insufficient. A contradiction in position without more is insufficient. The confidential communication must go to the very heart of the affirmative relief sought. Third, disclosure of the confidential communication must be the only means by which the aggrieved party may obtain the evidence. If any one of these requirements is lacking, the trial court must uphold the privilege.

C.

We next examine the facts of this case to determine whether the offensive use waiver guidelines were met. We conclude that in this case there has been no waiver of the attorney-client privilege.

Republic is not seeking affirmative relief. Republic did file a declaratory judgment action, but a declaratory judgment action is not necessarily an action for affirmative relief.

Republic seeks a declaration of its obligations with respect to the reinsurance proceeds. It also requests a declaration that it owed no duties to the Trevino plaintiffs, Culver, Canal, or Reginald Davis. Finally, it seeks an injunction that would prohibit the same parties from filing a lawsuit to recover the reinsurance proceeds. The unifying factor to the relief Republic seeks is that all of it is, in reality, defensive in nature. We reject the contentions of the real parties in interest that Republic's declaratory judgment is seeking the type of affirmative relief that would result in an offensive use waiver. Because we reach the conclusion that Republic is not seeking affirmative relief, we need not consider the other offensive use factors.

The trial court abused its discretion in ordering Republic to produce documents protected by the attorney-client privilege.

§ 5-3(I)(4). Eavesdropping

Inadvertent or intentional hearing of a confidential communication will not waive a privilege. Provided that the holder meets the confidential intent requirement, courts normally will prevent the eavesdropper from coming forward to disclose the privileged information.

§ 5-4. Comparison of Federal and Texas Privileges

	Texas (Civil and Criminal)	Federal
Recognized Source of Privileges	Constitution, Statute, Rules	Federal common law
Required Reports	Rule 502	Generally recognized
Lawyer-Client	Rule 503	Generally the same
Husband-Wife	Rule 504. Rule 504(b) includes a testimonial privilege in criminal cases	Recognizes communications and testimonial privileges; the latter in criminal cases
Other Family Privileges	Not recognized	Generally rejects parent-child & in-law privileges
Clergy-Penitent	Rule 505	Generally the same
Political Vote	Rule 506	Generally recognized
Trade Secrets	Rule 507	Generally the same
Identity of Informer	Rule 508	Generally the same
Physician-Patient	Rule 509; *Cf.* 509(b) specifically rejected for criminal cases	Generally not recognized; statutes may require some confidentiality
Mental Health	Civil—Rule 510 Crim—Rule 509(b) — Alcohol & Drug Abuse Communications	Recognized by Supreme Court *Jaffee v. Redmond*
Journalist	Recognized by Statute. Tex, Civ. Prac, & Rem. Code §§ 22.021-027; CCP Arts. 38.11 and 38.111	Generally recognized

§ 5-5. Problems & Questions

a. Ms. Emily Snirnflirt visits the law offices of Jones and Jones, in the Jones Business Tower, and speaks with a gentleman who introduces himself as Jeffrey Jones, a recently admitted member of the Texas Bar. Unbeknownst to Emily, he is lying. Ms. Snirnflirt tells Jones that she needs legal representation—she is named as a defendant in a personal injury action in which she allegedly ran into a parked vehicle badly injuring the occupants.

   She tells Jones that she had been drinking before the accident but that no one at the scene of the accident questioned her about that possibility and no BAT was conducted. She also confesses that she saw the car, realized that it was parked and deliberately rammed it because it looked like her husband's car. She says that if she sees his car she will do the same thing again. Jones tells her he will represent her and asks her to step into a nearby room and speak with the firm's law clerk who is supposed to start immediately researching the legal issues and preparing the file. She does so and relates the same information to the law clerk. She also tells the law clerk that she has a prior felony conviction for perjury. Meanwhile, outside the door, a secretary is listening at the door, hears the information, and immediately calls her husband with the information.

   What, if any, of the information provided by Ms. Snirnflirt is privileged?

b. After leaving Jones's office, Ms. Snirnflirt uses a public phone in the lobby of the office building to call her husband, from whom she has been legally separated for two years, and tells him what she did, begs for his mercy and says that she needs his help in the lawsuit. She says that she needs an alibi witness for the two hours preceding the accident when she was actually at the Black Katt drinking with some friends. He reluctantly agrees to do so. She also expresses to him the fear that someone will learn about her prior felony conviction. He assures her that he will protect the information.

   What, if any, of this information is privileged?

CHAPTER SIX

WITNESSES AND ISSUES OF CREDIBILITY

§ 6-1. In General

Article VI of the Federal Rules of Evidence regulates witness testimony. Generally, the provisions in Article VI can be divided into three categories: rules determining competency, rules governing impeachment, and miscellaneous provisions.

§ 6-2. Rules Determining Competency

§ 6-2(A). In General

Only individuals who meet the competency requirements found in Rules 601-606 may testify as witnesses. At common law, four factors determined a witness competency:

(1) The mental capacity to perceive through one's senses,
(2) The mental capacity to remember,
(3) The mental capacity to communicate, and
(4) The moral capacity for truthfulness.

Although the modern rules of evidence do not specifically list these factors, they still serve as the underlying principles behind the competency rules. And they may still be used to impeach a witness's credibility.

Note that Federal Rule of Evidence 601 recognizes that a state's competency rules will be applied in federal civil proceedings where state law applies with regard to an element of a claim or defense, i.e. in diversity proceedings. In a federal criminal proceeding, the state rules governing competency would not apply.

§ 6-2(B). Persons Who Lack Mental Capacity

Federal Rule of Evidence 601 presumes that a witness is competent, unless otherwise provided in the rules of evidence. This means that even a person suffering from mental delusions is competent to testify. A judge, however, could be asked to exclude such testimony on the grounds that the witness lacked personal knowledge, Rule 602, or was confusing, Rule 403, or would needlessly consume time or would embarrass the witness. Rule 611(a). Thus, in theory, a party may challenge any witness as incompetent upon a showing that the witness lacks one of the four common law capacities. For all practical purposes, however, the court will usually rule that a person's lack of ability to remember, for example, goes to the issue of credibility, not the ability to testify.

In contrast, Texas Rule of Evidence 601(a)(1) gives the trial court the authority to disqualify witnesses who in the judgment of the court are insane at the time of trial or were insane at the time they observed the facts about which they have been called to testify. This would be a decision under Rule 104(a).

Rule 601(a)(2) also gives the trial judge the authority to disqualify other persons who "lack sufficient intellect" to testify to the matters in the case.

§ 6-2(C). Children

Federal Rule of Evidence 601 presumes that a child witness is competent to testify. But Texas Rule of Evidence 601(a)(2) gives the court authority to disqualify children if they seem to lack sufficient intellect to relate the facts. This determination—a Rule 104(a) decision—could rest on the court's determination of whether the child meets the four common law criteria.

§ 6-2(D). Judges and Attorneys

Article VI also contains rules which prohibit presiding judges from testifying as witnesses in cases before them. *See* Rule 605. And although the rules of evidence do not address the issue, Codes of Professional Responsibility and Model Codes of Conduct generally prohibit attorneys from acting both as witnesses and counsel in the same case.

§ 6-2(E). Jurors

Although it is rare that an attorney has grounds to object, under Federal Rule 606(a), jurors are not competent to testify as a witness in the case in which they are sitting. And under Rule 606(b), jurors are not permitted to testify about certain aspects of their deliberations, i.e., any matter or statement which may have had an impact on their deliberations. Jurors, under the Federal Rule, may testify about whether any extraneous prejudicial information or outside influence was brought to bear upon their deliberations. The reason for this rule is that courts are very hesitant to impeach a jury's verdict.

The question of what amounts to extraneous prejudicial information is not always easy to divine. Does it mean that jurors cannot discuss their life experiences, or report what they heard on the radio about the case? What if one of the jurors falls asleep during the trial, or deliberations? That issue was addressed by the Supreme Court in *Tanner v. United States*.

TANNER v. UNITED STATES
483 U.S. 107 (1987)

O'CONNOR, J.

Petitioners William Conover and Anthony Tanner were convicted of conspiring to defraud the United States in violation of 18 U.S.C. § 371, and of committing mail fraud in violation of 18 U.S.C. § 1341. The United States Court of Appeals for the Eleventh Circuit affirmed the convictions. Petitioners argue that the District Court erred in refusing to admit juror testimony at a post-verdict hearing on juror intoxication during the trial. We affirm in part and remand.

I

* * * * *

The day before petitioners were scheduled to be sentenced, Tanner filed a motion, in which Conover subsequently joined, seeking continuance of the sentencing date, permission to interview jurors, an evidentiary hearing, and a new trial. According to an affidavit accompanying the motion, Tanner's attorney had received an unsolicited telephone call from one of the trial jurors, Vera Asbul. Juror Asbul informed Tanner's attorney that several of the jurors consumed alcohol during the lunch breaks at various times throughout the trial, causing them to sleep through the afternoons. The District Court continued the sentencing date, ordered the parties to file memoranda, and heard argument on the motion to interview jurors. The District Court concluded that juror testimony on intoxication was inadmissible under Federal Rule of Evidence 606(b) to impeach the jury's verdict. The District Court invited petitioners to call any nonjuror witnesses, such as courtroom personnel, in support of the motion for new trial. Tanner's counsel took the stand and testified that he had observed one of the jurors "in a sort of giggly mood" at one point during the trial but did not bring this to anyone's attention at the time.

Earlier in the hearing the judge referred to a conversation between defense counsel and the judge during the trial on the possibility that jurors were sometimes falling asleep. During that extended exchange the judge twice advised counsel to immediately inform the court if they observed jurors being inattentive, and suggested measures the judge would take if he were so informed:

"MR. MILBRATH [defense counsel]: But, in any event, I've noticed over a period of several days that a couple of jurors in particular have been taking long naps during the trial.

"THE COURT: Is that right. Maybe I didn't notice because I was—

"MR. MILBRATH: I imagine the Prosecutors have noticed that a time or two.

"THE COURT: What's your solution?

"MR. MILBRATH: Well, I just think a respectful comment from the Court that if any of them are getting drowsy, they just ask for a break or something might be helpful.

"THE COURT: Well, here's what I have done in the past—and, you have to do it very diplomatically, of course: I once said, I remember, 'I think we'll just let everybody stand up and stretch, it's getting a little sleepy in here,' I said, but that doesn't sound good in the record. "I'm going to—not going to take on that responsibility. If any of you think you see that happening, ask for a bench conference and come up and tell me about it and I'll figure out what to do about it, and I won't mention who suggested it.

"MR. MILBRATH: All right.

"THE COURT: But, I'm not going to sit here and watch. I'm—among other things, I'm not going to see—this is off the record. "(Discussion had off the record.). "This is a new thing to this jury, and I don't know how interesting it is to them or not; some of them look like they're pretty interested. And, as I say, if you don't think they are, come up and let me know and I'll figure how—either have a recess or—which is more than likely what I would do."

As the judge observed during the hearing, despite the above admonitions counsel did not bring the matter to the court again.

The judge also observed that in the past courtroom employees had alerted him to problems with the jury. "Nothing was brought to my attention in this case about anyone appearing to be intoxicated," the judge stated, adding, "I saw nothing that suggested they were."

Following the hearing the District Court filed an order stating that "[o]n the basis of the admissible evidence offered I specifically find that the motions for leave to interview jurors or for an evidentiary hearing at which jurors would be witnesses is not required or appropriate." The District Court also denied the motion for new trial..

While the appeal of this case was pending before the Eleventh Circuit, petitioners filed another new trial motion based on additional evidence of jury misconduct. In another affidavit, Tanner's attorney stated that he received an unsolicited visit at his residence from a second juror, Daniel Hardy. Despite the fact that the District Court had denied petitioners' motion for leave to interview jurors, two days after Hardy's visit Tanner's attorney arranged for Hardy to be interviewed by two private investigators. The interview was transcribed, sworn to by the juror, and attached to the new trial motion. In the interview Hardy stated that he "felt like ... the jury was on one big party." Hardy indicated that seven of the jurors drank alcohol during the noon recess. Four jurors, including Hardy, consumed between them "a pitcher to three pitchers" of beer during various recesses. Of the three other jurors who were alleged to have consumed alcohol, Hardy stated that on several occasions he observed two jurors having one or two mixed drinks during the lunch recess, and one other juror, who was also the foreperson, having a liter of wine on each of three occasions. Juror Hardy also stated that he and three other jurors smoked marijuana quite regularly during the trial. Moreover, Hardy stated that during the trial he observed one juror ingest cocaine five times and another juror ingest cocaine two or three times. One juror sold a quarter pound of marijuana to another juror during the trial, and took marijuana, cocaine, and drug paraphernalia into the courthouse. Hardy noted that some of the jurors were falling asleep during the trial, and that one of the jurors described himself to Hardy as "flying." Hardy stated that before he visited Tanner's attorney at his residence, no one had contacted him concerning the jury's conduct, and Hardy had not been offered anything in return for his statement. Hardy said that he came forward "to clear my conscience" and "because I felt ... that the people on the jury didn't have no business being on the jury. I felt ... that Mr. Tanner should have a better opportunity to get somebody that would review the facts right."

The District Court denied petitioners' motion for a new trial.

The Court of Appeals for the Eleventh Circuit affirmed. We granted certiorari to consider whether the District Court was required to hold an evidentiary hearing, including juror testimony, on juror alcohol and drug use during the trial.

II

Petitioners argue that the District Court erred in not ordering an additional evidentiary hearing at which jurors would testify concerning drug and alcohol use during the trial. Petitioners assert that, contrary to the holdings of the District Court and the Court of Appeals, juror testimony on ingestion of drugs or alcohol during the trial is not barred by Federal Rule of Evidence 606(b). Moreover, petitioners argue that whether or not authorized by Rule 606(b), an evidentiary hearing including juror testimony on drug and alcohol use is compelled by their Sixth Amendment right to trial by a competent jury.

By the beginning of this century, if not earlier, the near-universal and firmly established common-law rule in the United States flatly prohibited the admission of juror testimony to impeach a jury verdict.

Exceptions to the common-law rule were recognized only in situations in which an "extraneous influence," *Mattox v. United States*, 146 U.S. 140 (1892), was alleged to have affected the jury. In *Mattox*, this Court held admissible the testimony of jurors describing how they heard and read prejudicial information not admitted into evidence. The Court allowed juror testimony on influence by outsiders in *Parker v. Gladden*, 385 U.S. 363 (1966) (bailiff's comments on defendant), and *Remmer v. United States*, 347 U.S. 227 (1954) (bribe offered to juror). *See also Smith v. Phillips*, 455 U.S. 209 (1982) (juror in criminal trial had submitted an application for employment at the District Attorney's office). In situations that did not fall into this exception for external influence, however, the Court adhered to the common-law rule against admitting juror testimony to impeach a verdict.

Lower courts used this external/internal distinction to identify those instances in which juror testimony impeaching a verdict would be admissible. The distinction was not based on whether the juror was literally inside or outside the jury room when the alleged irregularity took place; rather, the distinction was based on the nature of the allegation. Clearly a rigid distinction based only on whether the event took place inside or outside the jury room would have been quite unhelpful. For example, under a distinction based on location a juror could not testify concerning a newspaper read inside the jury room. Instead, of course, this has been considered an external influence about which juror testimony is admissible. Similarly, under a rigid locational distinction jurors could be regularly required to testify after the verdict as to whether they heard and comprehended the judge's instructions, since the charge to the jury takes place outside the jury room. Courts wisely have treated allegations of a juror's inability to hear or comprehend at trial as an internal matter. *See Government of the Virgin Islands v. Nicholas*, 759 F.2d 1073 (CA3 1985); *Davis v. United States*, 47 F.2d 1071 (CA5 1931) (rejecting juror testimony impeaching verdict, including testimony that jurors had not heard a particular instruction of the court).

Substantial policy considerations support the common-law rule against the admission of jury testimony to impeach a verdict. As early as 1915 this Court explained the necessity of shielding jury deliberations from public scrutiny: "[L]et it once be established that verdicts solemnly made and publicly returned into court can be attacked and set aside on the testimony of those who took part in their publication and all verdicts could be, and many would be, followed by an inquiry in the hope of discovering something which might invalidate the finding. Jurors would be harassed and beset by the defeated party in an effort to secure from them evidence of facts which might establish misconduct sufficient to set aside a verdict. If evidence thus secured could be thus used, the result would be to make what was intended to be a private deliberation, the constant subject of public investigation—to the destruction of all frankness and freedom of discussion and conference." *McDonald v. Pless*, 238 U.S.264, 267-268 (1915).

The Court's holdings requiring an evidentiary hearing where extrinsic influence or relationships have tainted the deliberations do not detract from, but rather harmonize with, the weighty government interest in insulating the jury's deliberative process. *See Smith v. Phillips*, 455 U.S. 209 (1982) (juror in criminal trial had submitted an application for employment at the District Attorney's office); *Remmer v. United States*, 347 U.S. 227 (1954) (juror reported attempted bribe during trial and was subjected to investigation).

There is little doubt that post-verdict investigation into juror misconduct would in some instances lead to the invalidation of verdicts reached after irresponsible or improper juror behavior. It is not at all clear, however, that the jury system could survive such efforts to perfect it. Allegations of juror misconduct, incompetency, or inattentiveness, raised for the first time days, weeks, or months after the verdict, seriously disrupt the finality of the process. Moreover, full and frank discussion in the jury room, jurors' willingness to return an unpopular verdict, and the community's trust in a system that relies on the decisions of laypeople would all be undermined by a barrage of post-verdict scrutiny of juror conduct.

Federal Rule of Evidence 606(b) is grounded in the common-law rule against admission of jury testimony to impeach a verdict and the exception for juror testimony relating to extraneous influences.

Petitioners have presented no argument that Rule 606(b) is inapplicable to the juror affidavits and the further inquiry they sought in this case, and, in fact, there appears to be virtually no support for such a proposition. Rather, petitioners argue that substance abuse constitutes an improper "outside influence" about which jurors may testify under Rule 606(b). In our view the language of the Rule cannot easily be stretched to cover this circumstance. However severe their effect and improper their use, drugs or alcohol voluntarily ingested by a juror seems no more an "outside influence" than a virus, poorly prepared food, or a lack of sleep.

In any case, whatever ambiguity might linger in the language of Rule 606(b) as applied to juror intoxication is resolved by the legislative history of the Rule. In 1972, following criticism of a proposed rule that would have allowed considerably broader use of juror testimony to impeach verdicts, the Advisory Committee drafted the present version of Rule 606(b). This Court adopted the present version of Rule 606(b) and transmitted it to Congress.

[T]he legislative history demonstrates with uncommon clarity that Congress specifically understood, considered, and rejected a version of Rule 606(b) that would have allowed jurors to testify on juror conduct during deliberations, including juror intoxication. This legislative history provides strong support for the most reasonable reading of the language of Rule 606(b) — that juror intoxication is not an "outside influence" about which jurors may testify to impeach their verdict.

Finally, even if Rule 606(b) is interpreted to retain the common-law exception allowing post-verdict inquiry of juror incompetence in cases of "substantial if not wholly conclusive evidence of incompetency," the showing made by petitioners falls far short of this standard.

As described above, long-recognized and very substantial concerns support the protection of jury deliberations from intrusive inquiry. Petitioners' Sixth Amendment interests in an unimpaired jury, on the other hand, are protected by several aspects of the trial process. The suitability of an individual for the responsibility of jury service, of course, is examined during voir dire. Moreover, during the trial the jury is observable by the court, by counsel, and by court personnel. *See United States v. Provenzano*, 620 F.2d 985, 996-997 (CA3 1980) (marshal discovered sequestered juror smoking marijuana during early morning hours). Moreover, jurors are observable by each other, and may report inappropriate juror behavior to the court before they render a verdict. Finally, after the trial a party may seek to impeach the verdict by nonjuror evidence of misconduct. *See United States v. Taliaferro*, 558 F.2d 724 (CA4 1977) (court considered records of club where jurors dined, and testimony of marshal who accompanied jurors, to determine whether jurors were intoxicated during deliberations). Indeed, in this case the District Court held an evidentiary hearing giving petitioners ample opportunity to produce nonjuror evidence supporting their allegations.

In light of these other sources of protection of petitioners' right to a competent jury, we conclude that the District Court did not err in deciding, based on the inadmissibility of juror testimony and the clear insufficiency of the nonjuror evidence offered by petitioners, that an additional post-verdict evidentiary hearing was unnecessary.

PEÑA–RODRIGUEZ v. COLORADO
137 S.Ct. 855 (2017)|

Justice KENNEDY delivered the opinion of the Court.

The jury is a central foundation of our justice system and our democracy. Whatever its imperfections in a particular case, the jury is a necessary check on governmental power. The jury, over the centuries, has been an inspired, trusted, and effective instrument for resolving factual disputes and determining ultimate questions of guilt or innocence in criminal cases. Over the long course its judgments find acceptance in the community, an acceptance essential to respect for the rule of law. The jury is a tangible implementation of the principle that the law comes from the people.

Like all human institutions, the jury system has its flaws, yet experience shows that fair and impartial verdicts can be reached if the jury follows the court's instructions and undertakes deliberations that are honest, candid, robust, and based on common sense. A general rule has evolved to give substantial protection to verdict finality and to assure jurors that, once their verdict has been entered, it will not later be called into question based on the comments or conclusions they expressed during deliberations. This principle, itself centuries old, is often referred to as the no-impeachment rule. The instant case presents the question whether there is an exception to the no-impeachment rule when, after the jury is discharged, a juror comes forward with compelling evidence that another juror made clear and explicit statements indicating that racial animus was a significant motivating factor in his or her vote to convict.

I

State prosecutors in Colorado brought criminal charges against petitioner, Miguel Angel Peña–Rodriguez, based on the following allegations. In 2007, in the bathroom of a Colorado horse-racing facility, a man sexually assaulted two teenage sisters. The girls told their father and identified the man as an employee of the racetrack. The police located and arrested petitioner. Each girl separately identified petitioner as the man who had assaulted her.

The State charged petitioner with harassment, unlawful sexual contact, and attempted sexual assault on a child. Before the jury was empaneled, members of the venire were repeatedly asked whether they believed that they could be fair and impartial in the case. A written questionnaire asked if there was "anything about you that you feel would make it difficult for you to be a fair juror." The court repeated the question to the panel of prospective jurors and encouraged jurors to speak in private with the court if they had any concerns about their impartiality. Defense counsel likewise asked whether anyone felt that "this is simply not a good case" for them to be a fair juror. None of the empaneled jurors expressed any reservations based on racial or any other bias. And none asked to speak with the trial judge.

After a 3–day trial, the jury found petitioner guilty of unlawful sexual contact and harassment, but it failed to reach a verdict on the attempted sexual assault charge.

Following the discharge of the jury, petitioner's counsel entered the jury room to discuss the trial with the jurors. As the room was emptying, two jurors remained to speak with counsel in private. They stated that, during deliberations, another juror had expressed anti-Hispanic bias toward petitioner and petitioner's alibi witness. Petitioner's counsel reported this to the court and, with the court's supervision, obtained sworn affidavits from the two jurors.

The affidavits by the two jurors described a number of biased statements made by another juror, identified as Juror H.C. According to the two jurors, H.C. told the other jurors that he "believed the defendant was guilty because, in [H.C.'s] experience as an ex-law enforcement officer, Mexican men had a bravado that caused them to believe they could do whatever they wanted with women." The jurors reported that H.C. stated his belief that Mexican men are physically controlling of women because of their sense of entitlement, and further stated, " 'I think he did it because he's Mexican and Mexican men take whatever they want.' " According to the jurors, H.C. further explained that, in his experience, "nine times out of ten Mexican men were guilty of being aggressive toward women and young girls." . Finally, the jurors recounted that Juror H.C. said that he did not find petitioner's alibi witness credible because, among other things, the witness was " 'an illegal.' " (In fact, the witness testified during trial that he was a legal resident of the United States.)

After reviewing the affidavits, the trial court acknowledged H.C.'s apparent bias. But the court denied petitioner's motion for a new trial, noting that "[t]he actual deliberations that occur among the jurors are protected from inquiry under [Colorado Rule of Evidence] 606(b)." Like its federal counterpart, Colorado's Rule 606(b) generally prohibits a juror from testifying as to any statement made during deliberations in a proceeding inquiring into the validity of the verdict.

The Colorado Supreme Court affirmed. The prevailing opinion relied on two decisions of this Court rejecting constitutional challenges to the federal no-impeachment rule as applied to evidence of juror misconduct or bias. See *Tanner v. United States,* 483 U.S. 107 (1987); *Warger v. Shauers,* 135 S.Ct. 521 (2014). After reviewing those precedents, the court could find no "dividing line between different *types* of juror bias or misconduct," and thus no basis for permitting impeachment of the verdicts in petitioner's trial, notwithstanding H.C.'s apparent racial bias. This Court granted certiorari to decide whether there is a constitutional exception to the no-impeachment rule for instances of racial bias.

Juror H.C.'s bias was based on petitioner's Hispanic identity, which the Court in prior cases has referred to as ethnicity, and that may be an instructive term here. Yet we have also used the language of race when discussing the relevant constitutional principles in cases involving Hispanic persons. Petitioner and respondent both refer to race, or to race and ethnicity, in this more expansive sense in their briefs to the Court. This opinion refers to the nature of the bias as racial in keeping with the primary terminology employed by the parties and used in our precedents.

II

A

At common law jurors were forbidden to impeach their verdict, either by affidavit or live testimony. This rule originated in *Vaise v. Delaval,* 1 T.R. 11, 99 Eng. Rep. 944 (K.B. 1785). There, Lord Mansfield excluded juror testimony that the jury had decided the case through a game of chance. The Mansfield rule, as it came to be known, prohibited jurors, after the verdict was entered, from testifying either about their subjective mental processes or about objective events that occurred during deliberations.

American courts adopted the Mansfield rule as a matter of common law, though not in every detail. Some jurisdictions adopted a different, more flexible version of the no-impeachment bar known as the "Iowa rule." Under that rule, jurors were prevented only from testifying about their own subjective beliefs, thoughts, or motives during deliberations. Jurors could, however, testify about objective facts and events occurring during deliberations, in part because other jurors could corroborate that testimony.

An alternative approach, later referred to as the federal approach, stayed closer to the original Mansfield rule. Under this version of the rule, the no-impeachment bar permitted an exception only for testimony about events extraneous to the deliberative process, such as reliance on outside evidence—newspapers, dictionaries, and the like—or personal investigation of the facts.

The common-law development of the no-impeachment rule reached a milestone in 1975, when Congress adopted the Federal Rules of Evidence, including Rule 606(b). Congress, like the *McDonald* Court, rejected the Iowa rule. Instead it endorsed a broad no-impeachment rule, with only limited exceptions.

[Rule 606(b)] has substantial merit. It promotes full and vigorous discussion by providing jurors with considerable assurance that after being discharged they will not be summoned to recount their deliberations, and they will not otherwise be harassed or annoyed by litigants seeking to challenge the verdict. The rule gives stability and finality to verdicts.

B

Some version of the no-impeachment rule is followed in every State and the District of Columbia. Variations make classification imprecise, but, as a general matter, it appears that 42 jurisdictions follow the Federal Rule, while 9 follow the Iowa Rule. Within both classifications there is a diversity of approaches. Nine jurisdictions that follow the Federal Rule have codified exceptions other than those listed in Federal Rule 606(b). At least 16 jurisdictions, 11 of which follow the Federal Rule, have recognized an exception to the no-impeachment bar under the circumstances the Court faces here: juror testimony that racial bias played a part in deliberations. According to the parties and *amici,* only one State other than Colorado has addressed this issue and declined to recognize an exception for racial bias. *See Commonwealth v. Steele,* 599 Pa. 341, 377–379, 961 A.2d 786, 807-808 (2008).

The federal courts, for their part, are governed by Federal Rule 606(b), but their interpretations deserve further comment. Various Courts of Appeals have had occasion to consider a racial bias exception and have reached different conclusions. Three have held or suggested there is a constitutional exception for evidence of racial bias. See *United States v. Villar,* 586 F.3d 76 (C.A.1 2009) (holding the Constitution demands a racial-bias exception); *United States v. Henley,* 238 F.3d 1111 (C.A.9 2001) (finding persuasive arguments in favor of an exception but not deciding the issue); *Shillcutt v. Gagnon,* 827 F.2d 1155 (C.A.7 1987) (observing that in some cases fundamental fairness could require an exception). One Court of Appeals has declined to find an exception, reasoning that other safeguards inherent in the trial process suffice to protect defendants' constitutional interests. See *United States v. Benally,* 546 F.3d 1230 (C.A.10 2008). Another has suggested as much, holding in the habeas context that an exception for racial bias was not clearly established but indicating in dicta that no such exception exists. See *Williams v. Price,* 343 F.3d 223, 237–239 (C.A.3 2003) (Alito, J.). And one Court of Appeals has held that evidence of racial bias is excluded by Rule 606(b), without addressing whether the Constitution may at times demand an exception. See *Martinez v. Food City, Inc.,* 658 F.2d 369 (C.A.5 1981).

III

It must become the heritage of our Nation to rise above racial classifications that are so inconsistent with our commitment to the equal dignity of all persons. This imperative to purge racial prejudice from the administration of justice was given new force and direction by the ratification of the Civil War Amendments.

The duty to confront racial animus in the justice system is not the legislature's alone. Time and again, this Court has been called upon to enforce the Constitution's guarantee against state-sponsored racial discrimination in the jury system. In an effort to ensure that individuals who sit on juries are free of racial bias, the Court has held that the Constitution at times demands that defendants be permitted to ask questions about racial bias during *voir dire.*

The unmistakable principle underlying these precedents is that discrimination on the basis of race, odious in all aspects, is especially pernicious in the administration of justice. The jury is to be "a criminal defendant's fundamental 'protection of life and liberty against race or color prejudice. Permitting racial prejudice in the jury system damages "both the fact and the perception" of the jury's role as "a vital check against the wrongful exercise of power by the State

IV
A

This case lies at the intersection of the Court's decisions endorsing the no-impeachment rule and its decisions seeking to eliminate racial bias in the jury system. The two lines of precedent, however, need not conflict.

The stigma that attends racial bias may make it difficult for a juror to report inappropriate statements during the course of juror deliberations. It is one thing to accuse a fellow juror of having a personal experience that improperly influences her consideration of the case, as would have been required in *Warger.* It is quite another to call her a bigot.

The recognition that certain of the *Tanner* safeguards may be less effective in rooting out racial bias than other kinds of bias is not dispositive. All forms of improper bias pose challenges to the trial process. But there is a sound basis to treat racial bias with added precaution. A constitutional rule that racial bias in the justice system must be addressed—including, in some instances, after the verdict has been entered—is necessary to prevent a systemic loss of confidence in jury verdicts, a confidence that is a central premise of the Sixth Amendment trial right.

B

For the reasons explained above, the Court now holds that where a juror makes a clear statement that indicates he or she relied on racial stereotypes or animus to convict a criminal defendant, the Sixth Amendment requires that the no-impeachment rule give way in order to permit the trial court to consider the evidence of the juror's statement and any resulting denial of the jury trial guarantee.

Not every offhand comment indicating racial bias or hostility will justify setting aside the no-impeachment bar to allow further judicial inquiry. For the inquiry to proceed, there must be a showing that one or more jurors made statements exhibiting overt racial bias that cast serious doubt on the fairness and impartiality of the jury's deliberations and resulting verdict. To qualify, the statement must tend to show that racial animus was a significant motivating factor in the juror's vote to convict. Whether that threshold showing has been satisfied is a matter committed to the substantial discretion of the trial court in light of all the circumstances, including the content and timing of the alleged statements and the reliability of the proffered evidence.

The practical mechanics of acquiring and presenting such evidence will no doubt be shaped and guided by state rules of professional ethics and local court rules, both of which often limit counsel's post-trial contact with jurors. These limits seek to provide jurors some protection when they return to their daily affairs after the verdict has been entered. But while a juror can always tell counsel they do not wish to discuss the case, jurors in some instances may come forward of their own accord.

That is what happened here. In this case the alleged statements by a juror were egregious and unmistakable in their reliance on racial bias. Not only did juror H.C. deploy a dangerous racial stereotype to conclude petitioner was guilty and his alibi witness should not be believed, but he also encouraged other jurors to join him in convicting on that basis.

While the trial court concluded that Colorado's Rule 606(b) did not permit it even to consider the resulting affidavits, the Court's holding today removes that bar. When jurors disclose an instance of racial bias as serious as the one involved in this case, the law must not wholly disregard its occurrence.

C

As the preceding discussion makes clear, the Court relies on the experiences of the 17 jurisdictions that have recognized a racial-bias exception to the no-impeachment rule—some for over half a century—with no signs of an increase in juror harassment or a loss of juror willingness to engage in searching and candid deliberations.

The experience of these jurisdictions, and the experience of the courts going forward, will inform the proper exercise of trial judge discretion in these and related matters. This case does not ask, and the Court need not address, what procedures a trial court must follow when confronted with a motion for a new trial based on juror testimony of racial bias. The Court also does not decide the appropriate standard for determining when evidence of racial bias is sufficient to require that the verdict be set aside and a new trial be granted.

D

It is proper to observe as well that there are standard and existing processes designed to prevent racial bias in jury deliberations. The advantages of careful *voir dire* have already been noted. And other safeguards deserve mention.

Trial courts, often at the outset of the case and again in their final jury instructions, explain the jurors' duty to review the evidence and reach a verdict in a fair and impartial way, free from bias of any kind. Some instructions are framed by trial judges based on their own learning and experience. Model jury instructions likely take into account these continuing developments and are common across jurisdictions. Instructions may emphasize the group dynamic of deliberations by urging jurors to share their questions and conclusions with their colleagues.

Probing and thoughtful deliberation improves the likelihood that other jurors can confront the flawed nature of reasoning that is prompted or influenced by improper biases, whether racial or otherwise. These dynamics can help ensure that the exception is limited to rare cases.

The Nation must continue to make strides to overcome race-based discrimination. The progress that has already been made underlies the Court's insistence that blatant racial prejudice is antithetical to the functioning of the jury system and must be confronted in egregious cases like this one despite the general bar of the no-impeachment rule. It is the mark of a maturing legal system that it seeks to understand and to implement the lessons of history. The Court now seeks to strengthen the broader principle that society can and must move forward by achieving the thoughtful, rational dialogue at the foundation of both the jury system and the free society that sustains our Constitution.

The judgment of the Supreme Court of Colorado is reversed, and the case is remanded for further proceedings not inconsistent with this opinion.

[Justice THOMAS, ALITO, and THE CHIEF JUSTICE dissented]

The *Peña–Rodriguez* decision raises several questions: Should the racial bias exception be extended to civil cases as well? And what about instances where a juror exhibits bias during deliberations based on gender? Religion?

§ 6-2(F). Dead Man's Statutes or Rules

Some jurisdictions, through statute or court rule, limit the ability of parties in litigation involving estates from relating statements made by a decedent. The purpose of these provisions is to prevent one party from fraudulently claiming what a decedent said, when the other side has no real opportunity to disprove that matter. Although the federal rules do not include such a provision, Federal Rule of Evidence 601 recognizes that in civil actions, a state's competency of witnesses rule, e.g. a dead man's statute, might apply where an element of a claim or defense rests on state law.

In Texas, Rule of Evidence 601(b) specifically includes a "Dead Man's Rule" which limits testimony about uncorroborated oral statements made by a decedent, testator, intestate, or ward in civil cases by or against executors, administrators, or guardians.

In summary, that rule works like this: Assume that A and B entered into a contract and that during the performance of the contract A makes a number of oral statements to B. Before the contract is fully performed, A dies.

B later sues E, the executor of A's estate to recover for damages arising from A's failure to perform the contract. Thus the case involves an action "by or against executors...in which judgment may be rendered for or against them as such...".

At trial, B is not permitted to testify about A's (decedent) oral statements to B unless they are (1) corroborated or (2) E calls B to the stand and asks B about the statements.

At trial, E is not permitted to testify about A's (decedent) oral statements unless they are (1) corroborated or (2) B calls E to the stand and asks E about the statements.

Either party could call a disinterested witness (one who has no stake in the outcome of the trial) to testify about A's oral statements, whether corroborated or not. The Rule protects the parties from each other's testimony, but not from disinterested witnesses who happened to hear the statement. Nor does it protect the parties from a decedent's written statements.

§ 6-3. Examination of Witnesses

§ 6-3(A). In General

As noted in Chapter One, the normal progression of questioning is for the proponent to call his or her witness to the stand and pose non-leading direct examination questions. The opponent follows with cross-examination and possible impeachment of the witness. The proponent is then able to attempt to rehabilitate the credibility of his or her witness or clarify matters raised during cross-examination. Article VI of the Federal Rules of Evidence contain a number of specific rules which govern the questioning of witnesses during trial. Those rules are addressed in the following discussion.

§ 6-3(B). Exclusion of Witnesses

In order to keep the witnesses from listening to each other's testimony, Federal Rule of Evidence 615 recognizes the ability of the trial court to sequester, or exclude, those witnesses from the courtroom. The court must do so if requested by a party, and may do so *sua sponte*. Note that the Rule includes several exemptions or exceptions. For example, a party or an individual whose presence in the court room is essential will not be sequestered under this rule.

§ 6-3(C). Oaths or Affirmations

Even though presumed competent, witnesses must clear two additional hurdles before they can testify. They must take an oath or affirmation (as governed by Rule 603), and they must have "personal knowledge" of the matter which they will testify about. *See* Rule 602, discussed *infra*.

The requirement of an oath or affirmation focuses on what at common law was considered the moral capacity element of the competency requirements; a person was not considered competent to testify unless he or she expressed a belief in God and was willing to take an oath to tell the truth. Now, the requirement simply requires the witness to indicate through an oath, or affirmation, that he or she will tell the truth—without any statement concerning a belief, or unbelief, in God. Indeed, under Federal Rule of Evidence 610, a witness's religious beliefs are inadmissible on the issue of credibility.

Failure to take the oath or affirmation, however, may disqualify the witness from testifying. Note that the Rule permits the trial judge to use any form of oath or affirmation, as long as it awakens the conscience of the witness to testify truthfully. The witness is normally not free to choose the form of the oath.

§ 6-3(D). The Personal Knowledge Requirement

Federal Rule of Evidence 602 indicates that a witness may not testify as to any matter unless the witness has personal knowledge about that matter. The personal knowledge requirement helps ensure that the fact finder receives only reliable evidence and may be satisfied through the testimony of the witness. For example, during direct testimony about an automobile accident, the witness may relate that she saw, and heard, the collision. Personal knowledge can be obtained through any of the five senses. But hearsay testimony (X testifying about what Y told her) does not constitute personal knowledge and could be excluded as hearsay. Remembering the humorous distortions in the childhood game "telephone" makes the personal knowledge requirement and its link to the hearsay prohibition understandable. The most credible person to testify about the original statement uttered in the game would not be the last child in the telephone chain—it would be the first.

Whether a witness has the requisite personal knowledge remains a determination for the judge, and then the jury, under Rule 104(b). That is, the judge determines initially whether there is enough evidence to support a finding by a rational juror that the witness has personal knowledge about the matter in question.

§ 6-3(E). Use of Interpreters

In situations where a witness requires the assistance of an interpreter, Rule of Evidence 604 indicates that the interpreter must qualify as an expert under Rule 702, and must take an oath or affirmation to make a truthful translation of what the witness says.

§ 6-3(F). Form and Order of Questioning — Control by the Court

Federal Rule of Evidence 611 vests in the trial court vast authority to control the trial, including the examination of witnesses and the order of proof. Although the normal order of proof is for the party bearing the burden of proof to put on its case first, followed by the opponent's case, the court may in appropriate circumstances take a witness out of order.

The Rule also recognizes the judge's authority to control the flow, tempo, and scope of questioning—in order to save time, promote effective presentation of the evidence, and avoid the harassment and undue embarrassment of witnesses. See Rule 611(a).

Federal Rule 611 also directs the normal method of questioning; leading questions are normally not permitted on direct examination, unless the witness is hostile or identified with the opposite party. Ordinarily, the opponent is permitted to use leading questions on cross-examination. In federal court, the scope of cross-examination is limited to matters raised on direct examination, or matters touching on the witness's credibility. In contrast, in Texas courts, the scope of cross-examination is open to any relevant matter in the case. *See* Texas Rule 611.

§ 6-3(G). Voir Dire of Witnesses

The term "voir dire" is normally associated with counsel's questioning of potential jurors in order to determine if grounds for challenging the juror exist. But the term is also used to describe the opponent's ability to question a witness to determine if the witness is competent, *see* Rule 601, and has personal knowledge, *see* Rule 602. Most frequently it is used to challenge the qualifications of an expert witness or the basis of the expert's opinion. Because it effectively involves an out-of-order questioning of a witness, it is subject to the trial court's discretion under Federal Rule of Evidence 611. Unless the judge believes that the jury will hear otherwise inadmissible or unreliable evidence, the judge will normally require the opponent to wait until cross-examination to reveal the weaknesses in the witness's testimony.

§ 6-3(H). Questions by the Court and Jurors

Federal Rule of Evidence 614 allows the court either sua sponte or on the motion of a party to call and question witness. When the court calls a witness both parties have a right to cross-examine the court's witness. Additionally, either party may object, although the objection should be entered outside the presence of the jury. There is no Texas equivalent to Federal Rule 614.

§ 6-3(I). Refreshing a Witness's Memory

If a witness suffers a lapse of memory while testifying, counsel may use a writing, or some other object, to refresh the witness's memory; the writing or object does not normally become the piece of evidence. Instead, the witness's memory is jogged and he finishes testifying. Federal Rule of Evidence 612 addresses the question of whether, and to what extent, the opponent may examine, and use, the writing used to jog the witness's memory. Under the rule, the opponent has a right to see the writing being used in court. If it appears that a witness has refreshed his memory before testifying, the court in its discretion may order disclosure of the writing to the opponent. The Rule permits the proponent to show that some of the material in the writing is not related to the case and block that disclosure; once the opponent has the writing, he or she may offer it into evidence.

As noted in Federal Rule of Evidence 803(5), if counsel is unsuccessful in refreshing the witness's memory, it may be possible to read the actual contents of the writing itself to the jury, as a "past recollection recorded" hearsay exception.

§ 6-3(J). Production of a Witness's Prior Statements

Experienced trial counsel fully appreciate the value of having a witness's pretrial statements in front of them when they are examining or cross-examining a witness. That prior statement may serve as a helpful outline for direct examination and for the opponent, it may be a way to find inconsistencies in the witness's testimony. Such pretrial statements are normally produced during discovery. Although the Federal Rules of Evidence do not make specific allowance for production of such statements, *cf.* Fed. R. Evid. 612, Texas Rule of Evidence 615 explicitly provides, in criminal cases, for production of a witness's (other than a defendant) prior statement once they have testified on direct examination. Failure to produce a statement as required by the rule may result in striking the witness's direct testimony; if the prosecution refuses to produce the prior statement of one of its witnesses, the court may order a mistrial.

§ 6-4. Rules Governing Credibility Evidence

§ 6-4(A). In General

Federal Rules of Evidence 607 through 610 and 613 govern impeachment. Impeachment serves as the means by which an attorney calls a witness's *credibility* into question. Because juries are free to decide cases based upon which witness's testimony they believe, questions of credibility can be critical in a case. Undercutting the opposing witness's credibility, while developing, preserving, and where necessary, rehabilitating your own witness's credibility thus becomes an invaluable tool for both trial strategy and technique. Understanding the impeachment rules involves knowing who may impeach, what types of evidence are admissible to impeach, what foundation (if any) must be laid to impeach, when impeachment has occurred, and what types of evidence are admissible to rehabilitate a witness's credibility.

§ 6-4(B). The Stages and Types of Credibility Evidence

There are three main stages in credibility evidence: (1) bolstering; (2) impeachment; and (3) rehabilitation.

§ 6-4(B)(1). Stage 1 — Bolstering

Bolstering of a witness's credibility occurs when the party calling the witness attempts to bolster or increase the witness's credibility *before* it has been attacked by the opponent. Because such an attack may never occur, bolstering is generally impermissible because it may needlessly extend the trial. In effect, bolstering is a form of premature rehabilitation. The no-bolstering rule is reflected in Federal Rule of Evidence 608(a) which, insofar as character evidence is concerned, specifically indicates that evidence of truthful character evidence regarding a witness may not be introduced until the witness's character for truthfulness has been impugned.

Forms of bolstering may be permitted, however, in some limited circumstances. Some jurisdictions, for example, permit the prosecution in a sexual assault case to present evidence that the victim made a "fresh complaint" about the attack (to show a lack of fabrication) before the victim's credibility is actually attacked.

§ 6-4(B)(2). Stage 2 — Impeachment

Impeachment may occur through several commonly used techniques. One brand of impeachment focuses specifically on the witness's testimony in the case itself. The other brand of impeachment evidence is that which generally attacks the witness, as an untruthful person. Together, a witness may be impeached by one or more of the following methods:

(1) Impeachment through evidence of Bias
(2) Impeachment by Showing a Prior Inconsistent Statement
(3) Impeachment through Character for Untruthfulness
(4) Impeachment through proof of a Witness's Specific Acts
(5) Impeachment by proof that a Witness has Been Convicted
(6) Impeachment by evidence which contradicts a Witness's Testimony

(7)   Impeachment by proof that the Witness Lacks one of the Common-Law Elements of Competency

(8)   Impeachment by Omission

§ 6-4(B)(3). Stage 3 — Rehabilitation

Once a witness has been impeached, counsel may attempt to rehabilitate the witness through one of the following methods:

(1)   Conducting Redirect Examination.
(2)   Introducing the Witness's Prior Consistent Statements.
(3)   Corroborating the Witness's Testimony.
(4)   Introducing Evidence of the Witness's Truthful Character.
(5)   Introducing Expert Testimony on the Witness's Credibility.

§ 6-4(C). Who May Impeach?

Under Federal Rule 607 any party (including the party who called the witness) may impeach any witness. At the common law, a party calling a witness was considered to have vouched for the veracity of its own witness. Rule 607 abolished that "voucher rule."

§ 6-5. Impeachment — Bias

The Federal Rules of Evidence do not specifically address the issue of using bias to impeach a witness. Does that mean that counsel in federal court is not permitted to use bias to impeach a witness? The Supreme Court addressed that question in *United States v. Abel*.

UNITED STATES v. ABEL
469 U.S. 45 (1984)

Justice REHNQUIST delivered the opinion of the Court.

A divided panel of the Court of Appeals for the Ninth Circuit reversed respondent's conviction for bank robbery. The Court of Appeals held that the District Court improperly admitted testimony which impeached one of respondent's witnesses. We hold that the District Court did not err, and we reverse.

Respondent John Abel and two cohorts were indicted for robbing a savings and loan... The cohorts elected to plead guilty, but respondent went to trial. One of the cohorts, Kurt Ehle, agreed to testify against respondent and identify him as a participant in the robbery.

Respondent informed the District Court at a pretrial conference that he would seek to counter Ehle's testimony with that of Robert Mills. Mills was not a participant in the robbery but was friendly with respondent and with Ehle, and had spent time with both in prison. Mills planned to testify that after the robbery Ehle had admitted to Mills that Ehle intended to implicate respondent falsely, in order to receive favorable treatment from the Government. The prosecutor in turn disclosed that he intended to discredit Mills' testimony by calling Ehle back to the stand and eliciting from Ehle the fact that respondent, Mills, and Ehle were all members of the "Aryan Brotherhood," a secret prison gang that required its members always to deny the existence of the organization and to commit perjury, theft, and murder on each member's behalf.

Defense counsel objected to Ehle's proffered rebuttal testimony as too prejudicial to respondent. After a lengthy discussion in chambers the District Court decided to permit the prosecutor to cross-examine Mills about the gang, and if Mills denied knowledge of the gang, to introduce Ehle's rebuttal testimony concerning the tenets of the gang and Mills' and respondent's membership in it. The District Court held that the probative value of Ehle's rebuttal testimony outweighed its prejudicial effect, but that respondent might be entitled to a limiting instruction if his counsel would submit one to the court.

At trial Ehle implicated respondent as a participant in the robbery. Mills, called by respondent, testified that Ehle told him in prison that Ehle planned to implicate respondent falsely. When the prosecutor sought to cross- examine Mills concerning membership in the prison gang, the District Court conferred again with counsel outside of the jury's presence, and ordered the prosecutor not to use the term "Aryan Brotherhood" because it was unduly prejudicial. Accordingly, the prosecutor asked Mills if he and respondent were members of a "secret type of prison organization" which had a creed requiring members to deny its existence and lie for each other. When Mills denied knowledge of such an organization the prosecutor recalled Ehle.

Ehle testified that respondent, Mills, and he were indeed members of a secret prison organization whose tenets required its members to deny its existence and "lie, cheat, steal [and] kill" to protect each other. The District Court sustained a defense objection to a question concerning the punishment for violating the organization's rules. Ehle then further described the organization and testified that "in view of the fact of how close Abel and Mills were" it would have been "suicide" for Ehle to have told Mills what Mills attributed to him. Respondent's counsel did not request a limiting instruction and none was given.

The jury convicted respondent. On his appeal a divided panel of the Court of Appeals reversed.

We hold that the evidence showing Mills' and respondent's membership in the prison gang was sufficiently probative of Mills' possible bias towards respondent to warrant its admission into evidence. Thus it was within the District Court's discretion to admit Ehle's testimony, and the Court of Appeals was wrong in concluding otherwise.

Both parties correctly assume, as did the District Court and the Court of Appeals, that the question is governed by the Federal Rules of Evidence. But the Rules do not by their terms deal with impeachment for "bias," although they do expressly treat impeachment by character evidence and conduct, Rule 608, by evidence of conviction of a crime, Rule 609, and by showing of religious beliefs or opinion, Rule 610. Neither party has suggested what significance we should attribute to this fact. Although we are nominally the promulgators of the Rules, and should in theory need only to consult our collective memories to analyze the situation properly, we are in truth merely a conduit when we deal with an undertaking as substantial as the preparation of the Federal Rules of Evidence. In the case of these Rules, too, it must be remembered that Congress extensively reviewed our submission, and considerably revised it.

Before the present Rules were promulgated, the admissibility of evidence in the federal courts was governed in part by statutes or Rules, and in part by case law. This Court had held in *Alford v. United States*, 282 U.S. 687 (1931), that a trial court must allow some cross-examination of a witness to show bias. This holding was in accord with the overwhelming weight of authority in the state courts as reflected in Wigmore's classic treatise on the law of evidence. Our decision in *Davis v. Alaska*, 415 U.S. 308 (1974), holds that the Confrontation Clause of the Sixth Amendment requires a defendant to have some opportunity to show bias on the part of a prosecution witness.

With this state of unanimity confronting the drafters of the Federal Rules of Evidence, we think it unlikely that they intended to scuttle entirely the evidentiary availability of cross-examination for bias.

Rule 401 defines as "relevant evidence" evidence having any tendency to make the existence of any fact that is of consequence to the determination of the action more probable or less probable than it would be without the evidence. Rule 402 provides that all relevant evidence is admissible, except as otherwise provided by the United States Constitution, by Act of Congress, or by applicable rule. A successful showing of bias on the part of a witness would have a tendency to make the facts to which he testified less probable in the eyes of the jury than it would be without such testimony.

We think the lesson to be drawn from all of this is that it is permissible to impeach a witness by showing his bias under the Federal Rules of Evidence just as it was permissible to do so before their adoption.

Ehle's testimony about the prison gang certainly made the existence of Mills' bias towards respondent more probable. Thus it was relevant to support that inference. Bias is a term used in the "common law of evidence" to describe the relationship between a party and a witness which might lead the witness to slant, unconsciously or otherwise, his testimony in favor of or against a party. Bias may be induced by a witness's like, dislike, or fear of a party, or by the witness's self-interest. Proof of bias is almost always relevant because the jury, as finder of fact and weigher of credibility, has historically been entitled to assess all evidence which might bear on the accuracy and truth of a witness's testimony. The "common law of evidence" allowed the showing of bias by extrinsic evidence, while requiring the cross-examiner to "take the answer of the witness" with respect to less favored forms of impeachment.

Mills' and respondent's membership in the Aryan Brotherhood supported the inference that Mills' testimony was slanted or perhaps fabricated in respondent's favor. A witness's and a party's common membership in an organization, even without proof that the witness or party has personally adopted its tenets, is certainly probative of bias.

Respondent argues that even if the evidence of membership in the prison gang were relevant to show bias, the District Court erred in permitting a full description of the gang and its odious tenets. Respondent contends that the District Court abused its discretion under Federal Rule of Evidence 403, because the prejudicial effect of the contested evidence outweighed its probative value. In other words, testimony about the gang inflamed the jury against respondent, and the chance that he would be convicted by his mere association with the organization outweighed any probative value the testimony may have had on Mills' bias.

Respondent specifically contends that the District Court should not have permitted Ehle's precise description of the gang as a lying and murderous group. Respondent suggests that the District Court should have cut off the testimony after the prosecutor had elicited that Mills knew respondent and both may have belonged to an organization together. This argument ignores the fact that the type of organization in which a witness and a party share membership may be relevant to show bias. If the organization is a loosely knit group having nothing to do with the subject matter of the litigation, the inference of bias arising from common membership may be small or nonexistent. If the prosecutor had elicited that both respondent and Mills belonged to the Book of the Month Club, the jury probably would not have inferred bias even if the District Court had admitted the testimony. The attributes of the Aryan Brotherhood—a secret prison sect sworn to perjury and self-protection—bore directly not only on the fact of bias but also on the source and strength of Mills' bias. The tenets of this group showed that Mills had a powerful motive to slant his testimony towards respondent, or even commit perjury outright.

A district court is accorded a wide discretion in determining the admissibility of evidence under the Federal Rules. Assessing the probative value of common membership in any particular group, and weighing any factors counseling against admissibility is a matter first for the district court's sound judgment under Rules 401 and 403 and ultimately, if the evidence is admitted, for the trier of fact.

Before admitting Ehle's rebuttal testimony, the District Court gave heed to the extensive arguments of counsel, both in chambers and at the bench. In an attempt to avoid undue prejudice to respondent the court ordered that the name "Aryan Brotherhood" not be used. The court also offered to give a limiting instruction concerning the testimony, and it sustained defense objections to the prosecutor's questions concerning the punishment meted out to unfaithful members. These precautions did not prevent all prejudice to respondent from Ehle's testimony, but they did, in our opinion, ensure that the admission of this highly probative evidence did not unduly prejudice respondent. We hold there was no abuse of discretion under Rule 403 in admitting Ehle's testimony as to membership and tenets.

Respondent makes an additional argument based on Rule 608(b). That Rule allows a cross-examiner to impeach a witness by asking him about specific instances of past conduct, other than crimes covered by Rule 609, which are probative of his veracity or "character for truthfulness or untruthfulness." The Rule limits the inquiry to cross-examination of the witness, however, and prohibits the cross-examiner from introducing extrinsic evidence of the witness's past conduct.

Respondent claims that the prosecutor cross-examined Mills about the gang not to show bias but to offer Mills' membership in the gang as past conduct bearing on his veracity. This was error under Rule 608(b), respondent contends, because the mere fact of Mills' membership, without more, was not sufficiently probative of Mills' character for truthfulness. Respondent cites a second error under the same Rule, contending that Ehle's rebuttal testimony concerning the gang was extrinsic evidence offered to impugn Mills' veracity, and extrinsic evidence is barred by Rule 608(b).

It seems clear to us that the proffered testimony with respect to Mills' membership in the Aryan Brotherhood sufficed to show potential bias in favor of respondent; because of the tenets of the organization described, it might also impeach his veracity directly. But there is no rule of evidence which provides that testimony admissible for one purpose and inadmissible for another purpose is thereby rendered inadmissible; quite the contrary is the case. It would be a strange rule of law which held that relevant, competent evidence which tended to show bias on the part of a witness was nonetheless inadmissible because it also tended to show that the witness was a liar.

We intimate no view as to whether the evidence of Mills' membership in an organization having the tenets ascribed to the Aryan Brotherhood would be a specific instance of Mills' conduct which could not be proved against him by extrinsic evidence except as otherwise provided in Rule 608(b). It was enough that such evidence could properly be found admissible to show bias.

The judgment of the Court of Appeals is reversed.

———————————

Note that the Supreme Court specifically reminded that the right of a criminal defendant to cross-examine a witness about that witness's bias may actually override other rules which would exclude the evidence. *See Davis v. Alaska*, 415 U.S. 308 (1974).

An example of bias would be the relationship to a party, past relationships, or a personal or financial stake in the outcome of a case. In Texas, as with prior inconsistent statements, before using extrinsic evidence to expose bias or interest, the opponent during cross-examination must give the witness the circumstances which show the bias, and give the witness the opportunity to admit or deny the bias/interest. Tex. R. Evid. 613(b).

Finally, it is important to note that the rules regarding specific instances of conduct (SICs) (rules 404, 405, 608, 609) do not regulate the admissibility of SICs when the SICs are used to show bias or interest.

§ 6-6. Impeachment — Prior Inconsistent Statement

Federal Rule of Evidence 613 governs use of prior inconsistent statements. A prior inconsistent statement exists when a witness's testimony on the stand contradicts a statement the witness made prior to trial. For example X testifies in court: "The light was red." But, X in a police report, said: "The light was green." X's statement in the police report is a prior inconsistent statement and may be used to impeach X's credibility.

Note that a prior inconsistent statement is not considered hearsay if it is introduced to show simply that an inconsistent statement was made. If, on the other hand, it is admitted to show the truth of the matter asserted in the prior statement, the proponent will have to address the hearsay aspects of the statement

In Texas, before impeaching a witness because of a prior inconsistent statement, the opponent must inform the witness of the inconsistent statement's contents, when it was made, the place of the statement, the individual to whom the statement was made, and give the witness the opportunity to admit or deny the statement. If the witness admits making the prior inconsistent statement, extrinsic evidence of the statement (here, the police report) cannot be admitted into evidence. *See* Rule 613(a).

§ 6-6(A). The Methodology — Texas

In Texas, the formal steps for impeaching a witness through use of a prior inconsistent statement are as follows:

STEP 1: **Determine if There is an "Inconsistency"**

    a. A statement (written or oral) was made by the witness; or

    b. The witness was silent at a time when a reasonable person would have been expected to speak up (*Cf.* Criminal Cases); or

    c. The witness engaged in inconsistent acts (Probably not covered by Rule);

STEP 2: **Confirm the Testimony Given on Direct Examination**

STEP 3: **Lay the Foundation (Rule 613)**

The witness in Texas must be placed on notice of the upcoming impeachment: If the statement is oral, counsel should merely draw attention to the following elements. If statement is written, either use in same way as oral (without having witness read it) or have witness actually read it silently. In any event, the Rule requires counsel to show the written statement to opposing counsel upon request.

    a. Contents of Statement;

    b. Time and Place of Statements;

    c. Person to Whom Made; and

STEP 4: **Determine if Witness is Denying or Admitting Statement**

    a. It is sometimes difficult to determine if there is a denial; what if witness says that he does not remember or is evasive?

    b. If Witness unequivocally admits statement—STOP: Impeachment is complete.

    c. If Witness denies or is evasive, go to STEP 5.

STEP 5: **Introduce Extrinsic Evidence of Statement if Witness Denies Making the Statement or is Evasive**

    a. Offer testimony of another witness who heard statement, or

    b. Introduce Writing Including Statement (only pertinent portions?); Some courts may not let counsel actually introduce writing, but may instead permit counsel to read the statement to the jury.

Under Texas Rule 613(a)(3), the witness must be given the opportunity to explain or deny the statement. But the Rule does not require that that opportunity be provided by the impeaching party. In most cases, the witness will get that opportunity on redirect examination.

§ 6-6(B). Comparison Chart

The following chart compares the Federal and Texas Rules of Evidence regarding impeachment by prior inconsistent statement.

Impeachment by Prior Inconsistent Statements

Comparison of Federal and Texas Rules

	Federal Rule 613	Texas Rule 613
Types of Statements Which May be Used	— Explicit Statements; — Admission by Silence; *Cf.* Privilege Against Self-Incrimination — Opinions — Probably does not cover inconsist. conduct/acts	Same as Federal Rule
Foundation Required?	No particular foundation required; federal drafters rejected *Queen's Case*	Witness must be apprised of particulars of prior statement (contents, time, place, etc.). Follows *Queens Case.*
Extrinsic Evidence of Statement Permitted?	Yes. But witness (at some point) must be given opportunity to "deny or explain" statement and opposing counsel must be given opportunity to question the witness UNLESS interests of justice otherwise require	Yes. But witness must *first* be examined about the statement. Extrinsic evidence is admissible only if the witness fails to unequivocally admit the statement.
Must Witness be Shown Written Statement?	No. But must be shown to opposing counsel on request	No. But must be shown to opposing counsel on request
Does Rule Apply to Statements by Party-Opponent as Defined in Rule 801?	No	No

§ 6-7. Impeachment — Character for Untruthfulness

Under Federal Rule 608(a), reputation testimony and opinion testimony about a witness's character for untruthfulness are admissible to impeach a witness. This is usually accomplished by calling a witness who has (1) a personal opinion on the untruthfulness of another witness, who has already testified or (2) has heard about the other witness's reputation for untruthfulness. This form of impeachment focuses on the person, not on the person's specific testimony in the case. Using this form of impeachment can be presented as a three-step process:

- Step 1. A "Target Witness" (any witness or party in the case) testifies;
- Step 2. A "Character Witness" testifies (as opinion or reputation witness) about the untruthful character of the Target Witness under Rule 608(a); and
- Step 3. The counsel who called the Target Witness to the stand, can cross-examine the Character Witness through "Have you Heard" or "Did you Know" questions under Rule 405. Under that mode of questioning, the cross-examiner can inquire into the prior "truthful" acts of the Target Witness. But counsel is bound by the Character Witness's answers to those questions.

§ 6-8. Impeachment — Proof of Specific Incidents of Conduct (SICs)

Under Federal Rule of Evidence 608(b), the cross-examiner may ask the witness about a prior specific incident of conduct reflecting on the witness's character, if that act is probative of truthfulness or untruthfulness. The questioner, however, is stuck with the answer, i.e., he may not prove the act through extrinsic evidence if the act is admissible only for purposes of attacking the witness's character. Under the federal rule, if the witness's SIC is not being used to show the witness's character, then the limitation in Rule 608(b) does not apply. For example, the SIC might be admissible to show the witness's bias. In Texas, the cross-examiner is not permitted to even ask the witness about a "character-SIC."

But a witness's SIC may be inquired into if the SIC resulted in a conviction and is admissible under Texas Rule 609, if it shows a witness's bias, under Texas Rules 613, if it is otherwise admissible under Rule 404(b), or if the witness has made a blanket denial of any prior wrongdoing. Like character evidence, *supra*, this sort of impeachment evidence focuses on attacking the witness, not the witness's specific testimony.

§ 6-9. Impeachment — Proof of Conviction

Federal Rule of Evidence 609 governs the admissibility of a witness's prior conviction for purposes of impeachment. The logical relevancy of this evidence is that if a person has shown a propensity to ignore social norms on a prior occasion, the witness is less likely to follow the norms associated with taking an oath and promising to tell the truth at trial. In effect, this type of impeachment evidence focuses on the person, not necessarily the specific facts in the case; to that extent it is more like character evidence, discussed, *supra*.

Rule 609 sets out specific requirements for impeaching a witness with a prior conviction. The following chart reflects the major differences in the Federal and Texas versions of the rule.

FEDERAL RULE 609 VS. TEXAS RULE OF EVIDENCE 609

Provision	Federal Rule 609	Texas Rule 609
Crimes Covered	(a) Crime punishable by death or imprisonment for more than one year, under law of jurisdiction (b) "Crimen falsi" offenses	Felony or moral turpitude, regardless of punishment
Notice of Intent to Use	Only if conviction is more than 10 years old	In all cases, upon request by opponent
Balancing Tests	(a)(1) Accused—probative value outweighs prejudice Other witnesses—Rule 403 (a)(2) "Crimen falsi"—no balancing (b) Old convictions —probative value substantially outweighs prejudice	(a) For all witnesses and convictions, probative value must outweigh prejudice (b) Old convictions—probative value substantially outweighs prejudice
Finality of Conviction	Pending Appeal does not exclude	Pending Appeal excludes

One of the key provisions in both the Federal and Texas Rule 609 requires the proponent to give notice of that he or she intends to use a prior conviction for impeachment purposes. That obviously gives the opponent an opportunity to assess carefully whether to put a particular witness on the stand and if so, what tactics to use to soften the potential damage to the witness's credibility. That can be critical where the witness is the criminal defendant. And that raises the question of whether a defense counsel is entitled to know before the defendant even takes the stand whether the trial judge will permit the prosecution to use a defendant's prior conviction. In *Luce v. United States*, the Supreme Court addressed that issue.

LUCE v. UNITED STATES
469 U.S. 38 (1984)

Chief Justice BURGER delivered the opinion of the Court.

We granted certiorari to resolve a conflict among the Circuits as to whether the defendant, who did not testify at trial, is entitled to review of the District Court's ruling denying his motion to forbid the use of a prior conviction to impeach his credibility.

I

Petitioner was indicted on charges of conspiracy, and possession of cocaine with intent to distribute, in violation of 21 U.S.C. §§ 846 and 841(a)(1). During his trial in the United States District Court for the Western District of Tennessee, petitioner moved for a ruling to preclude the Government from using a 1974 state conviction to impeach him if he testified. There was no commitment by petitioner that he would testify if the motion were granted, nor did he make a proffer to the court as to what his testimony would be. In opposing the motion, the Government represented that the conviction was for a serious crime—possession of a controlled substance.

The District Court ruled that the prior conviction fell within the category of permissible impeachment evidence under Federal Rule of Evidence 609(a). The District Court noted, however, that the nature and scope of petitioner's trial testimony could affect the court's specific evidentiary rulings; for example, the court was prepared to hold that the prior conviction would be excluded if petitioner limited his testimony to explaining his attempt to flee from the arresting officers. However, if petitioner took the stand and denied any prior involvement with drugs, he could then be impeached by the 1974 conviction. Petitioner did not testify, and the jury returned guilty verdicts.

II

The United States Court of Appeals for the Sixth Circuit affirmed.

III

It is clear, of course, that had petitioner testified and been impeached by evidence of a prior conviction, the District Court's decision to admit the impeachment evidence would have been reviewable on appeal along with any other claims of error. The Court of Appeals would then have had a complete record detailing the nature of petitioner's testimony, the scope of the cross- examination, and the possible impact of the impeachment on the jury's verdict.

A reviewing court is handicapped in any effort to rule on subtle evidentiary questions outside a factual context. This is particularly true under Rule 609(a)(1), which directs the court to weigh the probative value of a prior conviction against the prejudicial effect to the defendant. To perform this balancing, the court must know the precise nature of the defendant's testimony, which is unknowable when, as here, the defendant does not testify.

Any possible harm flowing from a district court's in limine ruling permitting impeachment by a prior conviction is wholly speculative. The ruling is subject to change when the case unfolds, particularly if the actual testimony differs from what was contained in the defendant's proffer. Indeed even if nothing unexpected happens at trial, the district judge is free, in the exercise of sound judicial discretion, to alter a previous in limine ruling. On a record such as here, it would be a matter of conjecture whether the District Court would have allowed the Government to attack petitioner's credibility at trial by means of the prior conviction.

When the defendant does not testify, the reviewing court also has no way of knowing whether the Government would have sought to impeach with the prior conviction. If, for example, the Government's case is strong, and the defendant is subject to impeachment by other means, a prosecutor might elect not to use an arguably inadmissible prior conviction.

Because an accused's decision whether to testify "seldom turns on the resolution of one factor," a reviewing court cannot assume that the adverse ruling motivated a defendant's decision not to testify. In support of his motion a defendant might make a commitment to testify if his motion is granted; but such a commitment is virtually risk free because of the difficulty of enforcing it.

Even if these difficulties could be surmounted, the reviewing court would still face the question of harmless error. Were in limine rulings under Rule 609(a) reviewable on appeal, almost any error would result in the windfall of automatic reversal; the appellate court could not logically term "harmless" an error that presumptively kept the defendant from testifying. Requiring that a defendant testify in order to preserve Rule 609(a) claims will enable the reviewing court to determine the impact any erroneous impeachment may have had in light of the record as a whole; it will also tend to discourage making such motions solely to "plant" reversible error in the event of conviction.

* * * * *

We hold that to raise and preserve for review the claim of improper impeachment with a prior conviction, a defendant must testify. Accordingly, the judgment of the Court of Appeals is affirmed.

The question arises: If the defendant decides to take the stand and knows that a prior conviction may be used against him or her during cross-examination, is there any benefit to admitting the conviction during direct examination, and thus taking the "sting" away from the prosecution? And if the court has ruled *in limine* that the conviction is admissible, can the defendant testify about the conviction and then on appeal argue that the judge's ruling was incorrect?

Those issues were addressed by the Supreme Court in *Ohler v. United States*.

OHLER v. UNITED STATES
529 U.S. 753 (2000)

Chief Justice REHNQUIST delivered the opinion of the Court.

Maria Ohler drove a van from Mexico to California in July 1997. As she passed through the San Ysidro Port of Entry, a customs inspector noticed that someone had tampered with one of the van's interior panels. Inspectors searched the van and discovered approximately 81 pounds of marijuana. Ohler was arrested and charged with importation of marijuana and possession of marijuana with the intent to distribute. Before trial, the Government filed motions in limine seeking to admit Ohler's prior felony conviction as character evidence under Federal Rule of Evidence 404(b) and as impeachment evidence under Rule 609(a)(1). The District Court denied the motion to admit the conviction as character evidence, but reserved ruling on whether the conviction could be used for impeachment purposes. On the first day of trial, the District Court ruled that if Ohler testified, evidence of her prior conviction would be admissible under Rule 609(a)(1). She testified in her own defense, denying any knowledge of the marijuana. She also admitted on direct examination that she had been convicted of possession of methamphetamine in 1993. The jury found Ohler guilty of both counts…

On appeal, Ohler challenged the District Court's in limine ruling allowing the Government to use her prior conviction for impeachment purposes. The Court of Appeals for the Ninth Circuit affirmed, holding that Ohler waived her objection by introducing evidence of the conviction during her direct examination. We granted certiorari to resolve a conflict among the Circuits regarding whether appellate review of an in limine ruling is available in this situation.

Generally, a party introducing evidence cannot complain on appeal that the evidence was erroneously admitted. Ohler seeks to avoid the consequences of this well-established commonsense principle by invoking Rules 103 and 609 of the Federal Rules of Evidence. But neither of these Rules addresses the question at issue here. Rule 103 sets forth the unremarkable propositions that a party must make a timely objection to a ruling admitting evidence and that a party cannot challenge an evidentiary ruling unless it affects a substantial right. The Rule does not purport to determine when a party waives a prior objection, and it is silent with respect to the effect of introducing evidence on direct examination, and later assigning its admission as error on appeal.

Rule 609(a) is equally unavailing for Ohler; it merely identifies the situations in which a witness's prior conviction may be admitted for impeachment purposes. The Rule originally provided that admissible prior conviction evidence could be elicited from the defendant or established by public record during cross-examination, but it was amended in 1990 to clarify that the evidence could also be introduced on direct examination. According to Ohler, it follows from this amendment that a party does not waive her objection to the in limine ruling by introducing the evidence herself. However, like Rule 103, Rule 609(a) simply does not address this issue. There is no question that the Rule authorizes the eliciting of a prior conviction on direct examination, but it does no more than that.

Next, Ohler argues that it would be unfair to apply such a waiver rule in this situation because it compels a defendant to forgo the tactical advantage of preemptively introducing the conviction in order to appeal the in limine ruling. She argues that if a defendant is forced to wait for evidence of the conviction to be introduced on cross-examination, the jury will believe that the defendant is less credible because she was trying to conceal the conviction. The Government disputes that the defendant is unduly disadvantaged by waiting for the prosecution to introduce the conviction on cross-examination. First, the Government argues that it is debatable whether jurors actually perceive a defendant to be more credible if she introduces a conviction herself. Second, even if jurors do consider the defendant more credible, the Government suggests that it is an unwarranted advantage because the jury does not realize that the defendant disclosed the conviction only after failing to persuade the court to exclude it.

Whatever the merits of these contentions, they tend to obscure the fact that both the Government and the defendant in a criminal trial must make choices as the trial progresses. For example, the defendant must decide whether or not to take the stand in her own behalf. If she has an innocent or mitigating explanation for evidence that might otherwise incriminate, acquittal may be more likely if she takes the stand. A defendant has a further choice to make if she decides to testify, notwithstanding a prior conviction. The defendant must choose whether to introduce the conviction on direct examination and remove the sting or to take her chances with the prosecutor's possible elicitation of the conviction on cross-examination.

The Government, too, in a case such as this, must make a choice. If the defendant testifies, it must choose whether or not to impeach her by use of her prior conviction. Here the trial judge had indicated he would allow its use, but the Government still had to consider whether its use might be deemed reversible error on appeal. This choice is often based on the Government's appraisal of the apparent effect of the defendant's testimony. If she has offered a plausible, innocent explanation of the evidence against her, it will be inclined to use the prior conviction; if not, it may decide not to risk possible reversal on appeal from its use.

Due to the structure of trial, the Government has one inherent advantage in these competing trial strategies. Cross-examination comes after direct examination, and therefore the Government need not make its choice until the defendant has elected whether or not to take the stand in her own behalf and after the Government has heard the defendant testify. Petitioner's submission would deny to the Government its usual right to decide, after she testifies, whether or not to use her prior conviction against her. She seeks to short-circuit that decisional process by offering the conviction herself (and thereby removing the sting) and still preserve its admission as a claim of error on appeal.

Only when the government exercises its option to elicit the testimony is an appellate court confronted with a case where, under the normal rules of trial, the defendant can claim the denial of a substantial right if in fact the district court's in limine ruling proved to be erroneous. In our view, there is nothing "unfair," as petitioner puts it, about putting petitioner to her choice in accordance with the normal rules of trial.

Finally, Ohler argues that applying this rule to her situation unconstitutionally burdens her right to testify. She relies on *Rock v. Arkansas*, 483 U.S. 44 (1987), where we held that a prohibition of hypnotically refreshed testimony interfered with the defendant's right to testify. But here the rule in question does not prevent Ohler from taking the stand and presenting any admissible testimony which she chooses. She is of course subject to cross-examination and subject to impeachment by the use of a prior conviction. In a sense, the use of these tactics by the Government may deter a defendant from taking the stand.

For these reasons, we conclude that a defendant who preemptively introduces evidence of a prior conviction on direct examination may not on appeal claim that the admission of such evidence was error. The judgment of the Court of Appeals for the Ninth Circuit is therefore affirmed. It is so ordered.

---

§ 6-10. Impeachment — Contradictory Evidence

Counsel may impeach a witness, not by directly attacking the witness's credibility, but by presenting clearly contradictory (hopefully irrefutable) evidence. Doing so, at least indirectly presents a sort of swearing match between the witnesses.

§ 6-11. Impeachment — Lack of Element of Competency

As noted, *supra*, at the common law, courts applied four factors in determining whether a witness was competent to testify: Moral capacity; Mental capacity to observe; Mental capacity to recall; and Mental capacity to narrate. Although those four elements have generally been subsumed into other particular rules of evidence, the list serves as an aid in determining whether the witness's weakness in one of those elements is subject to attack at trial. For example, it may be shown that the witness could not have seen the accident because she was not in a position to see it. Or a witness's difficulty in remembering the details of an incident may cast doubt on the witness's credibility.

§ 6-12. Rehabilitation of Impeached Witness

Once a witness's credibility has been attacked, the counsel who called the witness normally attempts to rehabilitate the witness, although there is a school of thought that it may be better simply to ignore the opponent's attacks as though they did not really hurt. The following discussion briefly notes the various methods of rehabilitation.

§ 6-12(A). Rehabilitation — Conducting Redirect Examination

If a witness's credibility has been attacked during cross-examination, counsel may repair the damage by conducting redirect examination. During that examination counsel may attempt to ask the witness to explain inconsistencies or address points raised during the cross-examination.

§ 6-12(B). Rehabilitation — Prior Consistent Statements

A witness's prior consistent statements may be admissible under Federal Rule 801 to rebut any prior inconsistent statements or implications that the witness recently fabricated his or her testimony or has been subject to undue influence. Note, however, that the timing of the prior consistent statement is critical. The Supreme Court addressed that issue in *Tome v. United States*.

TOME v. UNITED STATES
513 U.S. 150 (1995)

Justice KENNEDY delivered the opinion of the Court, except as to Part IIB.

Various federal Courts of Appeals are divided over the evidence question presented by this case. At issue is the interpretation of a provision in the Federal Rules of Evidence bearing upon the admissibility of statements, made by a declarant who testifies as a witness, that are consistent with the testimony and are offered to rebut a charge of a "recent fabrication or improper influence or motive." Fed. Rule Evid. 801(d)(1)(B). The question is whether out-of-court consistent statements made after the alleged fabrication, or after the alleged improper influence or motive arose, are admissible under the Rule.

I

Petitioner Tome was charged in a one-count indictment with the felony of sexual abuse of a child, his own daughter, aged four at the time of the alleged crime. The case having arisen on the Navajo Indian Reservation, Tome was tried by a jury in the United States District Court for the District of New Mexico, where he was found guilty...

* * * * *

The prosecution's theory was that Tome committed sexual assaults upon the child while she was in his custody and that the crime was disclosed when the child was spending vacation time with her mother. The defense argued that the allegations were concocted so the child would not be returned to her father. At trial A.T., then six and one half years old, was the Government's first witness. For the most part, her direct testimony consisted of one- and two-word answers to a series of leading questions. Cross-examination took place over two trial days. The defense asked A.T. 348 questions. On the first day A.T. answered all the questions posed to her on general, background subjects.

The next day there was no testimony, and the prosecutor met with A.T. When cross-examination of A.T. resumed, she was questioned about those conversations but was reluctant to discuss them. Defense counsel then began questioning her about the allegations of abuse, and it appears she was reluctant at many points to answer. As the trial judge noted, however, some of the defense questions were imprecise or unclear. The judge expressed his concerns with the examination of A.T., observing there were lapses of as much as 40-55 seconds between some questions and the answers and that on the second day of examination the witness seemed to be losing concentration. The trial judge stated, "We have a very difficult situation here."

After A.T. testified, the Government produced six witnesses who testified about a total of seven statements made by A.T. describing the alleged sexual assaults.

A.T.'s out-of-court statements, recounted by the six witnesses, were offered by the Government under Rule 801(d)(1)(B). The trial court admitted all of the statements over defense counsel's objection, accepting the Government's argument that they rebutted the implicit charge that A.T.'s testimony was motivated by a desire to live with her mother. The court also admitted A.T.'s August 22d statement to her babysitter under Rule 803(24), and the statements to Dr. Kuper (and apparently also to Dr. Reich) under Rule 803(4) (statements for purposes of medical diagnosis). The Government offered the testimony of the social worker under both Rules 801(d)(1)(B) and 803(24), but the record does not indicate whether the court ruled on the latter ground. No objection was made to Dr. Spiegel's testimony. Following trial, Tome was convicted and sentenced to 12 years imprisonment.

* * * * *

The prevailing common-law rule for more than a century before adoption of the Federal Rules of Evidence was that a prior consistent statement introduced to rebut a charge of recent fabrication or improper influence or motive was admissible if the statement had been made before the alleged fabrication, influence, or motive came into being, but it was inadmissible if made afterwards. As Justice Story explained: "[W]here the testimony is assailed as a fabrication of a recent date ... in order to repel such imputation, proof of the antecedent declaration of the party may be admitted."

McCormick and Wigmore stated the rule in a more categorical manner: "The applicable principle is that the prior consistent statement has no relevancy to refute the charge unless the consistent statement was made before the source of the bias, interest, influence or incapacity originated." E. Cleary, MCCORMICK ON EVIDENCE § 49, p. 105 (2d ed. 1972). *See also* 4 J. Wigmore, EVIDENCE § 1128, p. 268 (J. Chadbourn rev. 1972). The question is whether Rule 801(d)(1)(B) embodies this temporal requirement. We hold that it does.

A

Rule 801 provides: "(d) Statements which are not hearsay.—A statement is not hearsay if— "(1) Prior statement by witness.—The declarant testifies at the trial or hearing and is subject to cross-examination concerning the statement, and the statement is ... "(B) consistent with the declarant's testimony and is offered to rebut an express or implied charge against the declarant of recent fabrication or improper influence or motive."

Rule 801 defines prior consistent statements as nonhearsay only if they are offered to rebut a charge of "recent fabrication or improper influence or motive." Fed. Rule Evid. 801(d)(1)(B). Noting the "troublesome" logic of treating a witness's prior consistent statements as hearsay at all (because the declarant is present in court and subject to cross-examination), the Advisory Committee decided to treat those consistent statements, once the preconditions of the Rule were satisfied, as nonhearsay and admissible as substantive evidence, not just to rebut an attack on the witness's credibility. A consistent statement meeting the requirements of the Rule is thus placed in the same category as a declarant's inconsistent statement made under oath in another proceeding, or prior identification testimony, or admissions by a party opponent.

The Rules do not accord this weighty, nonhearsay status to all prior consistent statements. To the contrary, admissibility under the Rules is confined to those statements offered to rebut a charge of "recent fabrication or improper influence or motive," the same phrase used by the Advisory Committee in its description of the "traditional" common law of evidence, which was the background against which the Rules were drafted. Prior consistent statements may not be admitted to counter all forms of impeachment or to bolster the witness merely because she has been discredited. In the present context, the question is whether A.T.'s out-of-court statements rebutted the alleged link between her desire to be with her mother and her testimony, not whether they suggested that A.T.'s in-court testimony was true. The Rule speaks of a party rebutting an alleged motive, not bolstering the veracity of the story told.

This limitation is instructive, not only to establish the preconditions of admissibility but also to reinforce the significance of the requirement that the consistent statements must have been made before the alleged influence, or motive to fabricate arose. That is to say, the forms of impeachment within the Rule's coverage are the ones in which the temporal requirement makes the most sense. A consistent statement that predates the motive is a square rebuttal of the charge that the testimony was contrived as a consequence of that motive. By contrast, prior consistent statements carry little rebuttal force when most other types of impeachment are involved.

There may arise instances when out-of-court statements that postdate the alleged fabrication have some probative force in rebutting a charge of fabrication or improper influence or motive, but those statements refute the charged fabrication in a less direct and forceful way. Evidence that a witness made consistent statements after the alleged motive to fabricate arose may suggest in some degree that the in-court testimony is truthful, and thus suggest in some degree that that testimony did not result from some improper influence; but if the drafters of Rule 801(d)(1)(B) intended to countenance rebuttal along that indirect inferential chain, the purpose of confining the types of impeachment that open the door to rebuttal by introducing consistent statements becomes unclear. If consistent statements are admissible without reference to the time frame we find imbedded in the Rule, there appears no sound reason not to admit consistent statements to rebut other forms of impeachment as well. Whatever objections can be leveled against limiting the Rule to this designated form of impeachment and confining the rebuttal to those statements made before the fabrication or improper influence or motive arose, it is clear to us that the drafters of Rule 801(d)(1)(B) were relying upon the common-law temporal requirement.

The underlying theory of the Government's position is that an out-of-court consistent statement, whenever it was made, tends to bolster the testimony of a witness and so tends also to rebut an express or implied charge that the testimony has been the product of an improper influence.

Congress could have adopted that rule with ease, providing, for instance, that "a witness's prior consistent statements are admissible whenever relevant to assess the witness's truthfulness or accuracy." The theory would be that, in a broad sense, any prior statement by a witness concerning the disputed issues at trial would have some relevance in assessing the accuracy or truthfulness of the witness's in- court testimony on the same subject. The narrow Rule enacted by Congress, however, cannot be understood to incorporate the Government's theory.

Our analysis is strengthened by the observation that the somewhat peculiar language of the Rule bears close similarity to the language used in many of the common law cases that describe the premotive requirement. "Rule 801(d)(1)(B) employs the precise language—'rebut[ting] ... charge[s] ... of recent fabrication or improper influence or motive'—consistently used in the panoply of pre-1975 decisions."

The language of the Rule, in its concentration on rebutting charges of recent fabrication, improper influence and motive to the exclusion of other forms of impeachment, as well as in its use of wording which follows the language of the common-law cases, suggests that it was intended to carry over the common-law pre-motive rule.

B

Our conclusion that Rule 801(d)(1)(B) embodies the common-law premotive requirement is confirmed by an examination of the Advisory Committee Notes to the Federal Rules of Evidence. We have relied on those well- considered Notes as a useful guide in ascertaining the meaning of the Rules. *See, e.g., Huddleston v. United States*, 485 U.S. 681, 688 (1988). Where, as with Rule 801(d)(1)(B), "Congress did not amend the Advisory Committee's draft in any way ... the Committee's commentary is particularly relevant in determining the meaning of the document Congress enacted." *Beech Aircraft Corp. v. Rainey*, 488 U.S. 153, at 165-166, n. 9 (1988). The Notes are also a respected source of scholarly commentary. Professor Cleary was a distinguished commentator on the law of evidence, and he and members of the Committee consulted and considered the views, criticisms, and suggestions of the academic community in preparing the Notes.

The Notes disclose a purpose to adhere to the common law in the application of evidentiary principles, absent express provisions to the contrary. The Notes give no indication, however, that Rule 801(d)(1)(B) abandoned the premotive requirement.

Throughout their discussion of the Rules, the Advisory Committee Notes rely on Wigmore and McCormick as authority for the common-law approach. In light of the categorical manner in which those authors state the premotive requirement it is difficult to imagine that the drafters, who noted the new substantive use of prior consistent statements, would have remained silent if they intended to modify the premotive requirement.

C

The Government's final argument in favor of affirmance is that the common-law premotive rule advocated by petitioner is inconsistent with the Federal Rules' liberal approach to relevancy and with strong academic criticism, beginning in the 1940's, directed at the exclusion of out-of-court statements made by a declarant who is present in court and subject to cross- examination. This argument misconceives the design of the Rules' hearsay provisions.

Hearsay evidence is often relevant. "The only way in which the probative force of hearsay differs from the probative force of other testimony is in the absence of oath, demeanor, and cross-examination as aids in determining credibility." That does not resolve the matter, however. Relevance is not the sole criterion of admissibility. Otherwise, it would be difficult to account for the Rules' general proscription of hearsay testimony (absent a specific exception), *see* Fed. Rule Evid. 802, let alone the traditional analysis of hearsay that the Rules, for the most part, reflect. That certain out- of-court statements may be relevant does not dispose of the question whether they are admissible.

The Government's reliance on academic commentators critical of excluding out- of-court statements by a witness is subject to like criticism. . . .

D

The case before us illustrates some of the important considerations supporting the Rule as we interpret it, especially in criminal cases. If the Rule were to permit the introduction of prior statements as substantive evidence to rebut every implicit charge that a witness's in-court testimony results from recent fabrication or improper influence or motive, the whole emphasis of the trial could shift to the out-of-court statements, not the in-court ones. The present case illustrates the point. . . .

We are aware that in some cases it may be difficult to ascertain when a particular fabrication, influence, or motive arose. Yet, as the Government concedes, a majority of common-law courts were performing this task for well over a century and the Government has presented us with no evidence that those courts, or the judicial circuits that adhere to the rule today, have been unable to make the determination. . . .

III

Courts must be sensitive to the difficulties attendant upon the prosecution of alleged child abusers. In almost all cases a youth is the prosecution's only eye witness. But "[t]his Court cannot alter evidentiary rules merely because litigants might prefer different rules in a particular class of cases." When a party seeks to introduce out-of- court statements that contain strong circumstantial indicia of reliability, that are highly probative on the material questions at trial, and that are better than other evidence otherwise available, there is no need to distort the requirements of Rule 801(d)(1)(B). If its requirements are met, Rule 803(24) exists for that eventuality. We intimate no view, however, concerning the admissibility of any of A.T.'s out-of-court statements under that section, or any other evidentiary principle. These matters, and others, are for the Court of Appeals to decide in the first instance.

Our holding is confined to the requirements for admission under Rule 801(d)(1)(B). The Rule permits the introduction of a declarant's consistent out-of-court statements to rebut a charge of recent fabrication or improper influence or motive only when those statements were made before the charged recent fabrication or improper influence or motive. These conditions of admissibility were not established here.

The judgment of the Court of Appeals for the Tenth Circuit is reversed, and the case is remanded for further proceedings consistent with this opinion.

Federal Rule 801(d)(1)(B), which was amended after the *Tome* decision, now provides that a prior consistent statement may be admitted for its truth if it is used to rehabilitate the "declarants" credibility as a witness when attacked on another ground..." It is not clear at this point whether the federal courts will apply the *Tome* timing requirement where the witness has been impeached on grounds other than showing a recent fabrication or improper motive.

§ 6-12(C). Rehabilitation — Corroborating Testimony

Just as an opponent may attack the credibility of a witness by introducing evidence which contradicts the witness's testimony, a witness's credibility may be bolstered or rehabilitated by introducing evidence which corroborates the witness's testimony. If the proponent offers too much corroborating, or cumulative, evidence about a witness or issue in the case, the opponent may be able to successfully block such repetitious testimony by making a Rule 403 objection.

§ 6-12(D). Rehabilitation — Evidence of Truthful Character

Under Rule 608(a), once a witness's character for truthfulness has been attacked through character evidence for untruthfulness, in the form of reputation or opinion evidence or otherwise (e.g., slashing cross-examination), counsel who called the witness is free to offer evidence of the witness's character for truthfulness.

§ 6-12(E). Introduce Expert Testimony

There is some authority for the proposition that if the credibility of a child-abuse victim has been attacked, the proponent may offer expert testimony to show that child abuse victims naturally tend to act in fairly predictable ways after such an act of abuse and that in the expert's opinion, the child in the case exhibits those same characteristics. The courts which have addressed this issue generally prohibit any attempt to use the expert as a sort of "human lie detector." That is, an expert may not be permitted to testify that in his or her expert opinion, the witness is telling the truth.

§ 6-13. Questions and Notes

a.   What is the logical relevance of credibility evidence under Rule 401? Specifically, what is the logical relevance of each type of credibility evidence, i.e., bias evidence, prior inconsistent statements, or contradiction?

b.   What, if any, extrinsic or intrinsic policy considerations govern the admissibility of the various types of credibility evidence?

c.   It is important to remember the potential role of Rules 403 and 105. The former serves as a safety-net objection for an opponent and the latter insures that the jury will consider the credibility evidence for its limited purpose.

§ 6-14. Problems

a. Using Rule 606(b), in the federal and Texas versions, determine whether the following pieces of information, learned in post-trial interviews of jurors in a criminal trial, are admissible. Assume that the following occurred during the jury's deliberations.

 1. The fact that the jury foreperson verbally threatened other jurors to vote to convict the defendant.

 2. Information that a juror shared her negative feelings about Catholics and the defendant in the case is a Catholic.

 3. The fact that a juror consumed alcohol during a lunch break and then fell asleep in the jury deliberation room.

 4. The fact that a juror conducted a Google search on road delays that had been introduced in the case, but did not tell any of the other jurors about it.

 5. The fact that one of the jurors received word that her minor child had been taken to the hospital and that as a result, she changed her vote to move things along during deliberations.

 6. The fact that one of the jurors received an email from a friend who related information about the criminal record of one of the defense witnesses, which had not been admitted at trial, and shared it with the other jurors.

 7. Information that the jury deliberately disregarded the judge's instructions not to consider evidence of the defendant's prior criminal record, which was offered at trial but not admitted.

 8. Information that the jury cast dice to decide whether the defendant was guilty.

 9. The fact that one of the jurors had received a phone message on her cell phone during deliberations—from an unknown source—threatening her family if she did not vote for acquittal.

b. Assume that the defendant in a criminal trial is being tried in 2020 for selling illegal drugs to an undercover agent in a criminal trial. Using Rule 609 in both the Federal and Texas versions, consider the admissibility of using the defendant's prior convictions to impeach him if he takes the stand:

 1. A 2015 Virginia conviction for simple assault and battery. He was charged with aggravated assault, a felony carrying a five-year penalty, but he pleaded not guilty. He was found guilty by a jury of the lesser, misdemeanor, offense of simple assault and battery. He was sentenced to six months confinement.

2. A federal perjury conviction in 2002. He had testified falsely in a federal drug trial. He attempted to plead guilty to a lesser offense, but the judge rejected the guilty plea. The federal perjury statute sets a base sentence of at least one year in confinement. His conviction was later overturned by a federal appeals court.

3. A 2011 Illinois conviction for the offense of transferring crack cocaine. He pleaded nolo contendere and was sentenced to five years confinement in the state penitentiary. He was released from confinement in 2013. Under Illinois law, the offense is considered a felony.

4. A 2018 Texas misdemeanor conviction for theft by deceit. He was found guilty and sentenced to a six-month prison sentence.

c. At a personal injury trial involving a traffic accident, Johnny Hernandez testifies for the defense that the plaintiff had told people at the scene of the accident that he was feeling just fine after the accident. The plaintiff wishes to cross-examine the defense witness on several matters. Using both the federal and Texas rules, decide whether the plaintiff may inquire into the following:

1. The fact that Hernandez was arrested, but not charged, for DUI, two years ago.

2. The fact that Hernandez and the plaintiff were once very good friends but had a falling out over a girlfriend several years before the accident. The girlfriend is now the plaintiff's wife.

3. The fact that Hernandez lied on his job application with HEB in 2018. Counsel has a copy of the false job application entries.

d. Assume that Mr. Bobby Norton has just finished testifying on direct examination in a personal injury case styled: *Bloomer v. LostsaTools*. He testified on behalf of Jackson Bloomer and stated that he was with Bloomer at the time he started up a rental chain saw that injured Bloomer. He also stated that he never heard anyone associated with the company give safety instructions or say anything about being careful with the chain saw.

You are representing the defendant, LotsaTools. You have in your possession an e-mail written by Mr. Norton to a hunting buddy, Charlie Winston, about the incident.

Be prepared to impeach Mr. Norton using that letter on cross-examination. The professor will play the role of Mr. Norton. The e-mail reads as follows:

From: BNorton@dmail.com

To: Charlieangel@bol.com

Sent: November 6, 2019 3:45 PM

Subject: Gene Pool Story!!!

Charlie:

Did you hear what happened to Jackson last weekend? That idiot cut his arm badly using a chain saw that he rented from that new place on Main Street—Lottatools or something like that. Needed 20 stitches in his arm. Lucky he did not cut it off.

I told him that he had no business renting a chain saw and that he needed to be careful. But you know Jackson. As always, he did not listen to the instructions the guy gave us.

The rental tool guy told Jackson that he needed to have the chain saw on the ground when he started it. But no, buckaroo Jackson decided to be a big man and hold it out as he pulled the cord.

See you on the course weekend?

e. At a trial involving a breach of contract on a land sale, *Anders v. Smith*, the plaintiff introduced evidence to show that Mary Smith decided not to go through with a land sale of her ranch to Larry Anders. Assume that Johnny Rogers, a defense witness, has just finished testifying on direct examination on behalf of the defendant, Mary Smith. She told Rogers that Anders breached the contract first. There was some evidence in the case, however, that Smith breached the contract because of her personal animus against Anders over a past personal relationship. When asked about that point during direct examination, Rogers testified that he never heard Ms. Smith make comments to him that she was going to get even with Larry Anders for dumping her several years earlier for another woman, Sally Wilson.

You are representing the plaintiff, Mr. Anders. You have in your possession a copy of an undated handwritten note by Rogers to another rancher, Nathan Norris, regarding the land deal. Assume it was produced during discovery.

Be prepared to impeach Mr. Rogers using his note on cross-examination. The professor will play the role of Mr. Rogers. The note reads as follows:

Nathan—

I guess you heard about the big lawsuit that Anders is bringing against Mary over her ranch at Kerrville.

I sure hope that Anders does not hear about her conversation with me a year ago. Mary said that she was going to get even with Larry Anders over his affair with Sally Wilson.

She said that he broke her heart and that she would never forget what he did.

Johnny

CHAPTER SEVEN

OPINION EVIDENCE & EXPERTS

§ 7-1. Introduction to Opinion Testimony

Article VII governs the admissibility of opinion testimony. Historically the courts have expressed a strong preference for in-court factual testimony relayed by witnesses with personal knowledge. Consequently, the rules governing the admissibility of opinion testimony, like the rules governing hearsay and best evidence, generally operate as rules of preference. Where necessity exists and reliability can be established, opinion testimony will be admissible provided that the proponent has adequately laid the applicable foundation. Two types of opinion testimony exist under Article VII—opinion testimony given by lay persons and opinion testimony given by experts.

§ 7-2. Lay Opinion Testimony — Rule 701

Lay opinion testimony is governed by Federal Rule of Evidence 701. Rule 701 allows a lay witness to give opinion testimony that is based on personal knowledge where the opinion will help the jury either understand the witness's own testimony or help the jury determine a fact issue. Personal knowledge serves as the foundation for lay opinion testimony, while the "helpfulness" requirement establishes the lay opinion's relevancy.

§ 7-2(A). Collective Facts and Skilled Observations

Lay opinion testimony may be offered to prove either a collective fact, or a skilled observation. Collective facts state a witness's conclusory opinion, rather than the numerous, complex, or potentially inarticulable facts upon which the opinion is based. An example of a collective fact opinion would be the speed of a car. Rather than setting forth the numerous elements which contribute to the witness's conclusion (i.e. "the wheels were spinning so fast I couldn't see the hub caps, the car reached the end of Mulberry street in the blink of an eye, four other cars were left in the dust, and I clocked it at 95 mph"), the witness simply states her conclusion ("The car was going very fast").

Skilled observations, on the other hand, usually come into play where witnesses, because of their familiarity with something, can form an opinion regarding its authenticity. For example, a husband could offer an opinion as to whether or not a particular document was written by his wife.

§ 7-2(B). The Scope of Lay Opinion Testimony

The scope of lay opinion testimony is limited by the personal knowledge and relevancy requirements, and the requirement that the opinion testimony not be based upon "scientific, technical, or other specialized knowledge within the scope of Rule 702." Under Rule 704, a lay opinion may even address the case's ultimate issue.

§ 7-3. Expert Opinion

Federal Rules of Evidence 702-706 govern the admissibility of expert testimony. Under Rule 702, expert testimony may be solicited when scientific, technical, or specialized knowledge would help the jury understand the evidence or determine a fact issue. Helpfulness serves as the initial threshold to admissibility. As with lay opinion testimony it is what establishes the testimony's relevancy.

§ 7-3(A). Laying the Foundation — Qualifying the Witness as an Expert

Before soliciting an expert opinion from a witness, the proponent must first lay the foundation by qualifying the witness as an expert. As governed by Rule 702, the proponent must show that the witness has the knowledge, skill, experience, training or education to testify as an expert. Also implicit in this foundation is that the witness meets the competency requirements of Rule 601. The proponent may then offer the witness as an expert to the court. Before entering an objection, the opponent may voir dire the witness regarding the witness's qualifications to serve as an expert.

§ 7-3(B). Opinion Testimony — Three Elements

Expert opinion testimony is potentially comprised of three elements: the theory, the underlying data, and the conclusion. The theory is the framework which supplies the guiding principles the expert will use to develop the opinion. The data are the facts the expert examines and uses as the basis for the opinion. The opinion is the expert's conclusion. Applying the given facts to the theoretical framework, the conclusion is what the expert believes the facts establish. Forming an expert opinion is similar to the way a law student develops an answer to a final exam question. The student applies legal principles (theories) to a given factual situation to form his or her answer (opinion).

§ 7-3(B)(1) The Underlying Theory

Nothing in the rules of evidence mandate that the expert lay out the guiding principles which he applied in forming the opinion. Having the expert state his theory, however, gives greater credibility to the expert's opinion testimony.

Assuming that a particular expert is capable of articulating the underlying theory, the question arises as to who should decide if the underlying theory is valid. This is particularly problematic where the proponent presents an "expert" who has propounded a new or novel scientific theory, which has not yet been tested by the scientific community. In addressing this issue most courts, until recently, applied what was commonly known as the *Frye* test. That test was first articulated in *Frye v. United States*, 293 F. 1013 (D.C. Cir. 1923), where the court addressed the admissibility of evidence derived from a forerunner of the polygraph test. The court said:

> Just when a scientific principle or discovery crosses the line between the experimental and demonstrable stages is difficult to define. Somewhere in this twilight zone the evidential force of the principle must be recognized, and while courts will go a long way in admitting expert testimony deduced from a well-recognized scientific principle or discovery, the thing from which the deduction is made must be

sufficiently established to have gained *general acceptance* in the particular field in which it belongs (emphasis added).

After the promulgation of the Federal Rules of Evidence, which do not specifically address the issue of expert testimony on scientific evidence, the question arose whether the rules had abrogated the familiar *Frye* test. The Supreme Court finally addressed that issue in *Daubert v. Merrell Dow Pharmaceuticals.*

DAUBERT v. MERRELL DOW PHARMACEUTICALS, INC.
506 U.S. 914 (1993)

Justice BLACKMUN delivered the opinion of the Court.

In this case we are called upon to determine the standard for admitting expert scientific testimony in a federal trial.

I

Petitioners Jason Daubert and Eric Schuller are minor children born with serious birth defects. They and their parents sued respondent in California state court, alleging that the birth defects had been caused by the mothers' ingestion of Bendectin, a prescription anti-nausea drug marketed by respondent. Respondent removed the suits to federal court on diversity grounds.

After extensive discovery, respondent moved for summary judgment, contending that Bendectin does not cause birth defects in humans and that petitioners would be unable to come forward with any admissible evidence that it does. In support of its motion, respondent submitted an affidavit of Steven H. Lamm, physician and epidemiologist, who is a well-credentialed expert on the risks from exposure to various chemical substances. Doctor Lamm stated that he had reviewed all the literature on Bendectin and human birth defects—more than 30 published studies involving over 130,000 patients. No study had found Bendectin to be a human teratogen (i.e., a substance capable of causing malformations in fetuses). On the basis of this review, Doctor Lamm concluded that maternal use of Bendectin during the first trimester of pregnancy has not been shown to be a risk factor for human birth defects.

Petitioners did not (and do not) contest this characterization of the published record regarding Bendectin. Instead, they responded to respondent's motion with the testimony of eight experts of their own, each of whom also possessed impressive credentials. These experts had concluded that Bendectin can cause birth defects. Their conclusions were based upon "in vitro" (test tube) and "in vivo" (live) animal studies that found a link between Bendectin and malformations; pharmacological studies of the chemical structure of Bendectin that purported to show similarities between the structure of the drug and that of other substances known to cause birth defects; and the "reanalysis" of previously published epidemiological (human statistical) studies.

The District Court granted respondent's motion for summary judgment. The court stated that scientific evidence is admissible only if the principle upon which it is based is "'sufficiently established to have general acceptance in the field to which it belongs.' " The court concluded that petitioners' evidence did not meet this standard.

The United States Court of Appeals for the Ninth Circuit affirmed. Citing *Frye v. United States*, 293 F. 1013, 1014 (1923), the court stated that expert opinion based on a scientific technique is inadmissible unless the technique is "generally accepted" as reliable in the relevant scientific community. The court declared that expert opinion based on a methodology that diverges "significantly from the procedures accepted by recognized authorities in the field ... cannot be shown to be 'generally accepted as a reliable technique.' "

We granted certiorari in light of sharp divisions among the courts regarding the proper standard for the admission of expert testimony.

II

A

In the 70 years since its formulation in the *Frye* case, the "general acceptance" test has been the dominant standard for determining the admissibility of novel scientific evidence at trial. Although under increasing attack of late, the rule continues to be followed by a majority of courts, including the Ninth Circuit.

* * * * *

The merits of the *Frye* test have been much debated, and scholarship on its proper scope and application is legion. Petitioners' primary attack, however, is not on the content but on the continuing authority of the rule. They contend that the *Frye* test was superseded by the adoption of the Federal Rules of Evidence. We agree.

We interpret the legislatively-enacted Federal Rules of Evidence as we would any statute. Rule 402 provides the baseline: "All relevant evidence is admissible, except as otherwise provided by the Constitution of the United States, by Act of Congress, by these rules, or by other rules prescribed by the Supreme Court pursuant to statutory authority. Evidence which is not relevant is not admissible." "Relevant evidence" is defined as that which has "any tendency to make the existence of any fact that is of consequence to the determination of the action more probable or less probable than it would be without the evidence." Rule 401. The Rule's basic standard of relevance thus is a liberal one.

Frye, of course, predated the Rules by half a century. In *United States v. Abel*, 469 U.S. 45 (1984), we considered the pertinence of background common law in interpreting the Rules of Evidence. We noted that the Rules occupy the field, but, quoting Professor Cleary, the Reporter, explained that the common law nevertheless could serve as an aid to their application:

> "'In principle, under the Federal Rules no common law of evidence remains. 'All relevant evidence is admissible, except as otherwise provided....' In reality, of course, the body of common law knowledge continues to exist, though in the somewhat altered form of a source of guidance in the exercise of delegated powers.'"

We found the common-law precept at issue in the *Abel* case entirely consistent with Rule 402's general requirement of admissibility, and considered it unlikely that the drafters had intended to change the rule. In *Bourjaily v. United States*, 483 U.S. 171 (1987), on the other hand, the Court was unable to find a particular common-law doctrine in the Rules, and so held it superseded.

Here there is a specific Rule that speaks to the contested issue. Rule 702, governing expert testimony, provides: "If scientific, technical, or other specialized knowledge will assist the trier of fact to understand the evidence or to determine a fact in issue, a witness qualified as an expert by knowledge, skill, experience, training, or education, may testify thereto in the form of an opinion or otherwise." Nothing in the text of this Rule establishes "general acceptance" as an absolute prerequisite to admissibility. Nor does respondent present any clear indication that Rule 702 or the Rules as a whole were intended to incorporate a "general acceptance" standard. The drafting history makes no mention of *Frye*, and a rigid "general acceptance" requirement would be at odds with the "liberal thrust" of the Federal Rules and their "general approach of relaxing the traditional barriers to 'opinion' testimony." *Beech Aircraft Corp. v. Rainey*, 488 U.S., at 169 (citing Rules 701 to 705). Given the Rules' permissive backdrop and their inclusion of a specific rule on expert testimony that does not mention "general acceptance," the assertion that the Rules somehow assimilated *Frye* is unconvincing. *Frye* made "general acceptance" the exclusive test for admitting expert scientific testimony. That austere standard, absent from and incompatible with the Federal Rules of Evidence, should not be applied in federal trials.

B

That the *Frye* test was displaced by the Rules of Evidence does not mean, however, that the Rules themselves place no limits on the admissibility of purportedly scientific evidence. Nor is the trial judge disabled from screening such evidence. To the contrary, under the Rules the trial judge must ensure that any and all scientific testimony or evidence admitted is not only relevant, but reliable.

The primary locus of this obligation is Rule 702, which clearly contemplates some degree of regulation of the subjects and theories about which an expert may testify. "If scientific, technical, or other specialized knowledge will assist the trier of fact to understand the evidence or to determine a fact in issue" an expert "may testify thereto." The subject of an expert's testimony must be "scientific ... knowledge." The adjective "scientific" implies a grounding in the methods and procedures of science. Similarly, the word "knowledge" connotes more than subjective belief or unsupported speculation. The term "applies to any body of known facts or to any body of ideas inferred from such facts or accepted as truths on good grounds." Of course, it would be unreasonable to conclude that the subject of scientific testimony must be "known" to a certainty; arguably, there are no certainties in science. But, in order to qualify as "scientific knowledge," an inference or assertion must be derived by the scientific method. Proposed testimony must be supported by appropriate validation— i.e., "good grounds," based on what is known. In short, the requirement that an expert's testimony pertain to "scientific knowledge" establishes a standard of evidentiary reliability.

Rule 702 further requires that the evidence or testimony "assist the trier of fact to understand the evidence or to determine a fact in issue." This condition goes primarily to relevance. "Expert testimony which does not relate to any issue in the case is not relevant and, ergo, non- helpful." The consideration has been aptly described by Judge Becker as one of "fit." "Fit" is not always obvious, and scientific validity for one purpose is not necessarily scientific validity for other, unrelated purposes. The study of the phases of the moon, for example, may provide valid scientific "knowledge" about whether a certain night was dark, and if darkness is a fact in issue, the knowledge will assist the trier of fact. However (absent creditable grounds supporting such a link), evidence that the moon was full on a certain night will not assist the trier of fact in determining whether an individual was unusually likely to have behaved irrationally on that night. Rule 702's "helpfulness" standard requires a valid scientific connection to the pertinent inquiry as a precondition to admissibility.

That these requirements are embodied in Rule 702 is not surprising. Unlike an ordinary witness, see Rule 701, an expert is permitted wide latitude to offer opinions, including those that are not based on first—hand knowledge or observation. Presumably, this relaxation of the usual requirement of first-hand knowledge—a rule which represents "a 'most pervasive manifestation' of the common law insistence upon 'the most reliable sources of information,' "—is premised on an assumption that the expert's opinion will have a reliable basis in the knowledge and experience of his discipline.

C

Faced with a proffer of expert scientific testimony, then, the trial judge must determine at the outset, pursuant to Rule 104(a), whether the expert is proposing to testify to (1) scientific knowledge that (2) will assist the trier of fact to understand or determine a fact in issue. This entails a preliminary assessment of whether the reasoning or methodology underlying the testimony is scientifically valid and of whether that reasoning or methodology properly can be applied to the facts in issue. We are confident that federal judges possess the capacity to undertake this review. Many factors will bear on the inquiry, and we do not presume to set out a definitive checklist or test. But some general observations are appropriate.

Ordinarily, a key question to be answered in determining whether a theory or technique is scientific knowledge that will assist the trier of fact will be whether it can be (and has been) tested. "Scientific methodology today is based on generating hypotheses and testing them to see if they can be falsified; indeed, this methodology is what distinguishes science from other fields of human inquiry."

Another pertinent consideration is whether the theory or technique has been subjected to peer review and publication. Publication (which is but one element of peer review) is not a sine qua non of admissibility; it does not necessarily correlate with reliability, and in some instances well-grounded but innovative theories will not have been published. Some propositions, moreover, are too particular, too new, or of too limited interest to be published. But submission to the scrutiny of the scientific community is a component of "good science," in part because it increases the likelihood that substantive flaws in methodology will be detected. The fact of publication (or lack thereof) in a peer-reviewed journal thus will be a relevant, though not dispositive, consideration in assessing the scientific validity of a particular technique or methodology on which an opinion is premised.

Additionally, in the case of a particular scientific technique, the court ordinarily should consider the known or potential rate of error, and the existence and maintenance of standards controlling the technique's operation. *See United States v. Williams*, 583 F.2d 1194, 1198 (CA2 1978) (noting professional organization's standard governing spectrographic analysis).

Finally, "general acceptance" can yet have a bearing on the inquiry. A "reliability assessment does not require, although it does permit, explicit identification of a relevant scientific community and an express determination of a particular degree of acceptance within that community." Widespread acceptance can be an important factor in ruling particular evidence admissible, and "a known technique that has been able to attract only minimal support within the community," may properly be viewed with skepticism.

The inquiry envisioned by Rule 702 is, we emphasize, a flexible one. Its overarching subject is the scientific validity—and thus the evidentiary relevance and reliability—of the principles that underlie a proposed submission. The focus, of course, must be solely on principles and methodology, not on the conclusions that they generate.

Throughout, a judge assessing a proffer of expert scientific testimony under Rule 702 should also be mindful of other applicable rules. Rule 703 provides that expert opinions based on otherwise inadmissible hearsay are to be admitted only if the facts or data are "of a type reasonably relied upon by experts in the particular field in forming opinions or inferences upon the subject." Rule 706 allows the court at its discretion to procure the assistance of an expert of its own choosing. Finally, Rule 403 permits the exclusion of relevant evidence "if its probative value is substantially outweighed by the danger of unfair prejudice, confusion of the issues, or misleading the jury...." Judge Weinstein has explained: "Expert evidence can be both powerful and quite misleading because of the difficulty in evaluating it. Because of this risk, the judge in weighing possible prejudice against probative force under Rule 403 of the present rules exercises more control over experts than over lay witnesses."

III

We conclude by briefly addressing what appear to be two underlying concerns of the parties and amici in this case. Respondent expresses apprehension that abandonment of "general acceptance" as the exclusive requirement for admission will result in a "free-for-all" in which befuddled juries are confounded by absurd and irrational pseudoscientific assertions. In this regard respondent seems to us to be overly pessimistic about the capabilities of the jury, and of the adversary system generally. Vigorous cross-examination, presentation of contrary evidence, and careful instruction on the burden of proof are the traditional and appropriate means of attacking shaky but admissible evidence.

Petitioners and, to a greater extent, their amici exhibit a different concern. They suggest that recognition of a screening role for the judge that allows for the exclusion of "invalid" evidence will sanction a stifling and repressive scientific orthodoxy and will be inimical to the search for truth. It is true that open debate is an essential part of both legal and scientific analyses. Yet there are important differences between the quest for truth in the courtroom and the quest for truth in the laboratory. Scientific conclusions are subject to perpetual revision. Law, on the other hand, must resolve disputes finally and quickly. We recognize that in practice, a gatekeeping role for the judge, no matter how flexible, inevitably on occasion will prevent the jury from learning of authentic insights and innovations. That, nevertheless, is the balance that is struck by Rules of Evidence designed not for the exhaustive search for cosmic understanding but for the particularized resolution of legal disputes.

IV

To summarize: "general acceptance" is not a necessary precondition to the admissibility of scientific evidence under the Federal Rules of Evidence, but the Rules of Evidence—especially Rule 702—do assign to the trial judge the task of ensuring that an expert's testimony both rests on a reliable foundation and is relevant to the task at hand. Pertinent evidence based on scientifically valid principles will satisfy those demands.

The issue of which test to apply in Texas cases was addressed by the Texas Court of Criminal Appeals in *Kelly v. State.*

KELLY v. STATE
824 S.W.2D 568 (Tex Crim. App. 1992)

CAMPBELL, Judge.

A jury found appellant, Barry Dean Kelly, guilty of murder and assessed his punishment at imprisonment for life. The Second Court of Appeals affirmed appellant's conviction. We granted appellant's petition for discretionary review, to determine whether the court of appeals erred in holding that the trial court did not abuse its discretion in admitting DNA "fingerprint" evidence at appellant's trial over his objection. We will affirm the judgment of the court of appeals.

Before trial, appellant filed a motion to suppress any expert testimony regarding DNA identification test results on the ground that such tests had "not gained general acceptance [as reliable] in the scientific community in which such testing belongs." At trial, after the State indicated its intention to offer expert testimony regarding a DNA identification test, the trial court conducted a hearing to determine the admissibility of such testimony. The hearing was conducted outside the presence of the jury, pursuant to Texas Rule of Criminal Evidence 104(a) and (c).

I. THE EXPERT TESTIMONY

Six witnesses testified at the suppression hearing—five for the State and one for the defense.

In brief, the testimony of the State's expert witnesses at the suppression hearing established the following: (1) it is generally accepted by molecular biologists that each person's DNA is unique and does not change during that person's lifetime; (2) the "restriction fragment length polymorphism" (RFLP) technique, generally accepted by molecular biologists as reliable, can be used to compare a known sample of DNA with an unknown sample of DNA to determine whether the two samples share certain molecular characteristics; (3) studies of sample populations can be used to determine reliably the frequencies, within the general population, of the molecular characteristics in question; (4) sufficient studies of sample populations have already been performed to allow reliable calculations concerning the frequencies, within the general population, of the molecular characteristics in question; (5) a false "match" of a known DNA sample with an unknown DNA sample is impossible with the RFLP technique; (6) reliable and generally accepted techniques are available to extract DNA from blood and semen stains; (7) Lifecodes Corporation utilized both a generally accepted DNA extraction technique and the RFLP technique to compare DNA from appellant's blood with DNA from a semen stain found at the home of Appellant's victim; (8) Lifecodes' test showed that appellant's DNA shared certain molecular characteristics with the semen stain DNA; (9) the RFLP analysis in this case was performed by Lifecodes in a scientifically acceptable manner.

John Thomas Castle, appellant's witness at the suppression hearing, testified that he had a B.S. degree in chemistry from Angelo State University in San Angelo, and that he was the owner-operator of Castle Forensic Laboratories in Dallas. He testified further that, in his opinion, the RFLP technique, at least as applied to forensic samples, was not generally accepted in the scientific community. He also questioned the reliability of Lifecodes' test results because, he claimed, Lifecodes had a policy of re-using certain laboratory materials.

At the conclusion of the testimony at the suppression hearing, appellant argued that DNA identification evidence was inadmissible under *Frye v. United States*, 293 F. 1013 (D.C.Cir.1923), because such evidence was, according to appellant, "not accepted [as reliable] in the scientific community and [by] the folks who deal with DNA." Appellant also argued that insufficient population studies had been conducted to make a DNA "match" meaningful. The State responded that the holding in *Frye* was not binding on Texas courts and that the evidence in question had been shown to be reliable and thus admissible under Texas Rule of Criminal Evidence 702.

[After the litigants concluded their arguments, the trial court admitted the evidence]

II. THE ARGUMENTS

Appellant argues now, as he did below, that the *Frye* "general acceptance" test governs the admissibility of scientific evidence in Texas courts and that the trial court abused its discretion in admitting the DNA evidence because, according to appellant, DNA identification tests—and Lifecodes' procedures in particular—are not generally accepted as reliable by any scientific community. In support of his argument, Appellant cites various authorities that have questioned the reliability of DNA identification testing.

The State counterargues that the "helpfulness" test of Rule 702 governs the admissibility of all expert testimony, scientific or otherwise, and that the DNA evidence at Appellant's trial was proven to be reliable and helpful and thus admissible under Rule 702.

* * * * *

IV. THE PRESENT VIABILITY OF THE *FRYE* TEST

To determine whether the court of appeals erred in holding that the trial court did not abuse its discretion, we must first determine what test governs the admissibility of novel scientific evidence in Texas criminal trials. We must then determine whether the trial court's decision admitting the DNA evidence was reasonable given the testimony at the suppression hearing and given the governing test of admissibility.

The test which some jurisdictions use with respect to the admission of novel scientific evidence is the test that was enunciated in *Frye*. The *Frye* court thus imposed a "general acceptance" test on the admissibility of scientific evidence.

Although this Court has never explicitly adopted the *Frye* test, on several occasions we have used a general acceptance test when reviewing lower court decisions regarding the admission of scientific evidence. In all those cases, however, the trials were held before the promulgation of the Texas Rules of Criminal Evidence.

Since the promulgation of the Rules in 1986, Rule 702 has governed the admission of all expert testimony.

We have recognized before that the "threshold determination" for a trial court to make regarding the admission of expert testimony is whether that testimony will help the trier of fact understand the evidence or determine a fact in issue. Thus, in a case such as this—where the trial court was faced with an offer of expert testimony on a scientific topic unfamiliar to lay jurors—the trial court's first task is to determine whether the testimony is sufficiently reliable and relevant to help the jury in reaching accurate results. "Unreliable scientific evidence simply will not assist the

[jury] to understand the evidence or accurately determine a fact in issue; such evidence obfuscates rather than leads to an intelligent evaluation of the facts."

If the trial judge determines that the proffered expert testimony is reliable (and thus probative and relevant), then she must next determine whether, on balance, that testimony might nevertheless be unhelpful to the trier of fact for other reasons. For example, even reliable and relevant expert testimony may be unhelpful if it is merely cumulative, or would confuse or mislead the jury, or would consume an inordinate amount of trial time. In short, if the trial judge determines that the proffered expert testimony is reliable and relevant, she must still decide whether the probative value of the testimony is outweighed by one or more of the factors identified in Rule 403.

Is the *Frye* general acceptance test still a part of Texas law? We conclude that it is not. First, there is no textual basis in Rule 702 for a special admissibility standard for novel scientific evidence. Second, as should be fairly obvious, scientific evidence may be shown reliable even though not yet generally accepted in the relevant scientific community.

V. PROOF OF RELIABILITY

How does the proponent of novel scientific evidence prove it to be reliable? As a matter of common sense, evidence derived from a scientific theory, to be considered reliable, must satisfy three criteria in any particular case: (a) the underlying scientific theory must be valid; (b) the technique applying the theory must be valid; and (c) the technique must have been properly applied on the occasion in question. *See generally* Tex.R.Crim.Evid. 705. Under Rule 104(a) and (c) and Rule 702, all three criteria must be proven to the trial court, outside the presence of the jury, before the evidence may be admitted. Factors that could affect a trial court's determination of reliability include, but are not limited to, the following: (1) the extent to which the underlying scientific theory and technique are accepted as valid by the relevant scientific community, if such a community can be ascertained; (2) the qualifications of the expert(s) testifying; (3) the existence of literature supporting or rejecting the underlying scientific theory and technique; (4) the potential rate of error of the technique; (5) the availability of other experts to test and evaluate the technique; (6) the clarity with which the underlying scientific theory and technique can be explained to the court; and (7) the experience and skill of the person(s) who applied the technique on the occasion in question.

VI. THE PROPONENT'S BURDEN OF PERSUASION

What burden of persuasion does the proponent of novel scientific evidence carry under Rule 702? Unfortunately, our rules of evidence do not prescribe the burden of persuasion or imply what burden might be appropriate. In *Zani v. State*, however, in addressing the burden of persuasion required of the proponent of posthypnotic testimony, we held that because of the "uncertainties inherent" in the evidence, "it [was] appropriate to require the proponent of such [evidence] to demonstrate ... by clear and convincing evidence, that such [evidence was] trustworthy." Although Zani was a pre-Rules case, we believe that its reasoning on this issue remains persuasive. Because of the difficulty laypersons have in evaluating the reliability of novel scientific testimony, we conclude it is appropriate for the burden of persuasion to be enhanced, i.e., that the burden be that of clear and convincing evidence rather than simply the preponderance of the evidence. In other words, before novel scientific evidence may be admitted under Rule 702, the proponent must persuade the trial court, by clear and convincing evidence, that the evidence is reliable and therefore relevant.

VII. SUMMARY

To summarize, under Rule 702 the proponent of novel scientific evidence must prove to the trial court, by clear and convincing evidence and outside the presence of the jury, that the proffered evidence is relevant. If the trial court is so persuaded, then the evidence should be admitted for the jury's consideration, unless the trial court determines that the probative value of the evidence is outweighed by some factor identified in Rule 403.

VIII. THE TRIAL COURT'S DECISION

We come finally to the question of whether the trial court abused its discretion in admitting the DNA evidence in the instant case. That is, we must determine whether the trial court's decision was "within the zone of reasonable disagreement" given the evidence presented at the suppression hearing and given the requirements of Rule 702.

The trial court was, of course, the sole judge of the weight and credibility of the evidence presented at the suppression hearing. Viewing that evidence in the light most favorable to the trial court's decision, we conclude that it was demonstrated by clear and convincing evidence that the scientific principle underlying the RFLP technique was valid, that the RFLP technique itself was valid, that the technique was properly applied in this case, and that the related population frequency studies were also valid and reliable.

———

Citing both *Daubert* and *Kelly*, the Texas Supreme Court finally addressed the issue of which test to apply to scientific evidence in *Du Pont v. Robinson*.

Du PONT de NEMOURS AND CO. INC., v. ROBINSON
923 S.W.2d 549 (Tex. 1995)

[The Plaintiffs brought a products liability action against a fungicide manufacturer, claiming that contaminated fungicide damaged orchard. The trial court excluded the testimony of plaintiffs' sole expert on causation. The Court of Appeals reversed and remanded, and further review was sought.]

GONZALEZ, Justice, delivered the opinion of the Court, in which PHILLIPS, Chief Justice, and HECHT, ENOCH and OWEN, Justices, join.

In this products liability case we determine the proper standard for the admission of scientific expert testimony under Rule 702 of the Texas Rules of Civil Evidence. The trial court excluded the testimony of an expert witness upon finding his opinions not scientifically reliable. The court of appeals reversed, holding that once a proponent establishes a witness's qualifications, the weight to be given the testimony and the credibility of the witness is to be determined by the trier of fact.

We hold that Rule 702 requires expert testimony to be relevant and reliable. Because the proponent of the testimony in this case failed to establish that the proffered testimony was scientifically reliable, the trial court did not abuse its discretion by excluding the expert witness. Accordingly, we reverse the judgment of the court of appeals and affirm that of the trial court.

I.

C.R. and Shirley Robinson sued E.I. du Pont de Nemours and Company (DuPont) for products liability, breach of warranty, and violations of the Texas Deceptive Trade Practices-Consumer Protection Act (DTPA). The Robinsons asserted that the application of Benlate 50 DF, a fungicide manufactured by DuPont, which they claim was contaminated, damaged their pecan orchard.

The Robinsons' sole expert witness on causation was Dr. Carl Whitcomb.

Dr. Whitcomb opined that Dupont contaminated Benlate during its manufacturing process with many things, including sulfonylurea (SU) herbicides, and that the application of contaminated Benlate damaged the Robinsons' pecan trees. One basis for his opinion was his inspection of the Robinsons' orchard in September 1992, conducted at the request of their attorney.

On October 3, 1992, Dr. Whitcomb reported his findings to the Robinsons' attorney. He based his opinion that contaminated Benlate damaged the Robinsons' pecan trees on a method called comparative symptomology.

Another basis for Dr. Whitcomb's opinion was an experiment he conducted in 1992, at the request of an attorney in Florida who represented clients asserting claims similar to the claims asserted by the Robinsons.

Another basis for Dr. Whitcomb's opinion was a laboratory analysis of ten boxes of Benlate (none of which were used by the Robinsons). The tests revealed that out of eighteen substances found in the Benlate samples, only five were common to all boxes. The tests did not reveal the presence of SU contaminants. He also admitted that, if free of contamination, Benlate was a good product.

Dr. Whitcomb also based his opinion on a review of reports of other plants treated with SU herbicides and one study involving the application of Benlate to cucumber plants. Lastly, Dr. Whitcomb relied upon some internal DuPont documents which concerned other claims against the company for damages caused by allegedly contaminated Benlate and a recall of several batches of Benlate due to contamination by the herbicide atrazine.

After deposing Dr. Whitcomb, DuPont filed a motion to exclude his testimony, alleging among other things that his opinions were speculative and unreliable. The trial court held a pretrial hearing on DuPont's motion and found that Dr. Whitcomb's testimony:

(1) was not grounded upon careful scientific methods and procedures;
(2) was not shown to be derived by scientific methods or supported by appropriate validation;
(3) was not shown to be based on scientifically valid reasoning and methodology;
(4) was not shown to have a reliable basis in the knowledge and experience of his discipline (horticulture);
(5) was not based on theories and techniques that had been subjected to peer review and publication;
(6) was essentially subjective belief and unsupported speculation;
(7) was not based on theories and techniques that the relevant scientific community had generally accepted; and
(8) was not based on a procedure reasonably relied upon by experts in the field.

Based on these findings, the trial court excluded Dr. Whitcomb's testimony, concluding that it was not reliable and would not fairly assist the trier of fact in understanding a fact in issue in the case.

The trial court granted DuPont's motion for a directed verdict. The Robinsons appealed the judgment, claiming that the trial court had abused its discretion by excluding their expert testimony.

The court of appeals reversed and remanded the case for a new trial.

* * * * *
II.
A.

As numerous courts and commentators have observed, the use of expert witnesses in litigation has become widespread. . . . In addition, the scientific theories about which these experts often testify have increased in complexity and have become more crucial to the outcome of the case. . .

Professional expert witnesses are available to render an opinion on almost any theory, regardless of its merit. . . .While many of these experts undoubtedly hold reliable opinions which are of invaluable assistance to the jury, there are some experts who "are more than willing to proffer opinions of dubious value for the proper fee."

Expert witnesses can have an extremely prejudicial impact on the jury, in part because of the way in which the jury perceives a witness labeled as an expert. Consequently, a jury more readily accepts the opinion of an expert witness as true simply because of his or her designation as an expert.

Added to the potentially prejudicial influence of the term expert is the difficulty inherent in evaluating scientific evidence. Jurors are often expected to understand complex testimony regarding arcane scientific concepts and are even asked to resolve issues on which the experts cannot agree. Because expert evidence can be hard to evaluate, it can be both powerful and misleading. Consequently, some commentators believe that "ostensibly scientific testimony may sway a jury even when as science it is palpably wrong."

In light of the increased use of expert witnesses and the likely prejudicial impact of their testimony, trial judges have a heightened responsibility to ensure that expert testimony show some indicia of reliability. . . .It is especially important that trial judges scrutinize proffered evidence for scientific reliability when it is based upon novel scientific theories, sometimes referred to as "junk science."

Concerns over the abusive use of the professional expert witness have led some commentators to call for the adoption of a reliability standard for Rule 702 of the Texas Rules of Civil Evidence.

B.

Rule 702 of the Texas Rules of Civil Evidence, which governs the admission of expert testimony, provides as follows:

If scientific, technical, or other specialized knowledge will assist the trier of fact to understand the evidence or to determine a fact in issue, a witness qualified as an expert by knowledge, skill, experience, training, or education, may testify thereto in the form of an opinion or otherwise.

Since the adoption of Rule 702 in 1983, this Court has not had occasion to address the proper standard for the admission of expert testimony. The courts of appeals, however, have been presented with this issue and have come to differing conclusions. Some courts of appeals have limited the trial court's inquiry to assessing the expert's qualifications. . . .Other courts have held that the proper inquiry for the admission of expert evidence is whether the underlying scientific principle is sufficiently reliable to be of assistance to the trier of fact.

We granted DuPont's application for writ of error to resolve the conflict between the courts of appeals by determining the appropriate standard for the admission of scientific expert testimony.

C.

In *Daubert v. Merrell Dow Pharmaceuticals, Inc.*, 509 U.S. 579, 589-90, (1993), the United States Supreme Court held that Rule 702 did not incorporate the Frye test, noting that Frye's restrictive "general acceptance" test was at odds with the liberal approach of the Federal Rules of Evidence. The Court enumerated four non-exclusive factors to aid trial judges in determining whether scientific evidence is relevant and reliable and thus admissible under Federal Rule of Evidence 702: (1) whether a theory or technique can be and has been tested (falsifiability); (2) whether the theory or technique has been subjected to peer review and publication; (3) the technique's known or potential rate of error; and (4) the general acceptance of the theory or technique by the relevant scientific community.

* * * * *

Since *Daubert*, one Texas court of appeals has adopted a combined reliability and relevancy standard for determining the admissibility of evidence offered pursuant to Rule 702 of the Texas Rules of Civil Evidence. Two courts of appeals have come to differing conclusions about whether a Daubert-type standard governs appellate reviews of the legal sufficiency of scientific expert testimony.

The Texas Court of Criminal Appeals also has held that scientific evidence offered pursuant to Rule 702 of the Texas Rules of Criminal Evidence must be relevant and reliable.. . . Under *Kelly*, factors affecting the trial court's determination of reliability include: (1) general acceptance of the theory and technique by the relevant scientific community; (2) the expert's qualifications; (3) the existence of literature supporting or rejecting the theory; (4) the technique's potential rate of error; (5) the availability of other experts to test and evaluate the technique; (6) the clarity with which the theory or technique can be explained to the trial court; and (7) the experience and skill of the person who applied the technique on the occasion in question.

D.

We are persuaded by the reasoning in *Daubert* and *Kelly*. Therefore, we hold that in addition to showing that an expert witness is qualified, Rule 702 also requires the proponent to show that the expert's testimony is relevant to the issues in the case and is based upon a reliable foundation. The trial court is responsible for making the preliminary determination of whether the proffered testimony meets the standards set forth today. See TEX.R.CIV.EVID. 104(a) (stating that the trial court is to decide preliminary questions concerning the admissibility of evidence).

Rule 702 contains three requirements for the admission of expert testimony: (1) the witness must be qualified; (2) the proposed testimony must be "scientific knowledge"; and (3) the testimony must "assist the trier of fact to understand the evidence or to determine a fact in issue." In order to constitute scientific knowledge which will assist the trier of fact, the proposed testimony must be relevant and reliable.

The requirement that the proposed testimony be relevant incorporates traditional relevancy analysis under Rules 401 and 402 of the Texas Rules of Civil Evidence. To be relevant, the proposed testimony must be "sufficiently tied to the facts of the case that it will aid the jury in resolving a factual dispute." Evidence that has no relationship to any of the issues in the case is irrelevant and does not satisfy Rule 702's requirement that the testimony be of assistance to the jury. It is thus inadmissible under Rule 702 as well as under Rules 401 and 402.

In addition to being relevant, the underlying scientific technique or principle must be reliable. Scientific evidence which is not grounded "in the methods and procedures of science" is no more than "subjective belief or unsupported speculation." Unreliable evidence is of no assistance to the trier of fact and is therefore inadmissible under Rule 702.

There are many factors that a trial court may consider in making the threshold determination of admissibility under Rule 702. These factors include, but are not limited to:

(1) the extent to which the theory has been or can be tested;
(2) the extent to which the technique relies upon the subjective interpretation of the expert,
(3) whether the theory has been subjected to peer review and/or publication;
(4) the technique's potential rate of error;
(5) whether the underlying theory or technique has been generally accepted as valid by the relevant scientific community; and
(6) the non-judicial uses which have been made of the theory or technique.

We emphasize that the factors mentioned above are non-exclusive. Trial courts may consider other factors which are helpful to determining the reliability of the scientific evidence. The factors a trial court will find helpful in determining whether the underlying theories and techniques of the proffered evidence are scientifically reliable will differ with each particular case.

If the trial judge determines that the proffered testimony is relevant and reliable, he or she must then determine whether to exclude the evidence because its probative value is outweighed by the "danger of unfair prejudice, confusion of the issues, or misleading the jury, or by considerations of undue delay, or needless presentation of cumulative evidence." TEX.R.CIV.EVID. 403.

We are confident that our trial courts will use great care when determining whether expert testimony is admissible under Rule 702. As the Supreme Court noted in Daubert, Rule 702 envisions a flexible inquiry focusing solely on the underlying principles and methodology, not on the conclusions they generate.

E.

The Robinsons contend that allowing the trial judge to assess the reliability of expert testimony violates their federal and state constitutional rights to a jury trial by infringing upon the jury's inherent authority to assess the credibility of witnesses and the weight to be given their testimony. We disagree. The right to a jury trial "was designed to preserve the basic institution of jury trial in only its most fundamental elements, not the great mass of procedural forms and details.". Moreover, under the standards enunciated today, the jury will continue to assess the weight and credibility of the proffered testimony.

The trial court's role is not to determine the truth or falsity of the expert's opinion. Rather, the trial court's role is to make the initial determination whether the expert's opinion is relevant and whether the methods and research upon which it is based are reliable. There is a difference between the reliability of the underlying theory or technique and the credibility of the witness who proposes to testify about it. An expert witness may be very believable, but his or her conclusions may be based upon unreliable methodology. As DuPont points out, a person with a degree should not be allowed to testify that the world is flat, that the moon is made of green cheese, or that the Earth is the center of the solar system.

* * * * *

IV.

Because Dr. Whitcomb's testimony and opinions were not reliable, we hold that the trial court did not abuse its discretion by excluding Dr. Whitcomb's testimony. Accordingly, we reverse the judgment of the court of appeals and affirm the judgment of the trial court.

CORNYN, Justice, joined by HIGHTOWER, GAMMAGE and SPECTOR, Justices, dissenting.[The dissenting opinion is omitted]

An issue not answered in the *Daubert-Kelly-Robinson* trilogy is whether the tests devised for the admissibility of opinion testimony on scientific evidence apply to all forms of expert testimony. The Supreme Court of the United States addressed that issue in *Kumho Tire Co v. Carmichael*.

KUMHO TIRE COMPANY v. CARMICHAEL
526 U.S. 137 (1999)

Justice BREYER delivered the opinion of the Court.

In Daubert v. Merrell Dow Pharmaceuticals, Inc., 509 U.S. 579 (1993), this Court focused upon the admissibility of scientific expert testimony. It pointed out that such testimony is admissible only if it is both relevant and reliable. And it held that the Federal Rules of Evidence "assign to the trial judge the task of ensuring that an expert's testimony both rests on a reliable foundation and is relevant to the task at hand." The Court also discussed certain more specific factors, such as testing, peer review, error rates, and "acceptability" in the relevant scientific community, some or all of which might prove helpful in determining the reliability of a particular scientific "theory or technique."

This case requires us to decide how *Daubert* applies to the testimony of engineers and other experts who are not scientists. We conclude that *Daubert*'s general holding—setting forth the trial judge's general "gatekeeping" obligation—applies not only to testimony based on "scientific" knowledge, but also to testimony based on "technical" and "other specialized" knowledge. We also conclude that a trial court may consider one or more of the more specific factors that *Daubert* mentioned when doing so will help determine that testimony's reliability. But, as the Court stated in *Daubert*, the test of reliability is "flexible," and *Daubert*'s list of specific factors neither necessarily nor exclusively applies to all experts or in every case. Rather, the law grants a district court the same broad latitude when it decides how to determine reliability as it enjoys in respect to its ultimate reliability determination. Applying these standards, we determine that the District Court's decision in this case—not to admit certain expert testimony—was within its discretion and therefore lawful.

I

On July 6, 1993, the right rear tire of a minivan driven by Patrick Carmichael blew out. In the accident that followed, one of the passengers died, and others were severely injured. In October 1993, the Carmichaels brought this diversity suit against the tire's maker and its distributor, whom we refer to collectively as Kumho Tire, claiming that the tire was defective. The plaintiffs rested their case in significant part upon deposition testimony provided by an expert in tire failure analysis, Dennis Carlson, Jr., who intended to testify in support of their conclusion.

Carlson's depositions relied upon certain features of tire technology that are not in dispute.

Carlson's testimony also accepted certain background facts about the tire in question. He assumed that before the blowout the tire had traveled far. He conceded that the tire tread had at least two punctures which had been inadequately repaired.

Despite the tire's age and history, Carlson concluded that a defect in its manufacture or design caused the blow-out. He rested this conclusion in part upon three premises which, for present purposes, we must assume are not in dispute: First, a tire's carcass should stay bound to the inner side of the tread for a significant period of time after its tread depth has worn away. Second, the tread of the tire at issue had separated from its inner steel-belted carcass prior to the accident. Third, this "separation" caused the blowout.

Carlson's conclusion that a defect caused the separation, however, rested upon certain other propositions, several of which the defendants strongly dispute. First, Carlson said that if a separation is not caused by a certain kind of tire misuse called "overdeflection" (which consists of underinflating the tire or causing it to carry too much weight, thereby generating heat that can undo the chemical tread/carcass bond), then, ordinarily, its cause is a tire defect. Second, he said that if a tire has been subject to sufficient overdeflection to cause a separation, it should reveal certain physical symptoms. These symptoms include (a) tread wear on the tire's shoulder that is greater than the tread wear along the tire's center, (b) signs of a "bead groove," where the beads have been pushed too hard against the bead seat on the inside of the tire's rim; (c) sidewalls of the tire with physical signs of deterioration, such as discoloration; and/or (d) marks on the tire's rim flange. Third, Carlson said that where he does not find at least two of the four physical signs just mentioned (and presumably where there is no reason to suspect a less common cause of separation), he concludes that a manufacturing or design defect caused the separation.

Carlson added that he had inspected the tire in question. He conceded that the tire to a limited degree showed greater wear on the shoulder than in the center, some signs of "bead groove," some discoloration, a few marks on the rim flange, and inadequately filled puncture holes (which can also cause heat that might lead to separation). But, in each instance, he testified that the symptoms were not significant, and he explained why he believed that they did not reveal overdeflection.

Kumho Tire moved the District Court to exclude Carlson's testimony on the ground that his methodology failed Rule 702's reliability requirement. The court agreed with Kumho that it should act as a *Daubert*-type reliability "gatekeeper," even though one might consider Carlson's testimony as "technical," rather than "scientific." The court then examined Carlson's methodology in light of the reliability-related factors that *Daubert* mentioned, such as a theory's testability, whether it "has been a subject of peer review or publication," the "known or potential rate of error," and the "degree of acceptance ... within the relevant scientific community." The District Court found that all those factors argued against the reliability of Carlson's methods, and it granted the motion to exclude the testimony (as well as the defendants' accompanying motion for summary judgment).

The plaintiffs, arguing that the court's application of the *Daubert* factors was too "inflexible," asked for reconsideration. And the Court granted that motion. It consequently affirmed its earlier order declaring Carlson's testimony inadmissible and granting the defendants' motion for summary judgment.

The Eleventh Circuit reversed. Kumho Tire petitioned for certiorari, asking us to determine whether a trial court "may" consider *Daubert*'s specific "factors" when determining the "admissibility of an engineering expert's testimony." We granted certiorari in light of uncertainty among the lower courts about whether, or how, *Daubert* applies to expert testimony that might be characterized as based not upon "scientific" knowledge, but rather upon "technical" or "other specialized" knowledge.

II

A

In *Daubert*, this Court held that Federal Rule of Evidence 702 imposes a special obligation upon a trial judge to "ensure that any and all scientific testimony ... is not only relevant, but reliable." The initial question before us is whether this basic gatekeeping obligation applies only to "scientific" testimony or to all expert testimony. We, like the parties, believe that it applies to all expert testimony.

For one thing, Rule 702 itself says:

"If scientific, technical, or other specialized knowledge will assist the trier of fact to understand the evidence or to determine a fact in issue, a witness qualified as an expert by knowledge, skill, experience, training, or education, may testify thereto in the form of an opinion or otherwise."

This language makes no relevant distinction between "scientific" knowledge and "technical" or "other specialized" knowledge. It makes clear that any such knowledge might become the subject of expert testimony. Hence, as a matter of language, the Rule applies its reliability standard to all "scientific," "technical," or "other specialized" matters within its scope. We concede that the Court in *Daubert* referred only to "scientific" knowledge. But as the Court there said, it referred to "scientific" testimony "because that [wa]s the nature of the expertise" at issue.

Neither is the evidentiary rationale that underlay the Court's basic *Daubert* "gatekeeping" determination limited to "scientific" knowledge. *Daubert* pointed out that Federal Rules 702 and

703 grant expert witnesses testimonial latitude unavailable to other witnesses on the "assumption that the expert's opinion will have a reliable basis in the knowledge and experience of his discipline." The Rules grant that latitude to all experts, not just to "scientific" ones.

Finally, it would prove difficult, if not impossible, for judges to administer evidentiary rules under which a gatekeeping obligation depended upon a distinction between "scientific" knowledge and "technical" or "other specialized" knowledge. There is no clear line that divides the one from the others. Disciplines such as engineering rest upon scientific knowledge. Pure scientific theory itself may depend for its development upon observation and properly engineered machinery. And conceptual efforts to distinguish the two are unlikely to produce clear legal lines capable of application in particular cases.

Neither is there a convincing need to make such distinctions. Experts of all kinds tie observations to conclusions through the use of what Judge Learned Hand called "general truths derived from ... specialized experience."

We conclude that *Daubert*'s general principles apply to the expert matters described in Rule 702. The Rule, in respect to all such matters, "establishes a standard of evidentiary reliability." It "requires a valid ... connection to the pertinent inquiry as a precondition to admissibility." And where such testimony's factual basis, data, principles, methods, or their application are called sufficiently into question, see Part III, infra, the trial judge must determine whether the testimony has "a reliable basis in the knowledge and experience of [the relevant] discipline."

B

The petitioners ask more specifically whether a trial judge determining the "admissibility of an engineering expert's testimony" may consider several more specific factors that *Daubert* said might "bear on" a judge's gate-keeping determination. These factors include:

—Whether a "theory or technique ... can be (and has been) tested";
—Whether it "has been subjected to peer review and publication";
—Whether, in respect to a particular technique, there is a high "known or potential rate of error" and whether there are "standards controlling the technique's operation"; and
-Whether the theory or technique enjoys "general acceptance" within a "relevant scientific community."

Emphasizing the word "may" in the question, we answer that question yes.

Engineering testimony rests upon scientific foundations, the reliability of which will be at issue in some cases. In other cases, the relevant reliability concerns may focus upon personal knowledge or experience.

Daubert itself is not to the contrary. It made clear that its list of factors was meant to be helpful, not definitive. Indeed, those factors do not all necessarily apply even in every instance in which the reliability of scientific testimony is challenged. It might not be surprising in a particular case, for example, that a claim made by a scientific witness has never been the subject of peer review, for the particular application at issue may never previously have interested any scientist. Nor, on the other hand, does the presence of *Daubert*'s general acceptance factor help show that an expert's testimony is reliable where the discipline itself lacks reliability, as, for example, do theories grounded in any so-called generally accepted principles of astrology or necromancy.

At the same time, and contrary to the Court of Appeals' view, some of *Daubert's* questions can help to evaluate the reliability even of experience-based testimony. In certain cases, it will be appropriate for the trial judge to ask, for example, how often an engineering expert's experience-based methodology has produced erroneous results, or whether such a method is generally accepted in the relevant engineering community. Likewise, it will at times be useful to ask even of a witness whose expertise is based purely on experience, say, a perfume tester able to distinguish among 140 odors at a sniff, whether his preparation is of a kind that others in the field would recognize as acceptable.

We must therefore disagree with the Eleventh Circuit's holding that a trial judge may ask questions of the sort *Daubert* mentioned only where an expert "relies on the application of scientific principles," but not where an expert relies "on skill or experience-based observation." We do not believe that Rule 702 creates a schematism that segregates expertise by type while mapping certain kinds of questions to certain kinds of experts. Life and the legal cases that it generates are too complex to warrant so definitive a match.

Rather, we conclude that the trial judge must have considerable leeway in deciding in a particular case how to go about determining whether particular expert testimony is reliable. That is to say, a trial court should consider the specific factors identified in *Daubert* where they are reasonable measures of the reliability of expert testimony.

C

The trial court must have the same kind of latitude in deciding how to test an expert's reliability, and to decide whether or when special briefing or other proceedings are needed to investigate reliability, as it enjoys when it decides whether or not that expert's relevant testimony is reliable. Our opinion in *Joiner* makes clear that a court of appeals is to apply an abuse-of-discretion standard when it "review[s] a trial court's decision to admit or exclude expert testimony." Indeed, the Rules seek to avoid "unjustifiable expense and delay" as part of their search for "truth" and the "jus[t] determin[ation]" of proceedings. Fed. Rule Evid. 102. Thus, whether *Daubert's* specific factors are, or are not, reasonable measures of reliability in a particular case is a matter that the law grants the trial judge broad latitude to determine. And the Eleventh Circuit erred insofar as it held to the contrary.

III

In sum, Rule 702 grants the district judge the discretionary authority, reviewable for its abuse, to determine reliability in light of the particular facts and circumstances of the particular case. The District Court did not abuse its discretionary authority in this case. Hence, the judgment of the Court of Appeals is

Reversed.

Still another question is whether the trial court should make any adjustments in the *Daubert-Kelly-Robinson* formula for the so-called "soft sciences" such as psychology or other human behavioral issues. The Texas Court of Criminal Appeals addressed that point in *Nenno v. State*.

NENNO v. STATE
970 S.W.2d 549 (Tex. Crim. App. 1998)

KELLER, Judge, delivered the opinion of the Court in which McCORMICK, Presiding Judge, and MEYERS, MANSFIELD, HOLLAND, and WOMACK, Judges, joined.

[The appellant was convicted and sentenced to death. On appeal, he challenged the admissibility of State expert testimony at the punishment stage on the question of his future dangerousness.]

* * * * *

C.   PUNISHMENT
1.   Expert testimony

In point of error one, appellant contends that the trial court erred in admitting expert testimony from Kenneth Lanning during the punishment stage of the trial. As explained in connection with point of error two, Lanning testified with regard to appellant's future dangerousness. Appellant contends that Lanning's testimony was inadmissible under [Rule] 702 because it failed to meet the three-pronged test announced in *Kelly v. State,* 824 S.W.2d 568 (Tex.Crim.App.1992). He also contends that the testimony was inadmissible under Tex.R.Crim. Evid. 403 because it merely duplicated the jury's knowledge and carried the prospect of unduly influencing the jury with an "expert" label.

Appellant contends that the State failed to show the validity of the scientific theories underlying Lanning's testimony or the validity of the method used for applying the theories. Appellant argues that this validity is lacking because the State failed to produce any evidence (1) that the theories underlying Lanning's testimony are accepted as valid by the relevant scientific community, (2) that the alleged literature on the theories supports his theories, (3) that there are specific data or published articles regarding the area of future dangerousness of prison inmates, (4) that his theories have been empirically tested, (5) that he has conducted any studies or independent research in the area of future dangerousness, or (6) that anyone else had tested or evaluated the theories upon which his testimony was based.

Although *Kelly* involved novel scientific evidence, we later concluded that the standard established in that case applied to *all* scientific evidence, whether or not it was novel. *Hartman v. State,* 946 S.W.2d 60, 62-63 (Tex.Crim.App.1997). The question we confront today is whether *Kelly* is applicable to *nonscientific* expert testimony (i.e. that involving technical or other specialized knowledge). The answer to that question is a qualified "yes." The general principles announced in *Kelly* (and *Daubert*) apply, but the specific factors outlined in those cases may or may not apply depending upon the context. We do not attempt, here, to develop a rigid distinction between "hard" science, "soft" sciences, or nonscientific testimony. The present case illustrates that the distinction between various types of testimony may often be blurred. The observations we make today apply to all types of expert testimony.

Courts must keep in mind the statement in *Daubert* that the inquiry is "a flexible one." The general approach of the Federal Rules — and by inference, the state rules that were patterned upon them — was to "relax the traditional barriers to opinion testimony." The Supreme Court, while setting out four factors relevant to scientific reliability, cautioned that "we do not presume to set out a definitive checklist or test." The factors listed were based upon "general observations" about the nature of scientific evidence. . And, the standard of evidentiary reliability set forth was derived from Rule 702's requirement that the expert's testimony pertain to "*scientific* knowledge" (emphasis added). While various federal circuits may sometimes purport to disagree with each other, a close examination of the cases shows a general agreement about two important propositions: (1) *Daubert* 's prescription that trial judges act as "gatekeepers" in determining the reliability of expert evidence applies to all forms of expert testimony, and (2) the four factors listed in *Daubert* do not necessarily apply outside of the hard science context; instead methods of proving reliability will vary, depending upon the field of expertise.

When addressing fields of study aside from the hard sciences, such as the social sciences or fields that are based primarily upon experience and training as opposed to the scientific method, *Kelly* 's requirement of reliability applies but with less rigor than to the hard sciences.   To speak of the validity of a "theory" or "technique" in these fields may be roughly accurate but somewhat misleading. The appropriate questions are: (1) whether the field of expertise is a legitimate one, (2) whether the subject matter of the expert's testimony is within the scope of that field, and (3) whether the expert's testimony properly relies upon and/or utilizes the principles involved in the field. These questions are merely an appropriately tailored translation of the *Kelly* test to areas outside of hard science. And, hard science methods of validation, such as assessing the potential rate of error or subjecting a theory to peer review, may often be inappropriate for testing the reliability of fields of expertise outside the hard sciences.

We turn then, to apply this test to Lanning's testimony. Lanning testified that his analysis was based upon his experience studying cases. He did not contend that he had a particular methodology for determining future dangerousness. Research concerning the behavior of offenders who sexually victimize children appears to be a legitimate field of expertise. Through interviews, case studies, and statistical research, a person may acquire, as a result of such experience, superior knowledge concerning the behavior of such offenders. Moreover, Lanning's testimony shows that future dangerousness is a subject that often surfaces during the course of research in this field. And, Lanning testified that he studied in excess of a thousand cases that concerned the issue of future dangerousness in some fashion. His research involved studying solved cases to attempt to understand the dynamics of what occurred. This research included personal interviews with inmates convicted of child sex offenses, examining the inmates' psychological records, and examining the facts of the offenses involved. Appellant complains about the lack of peer review. But the absence of peer review does not necessarily undercut the reliability of the testimony presented here. To the extent that a factfinder could decide that the absence of peer review cast doubt on the credibility of the testimony, such affects the weight of the evidence rather than its admissibility. We find the reliability of Lanning's testimony to be sufficiently established under Rule 702.

As for appellant's Rule 403 claim, the above discussion shows that Lanning's testimony did not merely duplicate the jury's knowledge because Lanning possessed superior knowledge concerning the behavior of offenders who sexually victimized children. We find that the trial court did not err in determining that the probative value of Lanning's testimony was not substantially outweighed by the danger of unfair prejudice. Point of error one is overruled.

* * * * *

The judgment of the trial court is affirmed.

§ 7-3(B)(2). Underlying Facts or Data

The facts upon which the expert bases an opinion are of three types: facts derived from personal knowledge, facts derived from trial data, and facts derived from outside sources. Suppose, for example, an attorney needs an expert witness to establish a plaintiff's injuries. The attorney's medical expert may base his opinion regarding the plaintiff's injures on:

- The expert's own physical examination of the plaintiff (facts derived from personal knowledge);
- The expert's in-court review of the plaintiff's medical file (facts given from trial data); or
- The expert's in-office review of another doctor's examination of the plaintiff (facts from outside sources).

When an expert bases his opinion upon facts derived from his or her personal knowledge, the expert witness complies with the personal knowledge requirement of Rule 602. Personal knowledge, however, is not a condition precedent to all types of expert opinion testimony. When an expert bases his opinion upon facts reviewed during trial, the facts need not have been admitted into evidence, although the data must be admissible. That is to say, that the proponent could introduce the facts into evidence if he chose to do so. An expert may derive an opinion from outside sources only if the facts could reasonably be relied on by other experts. Another doctor's medical report, for example, would fulfill this requirement because it is reasonable to assume that one doctor could (and would) rely on another doctor's medical report. This does not constitute hearsay under Rule 802 because the outside facts have not been used to prove the truth of the matter asserted, but serve only as the basis for the expert's opinion.

The expert need not disclose the facts upon which she bases her opinion, although the opponent has the right to solicit these facts during cross-examination. Also the court may require the expert to reveal the facts upon which the expert opinion is based. *See* Rule 705.

§ 7-3(B)(3). Scope of Expert Opinion Testimony

Experts may only testify when scientific, technical, or specialized knowledge is required to help the jury understand evidence, or decide an issue. With certain express exceptions, the expert's opinion may address any matter—even the ultimate issue—so long as the relevancy of the opinion can be established. Unlike lay opinion testimony, the expert is not limited to testifying to matters of which he has personal knowledge.

§ 7-4. Comparison Chart — Expert Testimony

	COMPARISON OF ADMISSIBILITY STANDARDS		
	Federal Rules of Evidence	**Texas Civil Cases**	**Texas Criminal Cases**
Who Decides?	Judge (Rule 104(a))	Judge (Rule 104(a))	Judge (Rule 104(a))
Standard for Admissibility	*Daubert*: Validity, i.e. reliability	*Robinson*: Validity, i.e., reliability	*Kelly*: Validity, i.e., reliability a. valid underlying scientific theory b. valid technique applying theory; & c. technique was properly applied
Burden of Proof	POE	POE	Clear and Convincing
Factors to Be Considered by Judge	(1) Has theory been tested? (2) Peer review? (3) Error rate & Standards? (4) Generally accepted?	(1) Extent of testing? (2) Degree of subject. application? (3) Peer review? (4) Error rate? (5) Generally accepted? (6) Nonjudicial uses of theory?	(1) Degree of acceptance? (2) Qual. of expert? (3) Exist. of Lit.? (4) Error rate? (5) Peer review? (6) Clarity of explanation? (7) Skill/experience of person applying?
Applies to What Sort of Evidence? (i.e. "hard" or "soft" science, junk science; or other specialized experience & technical knowledge)?	*Daubert* applies to all forms of expert testimony. *Kumho v. Carmichael*	*Daubert* applies to all forms of expert testimony. *Gammill v. Jack Williams Chev., Inc.*, 972 S.W.2d 713 (Tex. 1998) (case predates *Kumho*)	*Nenno v. State*, 970 S.W.2d 549 (Crim. App. 1998)(*Kelly* test applies to all scientific and nonscientific evidence—applies three-pronged test)

§ 7-5. Notes and Questions

a.   Study and compare the different tests used to determine if expert testimony on novel scientific evidence is admissible. Is there any real difference in Rule 702, *Frye*, *Daubert*, or the Texas case law? If so, what is it?

CHAPTER EIGHT

THE HEARSAY RULE: EXCLUSION, EXEMPTIONS & EXCEPTIONS

§ 8-1. The Hearsay Rule

§ 8-1(A). In General

The hearsay rule operates as a rule of exclusion. With certain express exemptions and exceptions, the hearsay rule, stated in Federal Rule 802, when invoked by a specific hearsay objection, will prevent certain types of testimony from being admitted at trial. The law of evidence prefers testimony which is the most reliable and trustworthy. In-court testimony by a witness is preferred because certain evidentiary safeguards (such as the oath requirement, the personal knowledge requirement, and the opponent's opportunity to cross-examine) help insure and promote the reliability of the witness's testimony. Evidence which either has not been, or cannot be held subject to these safeguards may not be as trustworthy, and thus may be excluded by the hearsay rule.

§ 8-1(B). The Reasons for the Hearsay Rule

Commentators generally agree that there are four reasons supporting the rule excluding hearsay. The first reason is that out-of-court statements are normally not under oath. A person's willingness to subject himself to charges of perjury or false statement generally reflects a willingness to tell the truth.

The second reason is that there may be error in the transmission of the statement. The person making the statement may misspeak or the hearer may err in hearing, remembering, or repeating the statement.

The third reason is the fact that the fact finder was not able to observe the declarant's demeanor at the time of the statement. In assessing a person's credibility it is sometimes important to watch their body language and eye contact. That is all missing if the jury only hears, or reads, the statement made by the declarant.

The final reason is normally considered to be the most important—the inability to cross-examine or confront the declarant at the time the statement was made. This factor is grounded on the assumption that a good cross-examiner could determine if the declarant was sincere, mistaken, lying, or truthful. Indeed, this factor is so important that one sees a convergence of the hearsay rule and the constitutional right to confrontation. Thus, even though a statement may qualify under one of the many hearsay exceptions, it may still be challenged on constitutional grounds.

§ 8-2. Hearsay Defined

Federal Rule 801(c) states that "Hearsay" means a statement that: (1) the declarant does not make while testifying at the current trial; and (2) a party offers in evidence to prove the truth of the matter asserted in the statement."

Thus, for a piece of testimony to be hearsay, it must be:

1)   A STATEMENT (written or oral verbal assertion or nonverbal conduct intended to be an assertion) (WOVA/NVC);

2)   Made by an OUT-OF-THIS-COURT DECLARANT (OTCD); and

3)   Is offered to prove the TRUTH OF THE MATTER ASSERTED (TOMA) in the statement (IS)

Reduced to an equation, the Federal Rule looks like this:

$$\textbf{S (WOVA/NVC) + OTCD + TOMA(IS) = H}$$

Each of these three elements must exist for a piece of evidence to qualify as hearsay. Should one of these elements be lacking, the testimony *is not* hearsay.

For reasons noted, *infra*, the Texas version varies slightly. First, the Texas version uses the word "expression" rather than assertion. And second, the TOMA element may be either express or implied by the declarant's statement. Thus, the Texas model is as follows:

$$\textbf{S (WOVE/NVC) + OTCD + TOMA (IS)(E/I) = H}$$

§ 8-3. The Hearsay Elements Analyzed

§8-3(A). Statement: Assertions & Expressions

A statement may be verbal (i.e., oral, written) or a non-verbal act if it is intended by the declarant as a substitute for a verbal statement. For example, a person's silent hand motion in response to a question, "Which way did they go?" would constitute a statement under Rule 801.

Under the Federal rules, a statement does not qualify under the definition unless the declarant intended it to be an "assertion." Thus, a nonassertive statement such as a question, command, or exclamation will normally not qualify as a statement under the Federal Rule because that rule uses the word "assertion" in defining statement. The federal courts, however, have concluded that such statements might fall within the hearsay definition if they are the functional equivalent of an assertive statement. For example, assume that Jones asks Smith if he is tired, and Smith responds: "Do bears live in the woods?" That question would normally be viewed in context as the functional equivalent of an assertive statement, "Yes, I am tired."

In contrast the Texas rule uses the term "expression." So questions and other non-declarative and non-assertive utterances might be considered statements. This raises the issue of whether an implied assertion by a declarant should be covered by the definition of hearsay. As noted, *supra*, one of the concerns about admitting hearsay statements is the declarant may have been under a mistaken belief at the time of making the statement. In theory, a witness's mistaken belief may be inquired into while on the stand. Admitting hearsay testimony denies that opportunity to the opponent. To guard against that, the drafters of the Texas rule expanded the definition of "Truth of the Matter Asserted" to include not only matters explicitly asserted, but also matters implied by the declarant's statement, if the probative value of the statement (i.e., the reason it is relevant to the case) flows from the belief of the declarant. These sorts of statements are normally referred to as "implied assertions." That is, the declarant says one thing, but it is the declarant's belief which the proponent wants the jury to believe as being true.

The seminal common law case on implied assertions is *Wright v. Doe D. Tatum*, an English case.

WRIGHT v. DOE D. TATUM
7 Ad. & El. 313, 112 Eng. Rep. 488 (Ex. 1837)

[The case arose from an action by Admiral Tatum, a legal heir of John Mardsen, a country gentleman and eccentric bachelor, who left property to a man named Wright in his will. Wright had risen from a position in Mardsen's employment and ended up being the latter's business manager. Tatum challenged the will on the ground that the testator, Mardsen, was not competent. The litigation covered eight years and resulted in 17 different opinions being written in two appellate courts. At trial, Wright offered letters received by Mardsen to show that he was mentally competent. The letter writers, i.e. the declarants, were acquaintances of Mardsen and were deceased at the time of trial. One of the letters asked Mardsen to ask his attorney to settle a case in order to avoid litigation. The others were of a more personal nature, written by friends familiar with each other. The theory of the proponent was that these letters would not have been written by someone who thought that the person receiving the letter was insane. The trial court excluded the letters. That ruling was challenged on appeal.]

Decision by PARKE, B:

The question for us to decide is, whether all or any of the three rejected letters were admissible evidence, on the issue raised in this case, for the purpose of shewing that Mr. Marsden was, from his majority in 1779 to and at the time of the making of the alleged will and codicil in 1822 and 1825, a person of sane mind and memory, and capable of making a will?

It is contended, on the part of the learned counsel for the plaintiff in error, that all were, on two grounds: First, that each of the three letters was evidence of an act done by the writers of them towards the testator, as being a competent person; and that such acts done were admissible evidence on this issue proprio vigore, without any act of recognition, or any act done thereupon by him.

Secondly, that in each of the three cases mentioned in the bill of exceptions, or at least in one of them, there was sufficient evidence of an act done by the testator, with reference to those letters respectively, to render their contents admissible evidence by way of explaining that act upon the principle laid down by the Court of King's Bench. I am of opinion upon a careful consideration of the case and the arguments on both sides, at this Bar, that none of the three letters were admissible, either on one ground or the other. It will be convenient, and facilitate the arrival at a just conclusion, to keep these two questions entirely distinct from each other.

First, then, were all or any of these letters admissible, on the issue in the case as acts done by the writers, assuming, for the sake of arguement, that there was no proof of any act done by the testator upon or relating to these letters or any of them— that is, would such letters or any of them be evidence of the testator's competence at the time of writing them, if sent to the testator's home and not opened or read by him?

Indeed this question is just the same as if the letters had been intercepted before their arrival at his house; for, in so, far as the writing and sending the letters by their respective writers were done by them towards the testator, those acts would in the two supposed cases be actually complete. It is argued that the letters would be admissible because they are evidence of the treatment of the testator as a competent person by individuals acquainted with his habits and personal character, not using the word treatment in a sense involving any conduct of the testator himself; that they are more than mere statements to a third person indicating an opinion of his competence by those persons; they are acts done towards the testator by them, which would not have been done if he had been incompetent, and from which, therefore a legitimate inference may, it is argued, be derived that he was so.

Each of the three letters, no doubt, indicates, that in the opinion of the writer the testator was a rational person. He is spoken of in respectful terms in all. Me. Ellershaw describes him as possessing hospitality and benevolent politeness; and Mr. Marton addresses him as competent to do business to the limited extent to which his letter calls upon him to act; and there is no question but that, if any one of those writers had been living, his evidence, founded on personal observation, that the testator possessed the qualities which justified the opinion expressed or implied in his letters would be admissible on this issue. But the point to be determined is, whether these letters are admissible as proof that he did possess these qualities?

I am of opinion that, according to the established principles of the law of evidence, the letters are all inadmissible for such purpose. One great principle in this law is, that all facts which are relevant to the issue may be proved; another is, that all such facts as have not been admitted by the party against whom they are offered, or some one under whom he claims, ought to be proved under the sanction of an oath (or its equivalent introduced by statute, a solemn affirmation), either on the trial of the issue or some other issue involving the same question between the same parties, or those to whom they are privy. To this rule certain exceptions have been recognised; some from very early times, on the ground of necessity or convenience; such as the proof of the quality and intention of acts by declarations accompanying them; or of pedigrees, and of public rights by the statement of deceased persons presumably well acquainted with the subject, as inhabitants of the district in the one case , or relations within certain limits in the other. Such also is the proof of possession by entries of deceased stewards or receivers charging themselves, or of facts of a public nature by public documents; within none of which exceptions is it contended that the present case be classed.

That the three letters were each of them written by the persons whose names they bear, and sent, at some time before they were found, to the testator's house, no doubt are facts, and those facts are proved on oath; and the letters are without doubt admissible on an issue in which the fact of sending such letters by those persons, and within that limit of time, is relevant to the matter in dispute; as, for instance, on a feigned issue to try the question whether such letters were sent to the testator's house or on any issue in which it is the material question whether such letters or any of them had been sent. Verbal declarations of the same parties are also facts, and in like manner admissible under the circumstances; and so would letters or declarations to third persons upon the like supposition.

But the question is, whether the contents of these letters are evidence of the fact to be proved upon this issue, — that is, the actual existence of the qualities which the testator is, in those letters, by implication, stated to possess: and those letters may be considered in this respect to be on the same footing as if they had contained a direct and positive statement that he was competent. For this purpose they are mere hearsay evidence, statements of the writers, not on oath, of the truth of the matter in question, with this addition, that they have acted upon the statements on the faith of their being true, by sending the letters to the testator. That the so acting cannot give a sufficient sanction for the truth of the statement is perfectly plain; for it is clear that, if the same statements had been made by parol or in writing to a third person, that would have been insufficient, and this is conceded by the learned counsel for the plaintiff in error. Yet in both cases there has been an acting on the belief of the truth, by making the statement, or writing and sending a letter to a third person; and what difference can it possibly make that this is an acting in the same nature by writing and sending the letter to the testator? It is admitted, and most properly, that you have no right to use in evidence the fact of the writing and sending a letter to a third person containing a statement of competence, on the ground that it affords an inference that such an act would not have been done unless the statement was true, or believed to be true, although such an inference no doubt would be raised in the conduct of the ordinary affairs of life, if the statement were made by a man of veracity. But it cannot be raised in a judicial inquiry; and if such an argument were admissible, it would lead to the indiscriminate admission of hearsay evidence of all manner of facts.

Further, it is clear that an acting to a much greater extent and degree upon such statements to a third person would not make the statements admissible. For example, if a wager to a large amount had been made as to the matter in issue by two third persons, the payment of that wager, however large the sum, would not be admissible to prove the truth of the matter in issue. You would not have had any right to present it to the jury as raising an inference to the truth of the fact, on the ground that otherwise the bet would not have been paid. It is, after all, nothing but the mere statement of that fact, with strong evidence of the belief of it by the party making it. Could it make any difference that the wager was between the third person and one of the parties to the suit? Certainly not. The payment by other underwriters on the same policy to the plaintiff could not be given in evidence to prove that the subject insured had been lost. Yet there is an act done, a payment strongly attesting the truth of the statement, which it implies, that there had been a loss. To illustrate this point still further, let us suppose a third person had betted a wager with Mr. Marsden that he could not solve some mathematical problem, the solution of which required a high degree of capacity; would payment of that wager to Mr. Marsden's banker be admissible evidence that he possessed that capacity? The answer is certain; it would not. It would be evidence of the fact of competence given by a third party not upon oath.

Let us suppose the parties who wrote these letters to have stated the matter therein contained, that is, their knowledge of his personal qualities and capacity for business, on oath before a magistrate, or in some judicial proceeding to which the plaintiff and defendant were not parties. No one could contend that such statement would be admissible on this issue; and yet there would have been an act done on the faith of the statement being true, and a very solemn one, which would raise in the ordinary conduct of affairs a strong belief in the truth of the statement, if the writers were faith-worthy. The acting in this case is of much less importance, and certainly is not equal to the sanction of an extra-judicial oath.

Many other instances of a similar nature, by way of illustration, were suggested by the learned counsel for the defendant in error, which, on the most cursory consideration, any one would at once declare to be inadmissible in evidence. Others were supposed on the part of the plaintiff in error, which, at first sight, have the appearance of being mere facts, and therefore admissible, though on further consideration they are open to precisely the same objection. Of the first description are the supposed cases of a letter by a third person to any one demanding a debt, which may be said to be a treatment of him as a debtor, being offered as proof that the debt was really due; a note, congratulating him on his high state of bodily vigor, being proposed as evidence of his being in good health; both of which are manifestly at first sight objectionable. To the latter class belong the supposed conduct of the family or relations of a testator, taking the same precautions in his absence as if he were a lunatic; his election, in his absence, to some high and responsible office; the conduct of a physical who permitted a will to be executed by a sick testator; the conduct of a deceased captain on a question of seaworthiness, who , after examining every part of the vessel, embarked in it with his family; all these, when deliberately considered, are, with reference to the matter in issue in each case, mere instances of hearsay evidence, mere statements, not on oath, but implied in or vouched by the actual conduct of persons by whose acts the litigant parties are not to be bound.

The conclusion at which I have arrived is, that proof of a particular fact, which is not of itself a matter in issue, but which is relevant only as implying a statement or opinion of a third person on the matter in issue, is inadmissible in all cases where such a statement or opinion of a third person on the matter in issue, is inadmissible in all cases where such a statement or opinion not on oath would be of itself inadmissible; and, therefore, in this case the letters which are offered only to prove the competence of the testator, that is the truth of the implied statements therein contained, were properly rejected, as the mere statement or opinion of the writer would certainly have been inadmissible. It is true that evidence of this description has been received in the Ecclesiastical Courts. But their rules of evidence are not the same in all respect as ours. Some greater laxity may be permitted in a Court which adjudicates both on the law and on the fact, and may be more safely trusted with the consideration of such evidence than a jury; and I would observe, also, that in no instance has the propriety of the reception of it even in the Spiritual Courts have been confirmed by the Courts of Delegates. I do not think, therefore, that we are bound by the authority of the cases referred to in the Ecclesiastical Courts.

[The judgment was affirmed, the judges being equally divided.]

———————————

Although the federal drafters rejected the rule in *Wright*, the Texas drafters adopted it in Texas Rule of Evidence 801(c).

§ 8-3(B). Out-of-Court Declarant

Two criteria must be met to satisfy this element. First, under both Federal and Texas rules, the declarant must be a person. A machine, instrument, or animal does not qualify as a declarant for hearsay purposes. It should be noted, however, that if a person created a document using a machine, for example a computer record, the out-of-court declarant requirement would be met for the computer record. The out-of-court declarant requirement would not be met, however, where a machine or instrument created the record itself, such as an ATM receipt.

Second, the declarant must have made the statement out-of-court, i.e., at a time and place other than while testifying in the case at bar. If Lucy testifies in court that "Yesterday, John told me Martin was sick," Lucy's testimony would meet the out-of-court declarant requirement. She was testifying to something that a person told her outside the courtroom—at a *time prior to her testimony.* If instead of Lucy, John had taken the witness stand and testified, "I told Lucy yesterday that Martin was sick," the out-of-court declarant requirement would still be met. At the time John made the statement to Lucy he was not testifying at trial. The same would hold true even if at the time John made the statement, he did so in another courtroom. One way of looking at this requirement is to translate it to mean an "out of this courtroom declarant."

The general rule can be stated in the maxim: "Once an out-of-court declarant, always an out-of-court declarant." This maxim generally holds true even when the out-of-court declarant becomes a witness at trial. Note, however, that an exemption to this concept exists under Texas Rule 801(e)(1) and Federal Rule 801(d)(1).

§ 8-3(C). Truth of the Matter Asserted

§ 8-3(C)(1). In General

A statement by an out-of-court declarant can only be excluded on hearsay grounds if the statement is offered to prove the truth of the matter asserted (TOMA) — in the statement — and not some other relevant issue. The key to determining whether TOMA exists, is being able to determine what the testimony has been offered to prove. In addressing this issue, the query should be: Why has the proponent solicited this particular testimony? For TOMA to exist, the statement must have been made to prove the truth of the statement's contents. Stated another way, if the proponent is not asking the jury to believe that the statement is true, it is not hearsay.

§ 8-3(C)(2). Examples of Nonhearsay Use (Non-TOMA Statements)

There are a number of instances in which an out-of-court statement may be relevant for a nonhearsay purpose—that is, the statement is being offered for some reason other than showing the truth of the matter asserted in the statement (TOMA). For example, suppose in a slip-and-fall case Mary was trying to prove she slipped and fell on a grape negligently left on the floor in the grocery store. Assume that Thelma, an eyewitness, were to testify: "I heard the Manager tell Carl, the clerk, that the grape was on the floor at aisle 36." "TOMA" would exist if Thelma's statement was introduced to prove that a grape was actually on the floor. However, if Thelma's testimony was relevant to show that the manager knew that the grape was on the floor, that Thelma was at the store that day, or explain why Thelma happened to be at aisle 36, TOMA would not exist and the testimony would be admissible for a nonhearsay purpose.

TOMA does not exist where a statement is offered to prove:

1)   Information acted upon, e.g., information provided to a police officer to show that probable cause existed to search the defendant's apartment.

2)   An operative fact, e.g., a whole host of legal documents (wills, search warrants, notice, etc.)

3)   To show the mental state of the statement's declarant, e.g., what the declarant was thinking.

4)   To show a prior inconsistent statement by the declarant.

§ 8-3(D) Definitional Analysis of Hearsay under the Federal and Texas Rules

The following chart briefly notes the basic definitional similarities and differences in the Texas and Federal rules.

	FEDERAL RULE 801	TEXAS RULE 801
OTCD says "It is cold outside" (Assertive Verbal Conduct)	Hearsay	Hearsay
When asked if it's cold outside, Person makes shivering motions (Assertive Nonverbal Conduct)	Hearsay	Hearsay
Person walks to closet and puts on extra heavy coat before going outside. (Nonassertive, Nonverbal Conduct)	Not Hearsay	Not Hearsay
OTCD tells friend " Wear your heavy coat today." (Nonassertive Verbal Conduct)	Not hearsay	Hearsay (Implied Assertion if Probative Value Flows from Belief of OTCD)
OTCD says "I am going to wear my heavy coat this morning" (Assertive Verbal Conduct, for other purposes)	Not hearsay	Hearsay (Implied Assertion if Probative Value Flows from Belief of OTCD)

§ 8-4. Exemptions to Hearsay Rule

The hearsay rule is not absolute. Federal Rule 801(d) lists the exemptions, or exclusions, to the hearsay rule. These exemptions do not constitute hearsay under the rules of evidence — even though the statements would otherwise satisfy the definition of hearsay. Additionally, Federal Rules 803-804 catalogue certain "exceptions" to the hearsay rule. Although these statements technically qualify as hearsay, their underlying reliability (and sometimes necessity) requires their admissibility.

Once it is determined that a piece of evidence qualifies as hearsay, those rules should be consulted to determine whether the evidence can be admitted as either a hearsay "exemption" or a hearsay "exception." If an exemption applies, the statement is not even considered to be hearsay, even if it is offered for the truth of the matter asserted. If, on the other hand, the statement is hearsay and does not qualify as a hearsay exemption, it may still be considered *admissible* hearsay under one of a number of exceptions to the hearsay rule.

This section focuses on the hearsay exemptions. Note that each exemption provision has its own foundation requirements that must be met before the evidence will be admissible.

§ 8-4(A). Prior Statements by Witness Now on Stand

Federal Rule 801(d)(1) indicates that certain prior out-of-court statements by a witness now on the stand will be considered nonhearsay. The exemption extends to a testifying witness's prior inconsistent statements, prior consistent statements, and a statement identifying a person.

§ 8-4(B). Party-Opponent Statements

Rule 801(d)(2) extends hearsay exemptions to those statements which were made by one of the parties to the case and are offered against that party by the opposing party. The rule extends to statements made by a party's spokesperson or one in the employment of the party who made the statement about a matter within the scope of that employment and to statements made by co-conspirators. A classic example of this exemption is a statement (even if intended to be exculpatory) made by a criminal defendant and offered into evidence against the defendant by the prosecution.

Statements falling within this exemption should not be confused with the exception admitting a person's "statement against interest." Those statements are discussed, *infra*.

In *Bourjaily v. United States*, the Supreme Court addressed the issue of what evidence could be considered by the trial judge in deciding whether a statement was admissible under the co-conspirator exemption in Rule 801.

In reading the case, note the Court's approach to interpreting the statutory language of the rule itself and also its approach to the Confrontation Clause challenge.

BOURJAILY v. UNITED STATES
483 U.S. 171 (1987)

Chief Justice REHNQUIST delivered the opinion of the Court.

Federal Rule of Evidence 801(d)(2)(E) provides: "A statement is not hearsay if ... [t]he statement is offered against a party and is ... a statement by a co-conspirator of a party during the course and in furtherance of the conspiracy." We granted certiorari to answer three questions regarding the admission of statements under Rule 801(d)(2)(E): (1) whether the court must determine by independent evidence that the conspiracy existed and that the defendant and the declarant were members of this conspiracy; (2) the quantum of proof on which such determinations must be based; and (3) whether a court must in each case examine the circumstances of such a statement to determine its reliability.

Petitioner was charged with conspiring to distribute cocaine and possession of cocaine with intent to distribute. The Government introduced, over petitioner's objection, Angelo Lonardo's telephone statements regarding the participation of the "friend" in the transaction. The District Court found that, considering the events in the parking lot and Lonardo's statements over the telephone, the Government had established by a preponderance of the evidence that a conspiracy involving Lonardo and petitioner existed, and that Lonardo's statements over the telephone had been made in the course of and in furtherance of the conspiracy. Accordingly, the trial court held that Lonardo's out-of-court statements satisfied Rule 801(d)(2)(E) and were not hearsay. Petitioner was convicted on both counts. The United States Court of Appeals for the Sixth Circuit affirmed. We affirm.

Before admitting a co-conspirator's statement over an objection that it does not qualify under Rule 801(d)(2)(E), a court must be satisfied that the statement actually falls within the definition of the Rule. There must be evidence that there was a conspiracy involving the declarant and the nonoffering party, and that the statement was made "during the course and in furtherance of the conspiracy." Federal Rule of Evidence 104(a) provides: "Preliminary questions concerning ... the admissibility of evidence shall be determined by the court." Petitioner and the Government agree that the existence of a conspiracy and petitioner's involvement in it are preliminary questions of fact that, under Rule 104, must be resolved by the court. The Federal Rules, however, nowhere define the standard of proof the court must observe in resolving these questions.

We are therefore guided by our prior decisions regarding admissibility determinations that hinge on preliminary factual questions. We have traditionally required that these matters be established by a preponderance of proof. Evidence is placed before the jury when it satisfies the technical requirements of the evidentiary Rules, which embody certain legal and policy determinations. The inquiry made by a court concerned with these matters is not whether the proponent of the evidence wins or loses his case on the merits, but whether the evidentiary Rules have been satisfied. Thus, the evidentiary standard is unrelated to the burden of proof on the substantive issues, be it a criminal case, see *In re Winship*, 397 U.S. 358 (1970), or a civil case. *See generally Colorado v. Connelly*, 479 U.S. 157 (1986). The preponderance standard ensures that before admitting evidence, the court will have found it more likely than not that the technical issues and policy concerns addressed by the Federal Rules of Evidence have been afforded due consideration. As in *Lego v. Twomey*, 404 U.S. 477, 488 (1972), we find "nothing to suggest that admissibility rulings have been unreliable or otherwise wanting in quality because not based on some higher standard." We think that our previous decisions in this area resolve the matter. . . . Therefore, we hold that when the preliminary facts relevant to Rule 801(d)(2)(E) are disputed, the offering party must prove them by a preponderance of the evidence.

Even though petitioner agrees that the courts below applied the proper standard of proof with regard to the preliminary facts relevant to Rule 801(d)(2)(E), he nevertheless challenges the admission of Lonardo's statements. Petitioner argues that in determining whether a conspiracy exists and whether the defendant was a member of it, the court must look only to independent evidence—that is, evidence other than the statements sought to be admitted. Petitioner relies on *Glasser v. United States*, 315 U.S. 60 (1942), in which this Court first mentioned the so-called "bootstrapping rule." The relevant issue in *Glasser* was whether Glasser's counsel, who also represented another defendant, faced such a conflict of interest that Glasser received ineffective assistance. Glasser contended that conflicting loyalties led his lawyer not to object to statements made by one of Glasser's co-conspirators. The Government argued that any objection would have been fruitless because the statements were admissible. The Court rejected this proposition: "[S]uch declarations are admissible over the objection of an alleged co-conspirator, who was not present when they were made, only if there is proof aliunde that he is connected with the conspiracy.... Otherwise, hearsay would lift itself by its own bootstraps to the level of competent evidence." Id. The Court revisited the bootstrapping rule in *United States v. Nixon*, 418 U.S. 683 1974), where again, in passing, the Court stated: "Declarations by one defendant may also be admissible against other defendants upon a sufficient showing, by independent evidence, of a conspiracy among one or more other defendants and the declarant and if the declarations at issue were in furtherance of that conspiracy." Read in the light most favorable to petitioner, *Glasser* could mean that a court should not consider hearsay statements at all in determining preliminary facts under Rule

801(d)(2)(E). Petitioner, of course, adopts this view of the bootstrapping rule. *Glasser*, however, could also mean that a court must have some proof aliunde, but may look at the hearsay statements themselves in light of this independent evidence to determine whether a conspiracy has been shown by a preponderance of the evidence. The Courts of Appeals have widely adopted the former view and held that in determining the preliminary facts relevant to co-conspirators' out-of-court statements, a court may not look at the hearsay statements themselves for their evidentiary value.

Both *Glasser* and *Nixon*, however, were decided before Congress enacted the Federal Rules of Evidence in 1975. These Rules now govern the treatment of evidentiary questions in federal courts. Rule 104(a) provides: "Preliminary questions concerning ... the admissibility of evidence shall be determined by the court.... In making its determination it is not bound by the rules of evidence except those with respect to privileges." Similarly, Rule 1101(d)(1) states that the Rules of Evidence (other than with respect to privileges) shall not apply to "[t]he determination of questions of fact preliminary to admissibility of evidence when the issue is to be determined by the court under rule 104." The question thus presented is whether any aspect of Glasser's bootstrapping rule remains viable after the enactment of the Federal Rules of Evidence.

Petitioner concedes that Rule 104, on its face, appears to allow the court to make the preliminary factual determinations relevant to Rule 801(d)(2)(E) by considering any evidence it wishes, unhindered by considerations of admissibility. That would seem to many to be the end of the matter. Congress has decided that courts may consider hearsay in making these factual determinations. Out-of-court statements made by anyone, including putative co-conspirators, are often hearsay. Even if they are, they may be considered, *Glasser* and the bootstrapping rule notwithstanding. But petitioner nevertheless argues that the bootstrapping rule, as most Courts of Appeals have construed it, survived this apparently unequivocal change in the law unscathed and that Rule 104, as applied to the admission of co-conspirator's statements, does not mean what it says. We disagree.

Petitioner claims that Congress evidenced no intent to disturb the bootstrapping rule, which was embedded in the previous approach, and we should not find that Congress altered the rule without affirmative evidence so indicating. It would be extraordinary to require legislative history to confirm the plain meaning of Rule 104. The Rule on its face allows the trial judge to consider any evidence whatsoever, bound only by the rules of privilege. We think that the Rule is sufficiently clear that to the extent that it is inconsistent with petitioner's interpretation of *Glasser* and *Nixon*, the Rule prevails.

Nor do we agree with petitioner that this construction of Rule 104(a) will allow courts to admit hearsay statements without any credible proof of the conspiracy, thus fundamentally changing the nature of the co-conspirator exception. Petitioner starts with the proposition that co-conspirators' out-of-court statements are deemed unreliable and are inadmissible, at least until a conspiracy is shown. Since these statements are unreliable, petitioner contends that they should not form any part of the basis for establishing a conspiracy, the very antecedent that renders them admissible.

Petitioner's theory ignores two simple facts of evidentiary life. First, out-of-court statements are only presumed unreliable. The presumption may be rebutted by appropriate proof. *See* Fed. Rule Evid. 803(24) (otherwise inadmissible hearsay may be admitted if circumstantial guarantees of trustworthiness demonstrated). Second, individual pieces of evidence, insufficient in themselves to prove a point, may in cumulation prove it. The sum of an evidentiary presentation may well be greater than its constituent parts. Taken together, these two propositions demonstrate that a piece of evidence, unreliable in isolation, may become quite probative when corroborated by other evidence. A per se rule barring consideration of these hearsay statements during preliminary fact finding is not therefore required. Even if out-of-court declarations by co-conspirators are presumptively unreliable, trial courts must be permitted to evaluate these statements for their evidentiary worth as revealed by the particular circumstances of the case. Courts often act as factfinders, and there is no reason to believe that courts are any less able to properly recognize the probative value of evidence in this particular area. The party opposing admission has an adequate incentive to point out the shortcomings in such evidence before the trial court finds the preliminary facts. If the opposing party is unsuccessful in keeping the evidence from the factfinder, he still has the opportunity to attack the probative value of the evidence as it relates to the substantive issue in the case. *See, e.g.*, Fed. Rule Evid. 806 (allowing attack on credibility of out-of-court declarant).

We think that there is little doubt that a co-conspirator's statements could themselves be probative of the existence of a conspiracy and the participation of both the defendant and the declarant in the conspiracy. Petitioner's case presents a paradigm. The out-of-court statements of Lonardo indicated that Lonardo was involved in a conspiracy with a "friend." The statements indicated that the friend had agreed with Lonardo to buy a kilogram of cocaine and to distribute it. The statements also revealed that the friend would be at the hotel parking lot, in his car, and would accept the cocaine from Greathouse's car after Greathouse gave Lonardo the keys. Each one of Lonardo's statements may itself be unreliable, but taken as a whole, the entire conversation between Lonardo and Greathouse was corroborated by independent evidence. The friend, who turned out to be petitioner, showed up at the prearranged spot at the prearranged time. He picked up the cocaine, and a significant sum of money was found in his car. On these facts, the trial court concluded, in our view correctly, that the Government had established the existence of a conspiracy and petitioner's participation in it.

We need not decide in this case whether the courts below could have relied solely upon Lonardo's hearsay statements to determine that a conspiracy had been established by a preponderance of the evidence. To the extent that *Glasser* meant that courts could not look to the hearsay statements themselves for any purpose, it has clearly been superseded by Rule 104(a). It is sufficient for today to hold that a court, in making a preliminary factual determination under Rule 801(d)(2)(E), may examine the hearsay statements sought to be admitted. As we have held in other cases concerning admissibility determinations, "the judge should receive the evidence and give it such weight as his judgment and experience counsel." *United States v. Matlock*, 415 U.S., at 175. The courts below properly considered the statements of Lonardo and the subsequent events in finding that the Government had established by a preponderance of the evidence that Lonardo was involved in a conspiracy with petitioner. We have no reason to believe that the District Court's factfinding of this point was clearly erroneous. We hold that Lonardo's out-of-court statements were properly admitted against petitioner.

We also reject any suggestion that admission of these statements against petitioner violated his rights under the Confrontation Clause of the Sixth Amendment. That Clause provides: "In all criminal prosecutions, the accused shall enjoy the right ... to be confronted with the witnesses against him." At petitioner's trial, Lonardo exercised his right not to testify. Petitioner argued that Lonardo's unavailability rendered the admission of his out-of-court statements unconstitutional since petitioner had no opportunity to confront Lonardo as to these statements. The Court of Appeals held that the requirements for admission under Rule 801(d)(2)(E) are identical to the requirements of the Confrontation Clause, and since the statements were admissible under the Rule, there was no constitutional problem. We agree.

Accordingly, we hold that the Confrontation Clause does not require a court to embark on an independent inquiry into the reliability of statements that satisfy the requirements of Rule 801(d)(2)(E).

The judgment of the Court of Appeals is affirmed.

Federal Rule of Evidence 801(d)(2) was amended in 1997 to reflect the results of *Bourjaily*. However, the drafters went further; the rule now states that the judge "must" consider the contents of the proffered statement itself (but not only the statement) in deciding whether it falls within the exemption. The amendment also extends to statements made by agents or employees.

§ 8-5. Hearsay Exceptions: Unavailability of Declarant Not Required

If a statement constitutes hearsay and there is no available hearsay exemption, the proponent may find an applicable hearsay exception in either Federal Rule of Evidence 803 or 804. The basic difference in the two rules is that in Rule 803, the proponent need not show that the declarant is unavailable. Under Rule 804, however, the unavailability of the declarant is an indispensable requirement.

The hearsay exceptions codify to a great extent common law recognition that certain out-of-court statements have indicia of reliability. Consider, for example, Rule 803(2) which covers excited utterances. The law generally recognizes that a declarant's excited utterance about a startling event is more likely to be free from deception. As with the exemptions, *supra*, each exception has its own set of foundation elements, which the proponent must be prepared to establish.

The following discussion addresses some of the more commonly encountered hearsay exceptions and some of the problems which the proponent is likely to encounter.

§ 8-5(A). Present Sense Impression

Federal Rule 803(1) indicates that a declarant's statement which describes what is currently taking place is admissible as a hearsay exception. The key element here is that the statement is being made contemporaneously with observing or otherwise sensing the event. If the declarant waits too long to make the statement, it will normally not be admissible under this exception.

§ 8-5(B). Excited Utterance

While the indicia of reliability under Rule 803(1) is contemporaneity, under Rule 803(2) it is the spontaneity of the declarant's statement. The statement may be in response to a question, but the proponent should be prepared to show that a particular startling event took place, the declarant observed it, and the statement, caused by the stress or excitement of that observation, relates to that startling event.

§ 8-5(C). Existing Mental, Emotional or Physical State

Rule 803(3) covers the declarant's existing condition. For example, the declarant says "I am angry" or "I hurt." The exception does not extend to past conditions, which might be covered in Rule 803(4), *infra*. The exception would include a statement evidencing an intent or plan to do something.

One of the problems that arises under this exception is the question of whether the declarant's statement of an intent to do something is admissible to show subsequent conduct. That issue was addressed in the important case of *Mutual Life Insurance Company v. Hillmon.*

MUTUAL LIFE INS. CO. v. HILLMON
145 U.S. 285 (1892)

[Sallie E. Hillmon brought an action against the Mutual Life Insurance Company on a policy of the life of her husband, John W. Hillmon, in the sum of $10,000, payable to her within 60 days after notice and proof of his death. The declaration alleged that Hillmon died on March 17, 1879, during the continuance of the policy, but that the defendant, though duly notified of the fact, had refused to pay the amount of the policy, or any part thereof; and the answer denied the death of Hillmon, and that Hillmon and others conspired to defraud the insurance company and falsely pretended and represented that Hillmon was dead, and that the produced body was in fact that of a man named Walters. In an effort to show that the body was that of Walters, the insurance company offered letters written by Walters to his sister and girlfriend. Those letters stated an intention to travel with Hillmon. After ruling on a procedural issue which required reversal of the case, the Court addressed the admissibility of those letters.]

Mr. Justice GRAY delivered the opinion of the court.

There is, however, one question of evidence so important, so fully argued at the bar, and so likely to arise upon another trial, that it is proper to express an opinion upon it.

This question is of the admissibility of the letters written by Walters on the first days of March, 1879, which were offered in evidence by the defendants, and excluded by the court. In order to determine the competency of these letters it is important to consider the state of the case when they were offered to be read.

The matter chiefly contested at the trial was the death of John W. Hillmon, the insured; and that depended upon the question whether the body found at Crooked Creek on the night of March 18, 1879, was his body or the body of one Walters.

Much conflicting evidence had been introduced as to the identity of the body. The plaintiff had also introduced evidence that Hillmon and one Brown left Wichita, in Kansas, on or about March 5, 1879, and traveled together through southern Kansas in search of a site for a cattle ranch; and that on the night of March 18th, while they were in camp at Crooked Creek, Hillmon was accidentally killed, and that his body was taken thence and buried. The defendants had introduced evidence, without objection, that Walters left his home and his betrothed in Iowa in March, 1878, and was afterwards in Kansas until March, 1879; that during that time he corresponded regularly with his family and his betrothed; that the last letters received from him were one received by his betrothed on March 3d, and postmarked at 'Wichita, March 2,' and one received by his sister about March 4th or 5th, and dated at Wichita a day or two before; and that he had not been heard from since.

The evidence that Walters was at Wichita on or before March 5th, and had not been heard from since, together with the evidence to identify as his the body found at Crooked Creek on March 18th, tended to show that he went from Wichita to Crooked Creek between those dates. Evidence that just before March 5th he had the intention of leaving Wichita with Hillmon would tend to corroborate the evidence already admitted, and to show that he went from Wichita to Crooked Creek with Hillmon. Letters from him to his family and his betrothed were the natural, if not the only attainable, evidence of his intention.

The position taken at the bar that the letters were competent evidence, within the rule stated in *Nicholls v. Webb*, 8 Wheat. 326, 337, as memoranda made in the ordinary course of business, cannot be maintained, for they were clearly not such.

But upon another ground suggested they should have been admitted. A man's state of mind or feeling can only be manifested to others by countenance, attitude, or gesture, or by sounds or words, spoken or written. The nature of the fact to be proved is the same, and evidence of its proper tokens is equally competent to prove it, whether expressed by aspect or conduct, by voice or pen. When the intention to be proved is important only as qualifying an act, its connection with that act must be shown, in order to warrant the admission of declarations of the intention. But whenever the intention is of itself a distinct and material fact in a chain of circumstances, it may be proved by contemporaneous oral or written declarations of the party.

The existence of a particular intention in a certain person at a certain time being a material fact to be proved, evidence that he expressed that intention at that time is as direct evidence of the fact as his own testimony that he then had that intention would be. After his death these can hardly be any other way of proving it, and while he is still alive his own memory of his state of mind at a former time is no more likely to be clear and true than a bystander's recollection of what he then said, and is less trustworthy than letters written by him at the very time and under circumstances precluding a suspicion of misrepresentation.

The letters in question were competent not as narratives of facts communicated to the writer by others, nor yet as proof that he actually went away from Wichita, but as evidence that, shortly before the time when other evidence tended to show that he went away, he had the intention of going, and of going with Hillmon, which made it more probable both that he did go and that he went with Hillmon than if there had been no proof of such intention. In view of the mass of conflicting testimony introduced upon the question whether it was the body of Walters that was found in Hillmon's camp, this evidence might properly influence the jury in determining that question.

The rule applicable to this case has been thus stated by this court: 'Wherever the bodily or mental feelings of an individual are material to be proved, the usual expressions of such feelings are original and competent evidence. Those expressions are the natural reflexes of what it might be impossible to show by other testimony. If there be such other testimony, this may be necessary to set the facts thus developed in their true light, and to give them their proper effect. As independent, explanatory, or corroborative evidence it is often indispensable to the due administration of justice. Such declarations are regarded as verbal acts, and are as competent as any other testimony, when relevant to the issue. Their truth or falsity is an inquiry for the jury.

In accordance with this rule, a bankrupt's declarations, oral or by letter, at or before the time of leaving or staying away from home, as to his reason for going abroad, have always been held by the English courts to be competent, in an action by his assignees against a creditor, as evidence that his departure was with intent to defraud his creditors, and therefore an act of bankruptcy.

In actions for criminal conversation, letters by the wife to her husband or to third persons are competent to show her affection towards her husband, and her reasons for living apart from him, if written before any misconduct on her part, and if there is no ground to suspect collusion. So letters from a husband to a third person, showing his state of feeling, affection, and sympathy for his wife, have been held by this court to be competent evidence, bearing on the validity of the marriage, when the legitimacy of their children is in issue.

Even in the probate of wills, which are required by law to be in writing, executed and attested in prescribed forms, yet, where the validity of a will is questioned for want of mental capacity, or by reason of fraud and undue influence, or where the will is lost, and it becomes necessary to prove its contents, written or oral evidence of declarations of the testator before the date of the will has been admitted, in Massachusetts and in England, to show his real intention as to the disposition of his property, although there has been a difference of opinion as to the admissibility, for such purposes, of his subsequent declarations.

Upon principle and authority, therefore, we are of opinion that the two letters were competent evidence of the intention of Walters at the time of writing them, which was a material fact bearing upon the question in controversy; and that for the exclusion of these letters, as well as for the undue restriction of the defendants' challenges, the verdicts must be set aside, and a new trial had.

Judgment reversed, and case remanded to the circuit court, with directions to set aside the verdict and to order a new trial.

---

§ 8-5(D). Statements for Purposes of Medical Diagnosis

Under Rule 803(4), the proponent may avoid the hearsay rule by showing that the offered statements were made in the course of obtaining a medical diagnosis or treatment. This exception would cover a declarant's "medical history" statements which reflect past feelings or conditions.

§ 8-5(E). Recorded Recollection

Federal Rule of Evidence 803(5) addresses the admissibility of a writing which reflects a past event recorded by the witness now on the stand. It is used where the witness cannot currently recall the event but is able to establish that he or she once did recall the details of the event and recorded it in writing. This exception relates to, but is distinct from, attempts by counsel to refresh the recollection of the witness. That topic is covered in Federal Rule 612 (writing used to refresh memory). The typical progression is for counsel to attempt to revive the witness's memory and if that fails lay the foundation for the writing which reflects the recorded recollection of the witness.

The following chart demonstrates the relationship of the two rules, in both the federal and Texas versions.

COMPARISON: PAST RECOLLECTION RECORDED — PRESENT MEMORY REFRESHED

	Present Memory Refreshed (Rule 612)	Past Recollection Recorded (Rule 803(5))
Writing Used As —	Used as "jogger" of memory	Is the Evidence itself
Trigger ?	Temporary Loss of Memory	Insufficient "Recollection"
Personal Knowledge	Implicit	Required by Rule
Introduced as an Exhibit By	Opponent, if at all	Read into evidence by Proponent & Introduced As Exhibit by Opponent, if at all
Production of Writing for Examination By Opponent	Civil Case • during testimony (right to examine) • before testifying (discretionary) Criminal Case • right to examine	N/A
If Proponent of Witness Fails to Produce Writing	Civil Case • Any order justice requires. Criminal Case • Any order justice requires; • If Gov. refuses, strike testimony or declare mistrial	N/A

§ 8-5(F). Business Records

The familiar business records exception to the hearsay rule is located in Rule 803(6). The basis for treating business records as an exception rests on the assumption that businesses have a duty to accurately and routinely record data pertinent to their activity; failure to do so may have an adverse impact on their ability to function.

One of the key elements to this exception is that the written record is recorded in the regular course of business. In the case of *Johnson v. Lutz*, the court addressed that element.

JOHNSON v. LUTZ
170 N.E. 517 (N.Y. 1930)

HUBBS, J.

This action is to recover damages for the wrongful death of the plaintiff's intestate, who was killed when his motorcycle came into collision with the defendants' truck at a street intersection. There was a sharp conflict in the testimony in regard to the circumstances under which the collision took place. A policeman's report of the accident filed by him in the station house was offered in evidence by the defendants under section 374-a of the Civil Practice Act, and was excluded. The sole ground for reversal urged by the appellants is that said report was erroneously excluded. That section reads: 'Any writing or record, whether in the form of an entry in a book or otherwise, made as a memorandum or record of any act, transaction, occurrence or event, shall be admissible in evidence in proof of said act, transaction, occurrence or event, if the trial judge shall find that it was made in the regular course of any business, and that it was the regular course of such business to make such memorandum or record at the time of such act, transaction, occurrence or event, or within a reasonable time thereafter. All other circumstances of the making of such writing or record, including lack of personal knowledge by the entrant or maker, may be shown to affect its weight, but they shall not affect its admissibility. The term business shall include business, profession, occupation and calling of every kind.'

Prior to the decision in the well-known case of *Vosburgh v. Thayer*, 12 Johns. 461, decided in 1815, shopbooks could not be introduced in evidence to prove an account. The decision in that case established that they were admissible where preliminary proof could be made that there were regular dealings between the parties; that the plaintiff kept honest and fair books; that some of the articles charged had been delivered; and that the plaintiff kept no clerk. At that time it might not have been a hardship to require a shopkeeper who sued to recover an account to furnish the preliminary proof required by that decision. Business was transacted in a comparatively small way, with few, if any, clerks.

Under modern conditions, the limitations upon the right to use books of account, memoranda, or records, made in the regular course of business, often resulted in a denial of justice, and usually in annoyance, expense, and waste of time and energy. A rule of evidence that was practical a century ago had become obsolete. The situation was appreciated, and attention was called to it by the courts and text-writers.

It is apparent that the Legislature enacted section 374-a to carry out the purpose announced in the report of the committee. That purpose was to secure the enactment of a statute which would afford a more workable rule of evidence in the proof of business transactions under existing business conditions.

In view of the history of section 374-a and the purpose for which it was enacted, it is apparent that it was never intended to apply to a situation like that in the case at bar. The memorandum in question was not made in the regular course of any business, profession, occupation, or calling. The policeman who made it was not present at the time of the accident. The memorandum was made from hearsay statements of third persons who happened to be present at the scene of the accident when he arrived. It does not appear whether they saw the accident and stated to him what they knew, or stated what some other persons had told them.

The purpose of the Legislature in enacting section 374-a was to permit a writing or record, made in the regular course of business, to be received in evidence, without the necessity of calling as witnesses all of the persons who had any part in making it, provided the record was made as a part of the duty of the person making it, or on information imparted by persons who were under a duty to impart such information. The amendment permits the introduction of shopbooks without the necessity of calling all clerks who may have sold different items of account. It was not intended to permit the receipt in evidence of entries based upon voluntary hearsay statements made by third parties not engaged in the business or under any duty in relation thereto. It was said, in *Mayor, etc., of New York City v. Second Ave. R. Co.*, 102 N. Y. 572, at page 581, 7 N. E. 905, 909, 55 Am. Rep. 839: 'It is a proper qualification of the rule admitting such evidence that the account must have been made in the ordinary course of business, and that it should not be extended so as to admit a mere private memorandum, not made in pursuance of any duty owing by the person making it, or when made upon information derived from another who made the communication casually and voluntarily, and not under the sanction of duty or other obligation.'

An important consideration leading to the amendment was the fact that in the business world credit is given to records made in the course of business by persons who are engaged in the business upon information given by others engaged in the same business as part of their duty.

Such entries are dealt with in that way in the most important undertakings of mercantile and industrial life. They are the ultimate basis of calculation, investment, and general confidence in every business enterprise. Nor does the practical impossibility of obtaining constantly and permanently the verification of every employee affect the trust that is given to such books. It would seem that expedients which the entire commercial world recognizes as safe could be sanctioned, and not discredited, by courts of justice. When it is a mere question of whether provisional confidence can be placed in a certain class of statements, there cannot profitably and sensibly be one rule for the business world and another for the court-room. The merchant and the manufacturer must not be turned away remodels because the methods in which the entire community places a just confidence are a little difficult to reconcile with technical judicial scruples on the part of the same persons who as attorneys have already employed and relied upon the same methods. In short, courts must here cease to be pedantic and endeavor to be practical.' 3 WIGMORE ON EVIDENCE (1923) § 1530, p. 278.

The Legislature has sought by the amendment to make the courts practical. It would be unfortunate not to give the amendment a construction which will enable it to cure the evil complained of and accomplish the purpose for which it was enacted. In construing it, we should not, however, permit it to be applied in a case for which it was never intended.

The judgment should be affirmed, with costs.

While the court in *Johnson* focused on the statements of a bystander—someone without a business motivation—it did not squarely address another sub-issue of whether the statements were made in the course of business. That raises the question: What actually constitutes regular course of business? The Supreme Court addressed that issue in *Palmer v. Hoffman*.

PALMER v. HOFFMAN
318 U.S. 109 (1943)

Mr. Justice DOUGLAS delivered the opinion of the Court.

This case arose out of a grade crossing accident which occurred in Massachusetts. Diversity of citizenship brought it to the federal District Court in New York. There were several causes of action. The District Court entered judgment on the verdict. The Circuit Court of Appeals affirmed, one judge dissenting. The case is here on a petition for a writ of certiorari which presents three points.

The accident occurred on the night of December 25, 1940. On December 27, 1940, the engineer of the train, who died before the trial, made a statement at a freight office of petitioners where he was interviewed by an assistant superintendent of the road and by a representative of the Massachusetts Public Utilities Commission. This statement was offered in evidence by petitioners under 28 U.S.C. § 695. They offered to prove (in the language of the Act) that the statement was signed in the regular course of business, it being the regular course of such business to make such a statement. Respondent's objection to its introduction was sustained.

We agree with the majority view below that it was properly excluded.

We may assume that if the statement was made 'in the regular course' of business, it would satisfy the other provisions of the Act. But we do not think that it was made 'in the regular course' of business within the meaning of the Act. The business of the petitioners is the railroad business. That business like other enterprises entails the keeping of numerous books and records essential to its conduct or useful in its efficient operation. Though such books and records were considered reliable and trustworthy for major decisions in the industrial and business world, their use in litigation was greatly circumscribed or hedged about by the hearsay rule—restrictions which greatly increased the time and cost of making the proof where those who made the records were numerous. It was that problem which started the movement towards adoption of legislation embodying the principles of the present Act. And the legislative history of the Act indicates the same purpose.

The engineer's statement which was held inadmissible in this case falls into quite a different category. It is not a record made for the systematic conduct of the business as a business. An accident report may affect that business in the sense that it affords information on which the management may act. It is not, however, typical of entries made systematically or as a matter of routine to record events or occurrences, to reflect transactions with others, or to provide internal controls. The conduct of a business commonly entails the payment of tort claims incurred by the negligence of its employees. But the fact that a company makes a business out of recording its employees' versions of their accidents does not put those statements in the class of records made 'in the regular course' of the business within the meaning of the Act. If it did, then any law office in the land could follow the same course, since business as defined in the Act includes the professions. We would then have a real perversion of a rule designed to facilitate admission of records which experience has shown to be quite trustworthy. Any business by installing a regular system for recording and preserving its version of accidents for which it was potentially liable could qualify those reports under the Act. The result would be that the Act would cover any system of recording events or occurrences provided it was 'regular' and though it had little or nothing to do with the management or operation of the business as such. Preparation of cases for trial by virtue of being a 'business' or incidental thereto would obtain the benefits of this liberalized version of the early shop book rule. The probability of trustworthiness of records because they were routine reflections of the day to day operations of a business would be forgotten as the basis of the rule. Regularity of preparation would become the test rather than the character of the records and their earmarks of acquired from their source and origin and the nature of their compilation. We cannot so completely empty the words of the Act of their historic meaning. If the Act is to be extended to apply not only to a 'regular course' of a business but also to any 'regular course' of conduct which may have some relationship to business, Congress not this Court must extend it. Such a major change which opens wide the door to avoidance of cross-examination should not be left to implication. Nor is it any answer to say that Congress has provided in the Act that the various circumstances of the making of the record should affect its weight not its admissibility. That provision comes into play only in case the other requirements of the Act are met.

In short, it is manifest that in this case those reports are not for the systematic conduct of the enterprise as a railroad business. Unlike payrolls, accounts receivable, accounts payable, bills of lading and the like these reports are calculated for use essentially in the court, not in the business. Their primary utility is in litigating, not in railroading.

It is, of course, not for us to take these reports out of the Act if Congress has put them in. But there is nothing in the background of the law on which this Act was built or in its legislative history which suggests for a moment that the business of preparing cases for trial should be included.

The several hundred years of history behind the Act indicate the nature of the reforms which it was designed to effect. It should of course be liberally interpreted so as to do away with the anachronistic rules which gave rise to its need and at which it was aimed. But 'regular course' of business must find its meaning in the inherent nature of the business in question and in the methods systematically employed for the conduct of the business as a business.

Affirmed.

---

§ 8-5(G). Public Records and Reports

Federal Rule of Evidence 803(8) covers another well-established exception to the hearsay rule—an exception for public records and reports. The indicia of reliability in this exception rests in large part on the fact that public offices have a duty to accurately collect, report, and record certain data. The exception covers a wide range of public documents.

Although Rule 803(8) seems to reflect well-established common law, subdivisions (A)(ii) and (A)(iii) place limitations on the ability of the government to introduce its own reports.

Subdivision (A)(ii) indicates that matters observed pursuant to a duty to do so may be admitted under the exception, unless the evidence is being offered during a criminal case and the matters were observed by police officers and other law enforcement personnel. No such limitation exists in Rule 803(6), *supra*. Subdivision (A)(iii) indicates that if the report or record contains factual conclusions resulting from an investigation, it may only be introduced during a civil case or during a criminal case, if offered by the defense against the government.

The limitation in Rule 803(8)(A)(ii), formerly Rule 803(8)(B), was the subject of *United States v. Oates*, 560 F.2d 45 (2d Cir. 1977). In *Oates*, the court took the minority position that if the offered police report was not admissible under Rule 803(8), it was not admissible under Rule 803(6). That is, the prosecution could not introduce the report through the backdoor of the business records exception.

In *Cole v. State*, the Texas Court of Criminal Appeals extended the *Oates* rationale to Texas criminal cases.

COLE v. STATE
839 S.W.2d 798 (Tex. Ct. Crim. App. 1990) (on rehearing)

OPINION ON STATE'S MOTION FOR REHEARING

PER CURIAM.

In our original opinion…, we addressed the "the sole issue of whether the court of appeals erred in holding that the trial court correctly admitted hearsay evidence concerning the results of chemical tests performed by an absent Department of Public Safety chemist pursuant to Rule 803(6) of the Texas Rules of Criminal Evidence". Based largely upon the Second Circuit's holding in *United States v. Oates*, 560 F.2d 45 (2nd Cir.1977), we held that the exclusionary provision contained in Texas Rule of Criminal Evidence 803(8)(B), the public records exception to the hearsay rule, precluded admission of the laboratory reports under Rule 803(6). The State filed a Motion for Rehearing, primarily asking that we reconsider our holding in light of widespread judicial and academic criticism leveled at the Oates decision. In this opinion, we will clarify portions of our original opinion in response to issues raised in the State's Motion for Rehearing.

I.
Admissibility of the Reports Under Rule 803(8)(B)

Before addressing the applicability of Rule 803(6), we initially concluded in our original opinion that the subject reports did not "satisfy the requirements of TRCE 803(8), since the reports were 'matters observed' by 'other law enforcement personnel.'" In its Motion for Rehearing, the State contends that DPS chemists are not "law enforcement personnel" within the meaning of Rule 803(8)(B). The State further asserts that the analysis and testing procedures conducted by chemists in a DPS laboratory are of an "unambiguous factual nature" and the reports are therefore not the type of documents intended to fall within the exclusionary provision of Rule 803(8)(B). After careful examination of the State's grounds for rehearing in this regard, we conclude the issue was correctly decided in our original opinion. However, in light of the State's Motion for Rehearing, further clarification is called for on this issue.

The State points to decisions of federal courts and other state courts which hold that certain types of documents are admissible because they are determined to be "routine, objective reports prepared by officials with no inherent motivation to distort the results." While we acknowledge the existence of considerable authority holding that chemical analyses and certain laboratory tests and reports are routine and objective in nature and therefore admissible, we are not convinced of the same here. Additionally, the opinions of many courts that hold laboratory reports to be generally objective and routine in nature are often inadequate in their consideration of the adversarial and investigatory context out of which many such scientific reports arise. . . .

The State's assertion that the analyses here were "objective, routine, scientific determinations of an unambiguous factual nature" implies that the conducting chemist-toxicologist merely fed data into a computer and mechanically read a printout of definitive results, absent any element of human error or individual interpretation. Examination of the testimony of Jim Thomas, the supervising chemist who testified at appellant's trial, reveals that at least the hair analysis conducted here was remarkably subjective in nature as well as remarkably imprecise and subject to individual interpretation. The following excerpts of Thomas' testimony are illustrative on this point.

When asked to describe what a forensic chemist does, Thomas testified that a forensic chemist analyzes data by making comparisons:

> A forensic chemist will take evidence that is admitted to our laboratory concerning a criminal investigation, this could be evidence such as trace evidence, like blood, or hair and fibers, glass, paint; we will take those samples, and usually it is a comparison with a known sample. *We will take one sample and compare it to the known sample.*(emphasis added by court).

* * * * * *

> Q. Let me ask you this, Mr. Thomas, in effect, what you did was put both these hairs under microscopes and look at them, didn't you?
> A. We have a comparison microscope to where you can put one sample on one side and one on the other and you view them simultaneously side by side.
> Q. So the purpose of the test is to eyeball and see if, in your opinion, they look alike?
> A. The purpose of the test is to look at the characteristics of each hair side by side, and see if they are comparable, that's right.

Language used by Thomas in describing the process involved in conducting a hair analysis reveals the imprecise nature of that process:

> The hair comparison is more of a comparison of characteristics, and *you are just seeing if there are any exclusions* to this having been the individual, or *whether it is still within the realm of possibility*, that hair being from an individual.

> As far as hair samples are concerned, there are variations of the characteristics within one individual's head of hair. Sometimes those variations themselves are specific enough where you can make a more positive conclusion, but since *there are so many variations within one individual and between individuals*, you are— with hairs, you are just taking one sample and comparing it to another sample, seeing how the characteristics compare microscopically, and *seeing if it is within the realm of possibility that this hair could have been contributed by this individual*, or whether the characteristics are such that you can exclude the individual. (emphasis added by court).

We cannot conclude that the reports here were "objective, routine, scientific determinations of an unambiguous factual nature."

The subjective nature of the testing process is not the lone factor for consideration in determining the admissibility of a report under Rule 803(8)(B)'s exclusionary provision. Substantial attention should be given to the adversarial context in which the relevant tests were conducted. A DPS laboratory is a uniquely litigious and prosecution-oriented environment. The subject reports appear on the letterhead of the "Department of Public Safety, Crime Laboratory Division", bearing the seal of the State of Texas to the right of the letterhead and a law enforcement insignia to the left. The "Prosecuting Attorney" was carbon copied on the reports and the reports close with the statement that "We are returning this evidence to the Lubbock Police Department property room", in an apparent effort to document the chain of custody. When asked to describe what a "forensic chemist" does, Thomas stated that "a forensic chemist will take evidence that is admitted to our laboratory *concerning a criminal investigation*.". (emphasis added by court). We conclude that we were wholly correct in holding in our original opinion that:

> The items upon which the tests were performed were collected as part of investigating a crime, and the reports prepared by the DPS chemist were unquestionably a product of evaluating the results of that investigation. Furthermore, and perhaps most importantly, the reports were not prepared for purposes independent of specific litigation, nor were they ministerial, objective observations of an unambiguous factual nature. Therefore, we find that the letter reports in the instant case fail to satisfy the requirements of TRCE 803(8)(B), since they constitute "matters observed" by "other law enforcement personnel," and are therefore inadmissible.

II.

Admissibility of the Reports Under Rule 803(6)

The second issue addressed in our original opinion was "whether hearsay evidence which does not qualify as an exception under TRCE 803(8) may nevertheless qualify under TRCE 803(6) as a business records exception". We held that "it would be inconsistent with the intended effect of [Rule 803(8)(B) to] allow such evidence to be admitted under TRCE 803(6) as a business record." We conclude this issue was correctly decided in our original opinion, but write to clarify our original opinion and address issues raised in the State's Motion for Rehearing. The State argues that a portion of the *Oates* opinion relied upon by this Court in our original opinion has since been retracted, points to considerable authority rejecting *Oates*' (and therefore our original opinion's) construction of Rules 803(6) and 803(8)(B), and asserts that our holding does not take into account all of the relevant legislative history.

In its lengthy opinion in *Oates*, the Second Circuit concluded that Congress intended that reports failing to qualify as admissible under 803(8)(B) are also inadmissible under 803(6) "or any of the other exceptions to the hearsay rule." We have re-examined the relevant legislative history and remain convinced that it supports our holding on original submission that documents inadmissible under 803(8)(B) may not be admitted under 803(6). However, we emphasize that our holding only pertains to the use of Rule 803(6) as a "back door" to evidence inadmissible under Rule 803(8)(B).

The State claims that our conclusions based upon the legislative history are "plainly contradicted by clear language in that history to the contrary." In support of its assertion, the State points to the following statement, made during discussions of Rule 803(5) and appearing in Senate and House Reports by the Committee on the Judiciary:

a memorandum or report, although barred by this Rule, would nonetheless be admissible if it came within another hearsay exception ... This principle is deemed applicable to all hearsay rules.

This statement reiterates the general rule that evidence which is inadmissible under one hearsay exception may often be admissible under another exception. We are not persuaded that a general statement made during discussions on Rule 803(5), should be construed to override congressional intent evidenced by specific statements made during discussions which addressed Rule 803(8)(B), the very rule at issue here. While we acknowledge the existence of that general rule, many, if not most, general rules are vulnerable to numerous exceptions thereto and we cannot ignore clear legislative intent to recognize such an exception.

The State also claims that statements made during congressional discussions on Rule 803(8) indicate that the Rule's exclusionary provision was only intended to "prevent the admission of offense reports in place of the testimony of the officer concerning his observations at the scene of the crime or arrest." We disagree with so narrow an interpretation of this provision. Rather than exclude only "offense reports" pertaining to observations at the scene of the crime or arrest, the plain language of Rule 803(8)(B) is broad in scope, excluding reports that set forth matters observed by law enforcement personnel. Moreover, although several statements in the legislative history refer to "offense reports" and the "policeman on the beat," the Rule's broad language, read in light of the legislative history as a whole, leads to the conclusion that Congress' broader concern was with the potentially prejudicial influence of an adversarial setting and with a defendant's confrontation rights.

Often in cases involving physical evidence, a prosecutor's decision to prosecute depends upon the results of a laboratory report. Here, the State's decision to prosecute appellant very likely turned upon the results of the subject reports. Accordingly, we think our original opinion correctly decided that the laboratory reports were the type of reports intended by Congress to be excluded from evidence in the absence of the conducting chemist.

We find the State's Motion for Rehearing without merit. The judgment of the court of appeals is reversed and this cause is remanded to that court for a harm analysis consistent with our original opinion and with this opinion, pursuant to TEX.R.APP.P. 81(b)(2).

It is important to note that in *Aguilar v. State*, 887 S.W.2d 27 (Tex. Crim. App. 1994) the Court of Criminal Appeals concluded that an expert witness could rely upon a lab report, which would be otherwise inadmissible under *Cole*, to form the basis for his opinion that the substance tested was contraband.

As noted by the courts in *Oates* and *Cole*, the hearsay exceptions in Rules 803(6) and (8) may be linked where the public agency completing the report may also be considered a business.

The following chart presents a comparison between the provisions in Texas Rules 803(6) and (8).

§ 8-5(H). Chart: Comparison of Texas Rules 803(6) and 803(8)

	Rule 803(6)	Rule 803(8)
Record, Data, or Writing?	Yes	Yes
Timing Requirement?	Yes (At or near time of event)	No
Regularity of Preparation?	Yes	No
Duty?	Yes (Business duty implied)	Yes (Explicitly stated)
Personal Knowledge?	Yes (Of informant or entrant)	Yes Implicit in rule
Limitations?	Yes (*Cole* limitation in criminal cases)	Yes (Matters observed by police) (Government investigations)
Authentication?	Rule 902(10)(Self-authenticating) Rule 901	Rule 902 Rule 901
Trustworthiness Veto?	Yes	Yes

§ 8-6. Hearsay Exceptions: Unavailability Required

If the proponent wishes to use one of the few exceptions in Rule 804, he or she will have to first establish that the person who made the offered statement is not available to testify at trial. Rule 804(a) lists the reasons for unavailability, e.g., refusal to testify, death, or incapacity to testify. Assuming that the judge concludes that the declarant is not available, the proponent must next establish the foundation for the exception relied upon.

Three exceptions in Federal Rule 804 are noted here.

§ 8-6(A). Former Testimony

A commonly encountered exception in Rule 804 is the "former testimony" exception. In effect, it is intended to cover those situations where the declarant gave sworn testimony at a prior proceeding and was subject to examination or cross-examination by the party against whom the statement is now being offered.

The prior proceeding may have been a trial, deposition, or other proceeding. The prior proceeding need not even be related to the present case.

The following chart demonstrates how the exception might work under the Texas counterpart to the federal rule.

COMPARISON CHART: RULE 804(b)(1)—FORMER TESTIMONY

	Texas Civil Case Rule 804(b)(1)	Texas Criminal Case Rule 804(b)(1)	Fed. R. Evid. 804(b)(1)
OTCD?	"Witness" at prior hearing, etc., who is now "unavailable" as a witness.	"Witness" at prior hearing, etc. who is now "unavailable" as a witness.	"Witness" at prior hearing, etc. who is now "unavailable" as a witness.
Statement?	"Testimony" as a witness at another trial or hearing of the current or different proceeding, or in deposition in another proceeding.	"Testimony" as a witness at a trial or hearing of the current or different proceeding or at a deposition (Chap 39, CCP)	"Testimony" as a witness at another a trial, hearing, or lawful deposition of the current or different proceeding
Against Whom Offered?	Same party or a person with a similar interest	Same party	Civil: Same party or predecessor in Interest Crim: Same party
Opportunity to Challenge or Present "Former Testimony"?	Party or person against whom offered had opport.. & similar motive to direct, cross-x or redirect OTCD at prior hearing	Party against whom offered had opport. & similar motive to direct, cross-x or redirect OTCD at prior hearing.	Party or person against whom offered had opport. & similar motive to direct, cross-x, or redirect OTCD at prior hearing.

§ 8-6(B). Dying Declarations.

Federal Rule of Evidence 804(b)(2) provides that a statement made under the belief of impending death may be treated as a hearsay exception. Note that although the exception may be used in any civil proceeding, its use in federal criminal cases is limited to homicide cases.

§ 8-6(C). Statements Against Interest

Under Federal Rule 804(b)(3), a declarant's statement may be admitted if the proponent can show that the statement was against the declarant's financial, criminal, or civil interest at the time the statement was made. The Texas counterpart to this rule is Rule 803(24), where unavailability of the declarant is not required.

The following chart demonstrates the differences between statements against interest and statements by opposing parties (formerly party admissions), two concepts which are often confused.

STATEMENTS BY AN OPPOSING PARTY (TX. RULE 801)
v.
STATEMENTS AGAINST INTEREST (TX. RULE 803(24))

	OPPOSING-PARTY STATEMENTS (Tex. R. Evid. 801(e))	**STATEMENTS AGAINST INTEREST (Tex. R. Evid. 803(24))**
Identity of "Out-of-This Court Declarant"	A Party in the Case (Personal, Adoptive, or Vicarious)	Any person — including a Party.
When is Statement Against Interest?	At time it is offered at trial	When it is made by OTCD
Who May offer it Into Evidence?	Party who did not make statement	Any Party
Must Declarant be Unavailable?	No	No. *Cf.* Fed. R. Evid. 804 .
Type of "Interest" Implicated in Statement	Not critical as long as the statement is being offered against the opposing party.	Rule specifies interests: (1) Financial (2) Civil/Crim. Liability (3) Social Stigma
Requirement of Corroboration?	Not required	Required in criminal cases where statement tends to expose OTCD to criminal liability

§ 8-6(D). Forfeiture by Wrongdoing

Under Federal Rule 804(b)(6), a party may introduce a hearsay statement made by an unavailable declarant if the opposing party caused the declarant's unavailability. Apparently, the form of the statement or the circumstances of its making are not critical under this hearsay exception, as long as the hearsay declarant is unavailable. Thus, the rationale of this exception is not based upon the traditional guarantees of trustworthiness or reliability. Instead the rule in effect tells a party that if they have caused the declarant's unavailability they have forfeited (or waived) the right to object to the proponent's introduction of the declarant's hearsay statement.

§ 8-7. The Federal Residual Hearsay Exception

The Federal Rules of Evidence contains a residual or as it is sometimes referred to as a "catch all" hearsay exception. Originally, Federal Rules 803(24) and 804(b)(5) contained separate residual hearsay exceptions—the former applied where the availability of the declarant was not important and the latter when the declarant's unavailability was required. In 1997, the two exceptions were blended into a new Federal Rule of Evidence 807. That rule provides:

Rule 807. Residual Exception

(a) In General. Under the following conditions, a hearsay statement is not excluded by the rule against hearsay even if the statement is not admissible under a hearsay exception in Rule 803 or 804:

> (1) the statement is supported by sufficient guarantees of trustworthiness—after considering the totality of circumstances under which it was made and evidence, if any, corroborating the statement; and

> (2) it is more probative on the point for which it is offered than any other evidence that the proponent can obtain through reasonable efforts.

(b) Notice. The statement is admissible only if the proponent gives an adverse party reasonable notice of the intent to offer the statement—including its substance and the declarant's name—so that the party has a fair opportunity to meet it. The notice must be provided in writing before the trial or hearing—or in any form during the trial or hearing if the court, for good cause, excuses a lack of earlier notice.

This exception is normally viewed as an exception of the last resort. The residual hearsay exception has been controversial and some federal courts are reluctant to admit a statement offered under this exception.

As noted in the rule, the proponent must establish five specific foundational elements: First, the offered statement must have circumstantial guarantees of trustworthiness that equal those exceptions in Rules 803 and 804. Second, the proffered statement must address a material fact. Third, the statement must be more probative on the issue than other evidence that is reasonably available to the proponent. Fourth, admitting the statement would promote the general purposes of the rules and the interests of justice. And fifth, the proponent is required to give advance notice to the opponent of an intent to rely upon the exception.

§ 8-8. The Hearsay Rule and the Right to Confrontation

The Sixth Amendment to the United States Constitution provides a criminal defendant with the right to confront his or her accusers, i.e., the prosecution witnesses. When the prosecution introduces a person's hearsay statement against the defendant, the Right to Confrontation may be implicated.

Until recently, the courts resolved the potential conflict between the hearsay exceptions, which permitted the prosecution to introduce an adverse declarant's out-of-court statements against a defendant and the constitutional right to confrontation by using a sort of formula. If the hearsay exception was considered to be "firmly rooted" (the courts had identified a number of them as being such) then no confrontation clause problem was present. On the other hand, if the prosecution was relying upon an exception that was not firmly rooted, then the prosecution had to first establish that the hearsay declarant was unavailable and that the statement was otherwise trustworthy, or "reliable."

But in the landmark decision, *Crawford v. Washington*, the Court signaled that the foregoing formula would no longer apply in those criminal cases where the prosecution was relying on "testimonial" hearsay. In those cases, the prosecution must establish that the hearsay declarant is unavailable to testify and that the defendant had an opportunity to cross-examine the declarant at the time of the statement. According to the Court, statements to police officers during an interrogation are considered to be testimonial in nature.

CRAWFORD v. WASHINGTON
541 U.S. 36 (2004)

Justice SCALIA delivered the opinion of the Court.

[The defendant petitioner, Michael Crawford, was convicted for stabbing a man who had allegedly tried to rape his wife, Sylvia. As part of its case, the prosecution relied on the state's hearsay exception for statements against penal interest and played a tape of Sylvia's statement to the police in which she described the stabbing, which varied to some extent from Crawford's version of the events. Crawford unsuccessfully objected to his wife's out-of-court statements on the ground that admitting them violated his Sixth Amendment confrontation rights; Crawford had no chance to cross-examine her, either at the police interview or at the trial itself, because she invoked the marital privilege. The Washington Supreme Court relied on earlier Supreme Court authority and affirmed his conviction stating that although Sylvia's statement did not fall within a firmly rooted hearsay exception, it nonetheless was reliable. The question before the Supreme Court was whether this procedure complied with the Sixth Amendment's guarantee that, "[i]n all criminal prosecutions, the accused shall enjoy the right ... to be confronted with the witnesses against him."]

II

The Sixth Amendment's Confrontation Clause provides that, "[i]n all criminal prosecutions, the accused shall enjoy the right ... to be confronted with the witnesses against him." We have held that this bedrock procedural guarantee applies to both federal and state prosecutions. *Pointer v. Texas,* 380 U.S. 400, 406 (1965). As noted above, *Ohio v. Roberts* says that an unavailable witness's out-of-court statement may be admitted so long as it has adequate indicia of reliability—i.e., falls within a "firmly rooted hearsay exception" or bears "particularized guarantees of trustworthiness." 448 U.S., at 66. Petitioner argues that this test strays from the original meaning of the Confrontation Clause and urges us to reconsider it.

A

The Constitution's text does not alone resolve this case. One could plausibly read "witnesses against" a defendant to mean those who actually testify at trial, those whose statements are offered at trial, or something in-between. We must therefore turn to the historical background of the Clause to understand its meaning.

[Justice Scalia's opinion includes an extensive historical review of the right to confront one's accusers, starting in Roman times.]

The most notorious instances of civil-law examination occurred in the great political trials of the 16th and 17th centuries. One such was the 1603 trial of Sir Walter Raleigh for treason. Lord Cobham, Raleigh's alleged accomplice, had implicated him in an examination before the Privy Council and in a letter. At Raleigh's trial, these were read to the jury. Raleigh argued that Cobham had lied to save himself: "Cobham is absolutely in the King's mercy; to excuse me cannot avail him; by accusing me he may hope for favour." Suspecting that Cobham would recant, Raleigh demanded that the judges call him to appear, arguing that "[t]he Proof of the Common Law is by witness and jury: let Cobham be here, let him speak it. Call my accuser before my face ...." The judges refused, and, despite Raleigh's protestations that he was being tried "by the Spanish Inquisition," the jury convicted, and Raleigh was sentenced to death.

One of Raleigh's trial judges later lamented that "the justice of England has never been so degraded and injured as by the condemnation of Sir Walter Raleigh." Through a series of statutory and judicial reforms, English law developed a right of confrontation that limited these abuses. For example, treason statutes required witnesses to confront the accused "face to face" at his arraignment. Courts, meanwhile, developed relatively strict rules of unavailability, admitting examinations only if the witness was demonstrably unable to testify in person. Several authorities also stated that a suspect's confession could be admitted only against himself, and not against others he implicated.

One recurring question was whether the admissibility of an unavailable witness's pretrial examination depended on whether the defendant had had an opportunity to cross-examine him.

B

Controversial examination practices were also used in the Colonies. John Adams, defending a merchant in a high-profile admiralty case, argued: "Examinations of witnesses upon Interrogatories, are only by the Civil Law. Interrogatories are unknown at common Law, and Englishmen and common Lawyers have an aversion to them if not an Abhorrence of them."

Many declarations of rights adopted around the time of the Revolution guaranteed a right of confrontation. The proposed Federal Constitution, however, did not....The First Congress responded by including the Confrontation Clause in the proposal that became the Sixth Amendment.

* * * * *

III

This history supports two inferences about the meaning of the Sixth Amendment.

A

First, the principal evil at which the Confrontation Clause was directed was the civil-law mode of criminal procedure, and particularly its use of *ex parte* examinations as evidence against the accused. It was these practices that the Crown deployed in notorious treason cases like Raleigh's; that the Marian statutes invited; that English law's assertion of a right to confrontation was meant to prohibit; and that the founding-era rhetoric decried. The Sixth Amendment must be interpreted with this focus in mind.

Accordingly, we once again reject the view that the Confrontation Clause applies of its own force only to in-court testimony, and that its application to out-of-court statements introduced at trial depends upon "the law of Evidence for the time being." Leaving the regulation of out-of-court statements to the law of evidence would render the Confrontation Clause powerless to prevent even the most flagrant inquisitorial practices. Raleigh was, after all, perfectly free to confront those who read Cobham's confession in court.

This focus also suggests that not all hearsay implicates the Sixth Amendment's core concerns. An off-hand, overheard remark might be unreliable evidence and thus a good candidate for exclusion under hearsay rules, but it bears little resemblance to the civil-law abuses the Confrontation Clause targeted. On the other hand, *ex parte* examinations might sometimes be admissible under modern hearsay rules, but the Framers certainly would not have condoned them.

The text of the Confrontation Clause reflects this focus. It applies to "witnesses" against the accused—in other words, those who "bear testimony." "Testimony," in turn, is typically "[a] solemn declaration or affirmation made for the purpose of establishing or proving some fact." An accuser who makes a formal statement to government officers bears testimony in a sense that a person who makes a casual remark to an acquaintance does not. The constitutional text, like the history underlying the common-law right of confrontation, thus reflects an especially acute concern with a specific type of out-of-court statement.

Various formulations of this core class of "testimonial" statements exist…These formulations all share a common nucleus and then define the Clause's coverage at various levels of abstraction around it. Regardless of the precise articulation, some statements qualify under any definition—for example, *ex parte* testimony at a preliminary hearing.

Statements taken by police officers in the course of interrogations are also testimonial under even a narrow standard. Police interrogations bear a striking resemblance to examinations by justices of the peace in England. The statements are not *sworn* testimony, but the absence of oath was not dispositive. Cobham's examination was unsworn, yet Raleigh's trial has long been thought a paradigmatic confrontation violation, Under the Marian statutes, witnesses were typically put on oath, but suspects were not. Yet Hawkins and others went out of their way to caution that such unsworn confessions were not admissible against anyone but the confessor.

That interrogators are police officers rather than magistrates does not change the picture either.

In sum, even if the Sixth Amendment is not solely concerned with testimonial hearsay, that is its primary object, and interrogations by law enforcement officers fall squarely within that class.

B

The historical record also supports a second proposition: that the Framers would not have allowed admission of testimonial statements of a witness who did not appear at trial unless he was unavailable to testify, and the defendant had had a prior opportunity for cross-examination. The text of the Sixth Amendment does not suggest any open-ended exceptions from the confrontation requirement to be developed by the courts. Rather, the "right ... to be confronted with the witnesses against him," Amdt. 6, is most naturally read as a reference to the right of confrontation at common law, admitting only those exceptions established at the time of the founding. As the English authorities above reveal, the common law in 1791 conditioned admissibility of an absent witness's examination on unavailability and a prior opportunity to cross-examine. The Sixth Amendment therefore incorporates those limitations. The numerous early state decisions applying the same test confirm that these principles were received as part of the common law in this country.

We do not read the historical sources to say that a prior opportunity to cross-examine was merely a sufficient, rather than a necessary, condition for admissibility of testimonial statements. They suggest that this requirement was dispositive, and not merely one of several ways to establish reliability. This is not to deny, as the Chief Justice notes, that "[t]here were always exceptions to the general rule of exclusion" of hearsay evidence. Several had become well established by 1791. But there is scant evidence that exceptions were invoked to admit *testimonial* statements against the accused in a *criminal* case. Most of the hearsay exceptions covered statements that by their nature were not testimonial—for example, business records or statements in furtherance of a conspiracy. We do not infer from these that the Framers thought exceptions would apply even to prior testimony.

IV

Our case law has been largely consistent with these two principles. Our leading early decision, for example, involved a deceased witness's prior trial testimony. *Mattox v. United States,* 156 U.S. 237 (1895). In allowing the statement to be admitted, we relied on the fact that the defendant had had, at the first trial, an adequate opportunity to confront the witness: "The substance of the constitutional protection is preserved to the prisoner in the advantage he has once had of seeing the witness face to face, and of subjecting him to the ordeal of a cross-examination. This, the law says, he shall under no circumstances be deprived of ...."

Our cases have thus remained faithful to the Framers' understanding: Testimonial statements of witnesses absent from trial have been admitted only where the declarant is unavailable, and only where the defendant has had a prior opportunity to cross-examine.

V

Although the results of our decisions have generally been faithful to the original meaning of the Confrontation Clause, the same cannot be said of our rationales. *Ohio v. Roberts* conditions the admissibility of all hearsay evidence on whether it falls under a "firmly rooted hearsay exception" or bears "particularized guarantees of trustworthiness." 448 U.S., at 66. This test departs from the historical principles identified above in two respects. First, it is too broad: It applies the same mode of analysis whether or not the hearsay consists of *ex parte* testimony. This often results in close constitutional scrutiny in cases that are far removed from the core concerns of the Clause. At the same time, however, the test is too narrow: It admits statements that *do* consist of *ex parte* testimony upon a mere finding of reliability. This malleable standard often fails to protect against paradigmatic confrontation violations.

Members of this Court and academics have suggested that we revise our doctrine to reflect more accurately the original understanding of the Clause. They offer two proposals: First, that we apply the Confrontation Clause only to testimonial statements, leaving the remainder to regulation by hearsay law—thus eliminating the overbreadth referred to above. Second, that we impose an absolute bar to statements that are testimonial, absent a prior opportunity to cross-examine—thus eliminating the excessive narrowness referred to above.

This case does, however, squarely implicate the second proposal.

A

Where testimonial statements are involved, we do not think the Framers meant to leave the Sixth Amendment's protection to the vagaries of the rules of evidence, much less to amorphous notions of "reliability." Certainly none of the authorities discussed above acknowledges any general reliability exception to the common-law rule. Admitting statements deemed reliable by a judge is fundamentally at odds with the right of confrontation. To be sure, the Clause's ultimate goal is to ensure reliability of evidence, but it is a procedural rather than a substantive guarantee. It commands, not that evidence be reliable, but that reliability be assessed in a particular manner: by testing in the crucible of cross-examination. The Clause thus reflects a judgment, not only about the desirability of reliable evidence (a point on which there could be little dissent), but about how reliability can best be determined.

The *Roberts* test allows a jury to hear evidence, untested by the adversary process, based on a mere judicial determination of reliability. It thus replaces the constitutionally prescribed method of assessing reliability with a wholly foreign one. In this respect, it is very different from exceptions to the Confrontation Clause that make no claim to be a surrogate means of assessing reliability. For example, the rule of forfeiture by wrongdoing (which we accept) extinguishes confrontation claims on essentially equitable grounds; it does not purport to be an alternative means of determining reliability.

The Raleigh trial itself involved the very sorts of reliability determinations that *Roberts* authorizes. In the face of Raleigh's repeated demands for confrontation, the prosecution responded with many of the arguments a court applying *Roberts* might invoke today: that Cobham's statements were self-inculpatory, that they were not made in the heat of passion, and that they were not "extracted from [him] upon any hopes or promise of Pardon." It is not plausible that the Framers' only objection to the trial was that Raleigh's judges did not properly weigh these factors before sentencing him to death. Rather, the problem was that the judges refused to allow Raleigh to confront Cobham in court, where he could cross-examine him and try to expose his accusation as a lie.

Dispensing with confrontation because testimony is obviously reliable is akin to dispensing with jury trial because a defendant is obviously guilty. This is not what the Sixth Amendment prescribes.

B

The legacy of *Roberts* in other courts vindicates the Framers' wisdom in rejecting a general reliability exception. The framework is so unpredictable that it fails to provide meaningful protection from even core confrontation violations.

Reliability is an amorphous, if not entirely subjective, concept. There are countless factors bearing on whether a statement is reliable; the nine-factor balancing test applied by the Court of Appeals below is representative.

To add insult to injury, some of the courts that admit untested testimonial statements find reliability in the very factors that *make* the statements testimonial. As noted earlier, one court relied on the fact that the witness's statement was made to police while in custody on pending charges—the theory being that this made the statement more clearly against penal interest and thus more reliable. Other courts routinely rely on the fact that a prior statement is given under oath in judicial proceedings. That inculpating statements are given in a testimonial setting is not an antidote to the confrontation problem, but rather the trigger that makes the Clause's demands most urgent. It is not enough to point out that most of the usual safeguards of the adversary process attend the statement, when the single safeguard missing is the one the Confrontation Clause demands.

C

We readily concede that we could resolve this case by simply reweighing the "reliability factors" under *Roberts* and finding that Sylvia Crawford's statement falls short. But we view this as one of those rare cases in which the result below is so improbable that it reveals a fundamental failure on our part to interpret the Constitution in a way that secures its intended constraint on judicial discretion. Moreover, to reverse the Washington Supreme Court's decision after conducting our own reliability analysis would perpetuate, not avoid, what the Sixth Amendment condemns. The Constitution prescribes a procedure for determining the reliability of testimony in criminal trials, and we, no less than the state courts, lack authority to replace it with one of our own devising.

Where nontestimonial hearsay is at issue, it is wholly consistent with the Framers' design to afford the States flexibility in their development of hearsay law—as does *Roberts,* and as would an approach that exempted such statements from Confrontation Clause scrutiny altogether. Where testimonial evidence is at issue, however, the Sixth Amendment demands what the common law required: unavailability and a prior opportunity for cross-examination. We leave for another day any effort to spell out a comprehensive definition of "testimonial." Whatever else the term covers, it applies at a minimum to prior testimony at a preliminary hearing, before a grand jury, or at a former trial; and to police interrogations. These are the modern practices with closest kinship to the abuses at which the Confrontation Clause was directed.

In this case, the State admitted Sylvia's testimonial statement against petitioner, despite the fact that he had no opportunity to cross-examine her. That alone is sufficient to make out a violation of the Sixth Amendment. *Roberts* notwithstanding, we decline to mine the record in search of indicia of reliability. Where testimonial statements are at issue, the only indicium of reliability sufficient to satisfy constitutional demands is the one the Constitution actually prescribes: confrontation.

The judgment of the Washington Supreme Court is reversed, and the case is remanded for further proceedings not inconsistent with this opinion. *It is so ordered.*

Chief Justice REHNQUIST, with whom Justice O'CONNOR joins, concurring in the judgment.

I dissent from the Court's decision to overrule *Ohio v. Roberts,* 448 U.S. 56 (1980). I believe that the Court's adoption of a new interpretation of the Confrontation Clause is not backed by sufficiently persuasive reasoning to overrule long-established precedent. Its decision casts a mantle of uncertainty over future criminal trials in both federal and state courts, and is by no means necessary to decide the present case.

The Court's distinction between testimonial and nontestimonial statements, contrary to its claim, is no better rooted in history than our current doctrine.

I am also not convinced that the Confrontation Clause categorically requires the exclusion of testimonial statements.

Exceptions to confrontation have always been derived from the experience that some out-of-court statements are just as reliable as cross-examined in-court testimony due to the circumstances under which they were made.

Indeed, cross-examination is a tool used to flesh out the truth, not an empty procedure. See *Kentucky v. Stincer,* 482 U.S. 730, 737 (1987) ("The right to cross-examination, protected by the Confrontation Clause, thus is essentially a 'functional' right designed to promote reliability in the truth-finding functions of a criminal trial"); *see also Maryland v. Craig,* 497 U.S. 836, 845 (1990) ("The central concern of the Confrontation Clause is to ensure the reliability of the evidence against a criminal defendant by subjecting it to rigorous testing in the context of an adversary proceeding before the trier of fact"). By creating an immutable category of excluded evidence, the Court adds little to a trial's truth-finding function and ignores this longstanding guidance.

To its credit, the Court's analysis of "testimony" excludes at least some hearsay exceptions, such as business records and official records. To hold otherwise would require numerous additional witnesses without any apparent gain in the truth-seeking process. Likewise to the Court's credit is its implicit recognition that the mistaken application of its new rule by courts which guess wrong as to the scope of the rule is subject to harmless-error analysis.

———————————

The Court's opinion in *Crawford* leaves at least two unanswered questions:

- What exactly is "testimonial hearsay?"

- What test should be used for non-testimonial hearsay in determining whether the Confrontation Clause has been implicated? The firmly rooted exception formula outlined above? Or something else?

In *Davis v. Washington,* 547 U.S. 813 (2006), the Supreme Court further refined the definition of testimonial hearsay as it pertains to statements made to police officers during an questioning. The Court stated that "statements made to police "under circumstances objectively indicating that the primary purpose of the interrogation is to enable police assistance to meet an ongoing emergency" are not testimonial and thus not subject to the Confrontation Clause. The Court added, however, that such "statements are testimonial "when the circumstances objectively indicate that . . . the primary purpose of the interrogation is to establish or prove past events potentially relevant to later criminal prosecution."

In *Melendez-Diaz v. Massachusetts*, 557 U.S. 305 (2009), the Supreme Court again addressed the interplay of hearsay and the Confrontation Clause—in the context of laboratory analysis certificates: The defendant was convicted in state court of distributing and trafficking in cocaine. Over his *Crawford v. Washington* objection, the trial judge admitted three "certificates of analysis" showing the results of the forensic analysis performed on substances seized in connection with the defendant's arrest. The certificates were sworn before a notary public by analysts at the State Laboratory Institute of the Massachusetts Department of Public Health, as required under state law. Writing for the 5-4 majority, Justice Scalia concluded that there was little doubt that the documents fell within the 'core class of testimonial statements'" described in *Crawford*. The Court rejected the State's argument that the analysts were not "accusatory" witnesses and thus were not subject to confrontation and concluded that the text of the Sixth Amendment "contemplates two classes of witnesses – those against the defendant and those in his favor." It also rejected the arguments that the analysts were not conventional witnesses and did not offer testimony prone to distortion or manipulation and therefore were not subject to confrontation. Justice Kennedy wrote for the dissenters and argued that the Court ignored 90 years of precedent in which scientific analysis could be introduced without testimony from the analyst who produced it. He also raised serious questions about which analysts must be produced, and argued that the Court's decision imposed unnecessary and costly burdens on both state and federal criminal justice systems. More recently, in *Bullcoming v. New Mexico*, 131 S.Ct 2705 (2011) the Court held that introducing the results through the testimony of a lab technician who had not run the drug tests himself, was also testimonial hearsay.

Some Federal and Texas courts held, post-*Crawford*, that if the trial court finds that the hearsay statement is not "testimonial" the court should continue by applying the *Roberts* test. In *Whorton v. Bocking*, 549 U.S. 406 (2007), however, the Court addressed the question of whether *Crawford* was retroactive. Writing for the Court, Justice Alito wrote that *Crawford* was "flatly inconsistent with *Roberts*, which it overruled."

§ 8-9. Problems

a.   Hearsay Problems I

Assume that at trial in 2021 the weather conditions on August 10 , 2019 in San Antonio are relevant under Rule 401 and that counsel wishes to establish that it was raining and very hot on that date. Assume that "A" is a nonparty witness who takes the stand to testify.

Using Texas Rule 801(a)–(e) and Federal Rule of Evidence 801(a)–(c), decide whether the following pieces of evidence constitute hearsay under the Texas and Federal versions. Be prepared to explain your reasoning.

1. Counsel offers into evidence A's affidavit in which he stated, under oath, that on August 10th, it had rained very hard in the afternoon.

2. A testifies that on the afternoon of August10th he saw B walk out the door wearing a raincoat.

3. A testifies that on the evening of August 10th he "read his digital rain gauge and it showed that .45 inches of rain had fallen."

4. A testifies that he watched the cable television news broadcast on the evening of August 10th and that the weatherman said "about a half inch of rain had fallen when scattered showers passed through the city."

5. A testifies that on August 10th, B called A on his cell phone and said: "It's raining."

6. A testifies at trial that late on the afternoon of August 10th, he asked B if it was raining and B responded by saying: "Do bears live in the woods?"

7. A testifies at trial that he remembers that "it was cold and hot" on August 10th.

8. A testifies that he read in the newspaper on August 11th that the previous day's rainfall had measured .45 inches at the airport.

9. A testifies that on August 10th, B sent him an email and told A, "WEAR SOMETHING VERY WARM TODAY!!"

10. Counsel offers into evidence A's deposition taken in the case in which he stated, under oath, that on August 10th it was very hot and rainy.

11. Counsel asks A why he carried his raincoat when he left work on February 10th, and A responds, "Because D told me that it was raining."

12. A testifies that on August 10th he overheard B say to D, "I'm going to use my new umbrella this afternoon."

13. Counsel offers into evidence A's former testimony from a prior state trial in Arizona, in which he testified under oath that on August 10th, it rained in San Antonio.

b. Hearsay Problems II

Assume that the question of whether it was hot on August 10th is relevant to an issue in the trial. Using the Texas and Federal versions of Rule(s) 801, decide whether the following information, to be provided by A at trial, is hearsay. Also determine if you would need additional facts before deciding whether the statement is hearsay or not.

1. A testifies that it was hot on August 20th and evidence is offered that he said the same thing on two later occasions.

_____ Hearsay

_____ Not Hearsay

Reasoning:

2.   A testifies that it was hot on August 20th. Opposing counsel offers evidence that two days later A told another person that it was not hot on August 20th.

        _____ Hearsay

        _____ Not Hearsay

        Reasoning:

3.   Counsel uses A to authenticate a desk calendar entry for Aug. 20th that A had written which stated "hotter than ever today" and then attempts to introduce the writing.

        _____ Hearsay

        _____ Not Hearsay

        Reasoning:

4.   Counsel offers into evidence an official weather report, obtained from the National Weather Service, which indicates that it was 102 degrees on August 20th.

        _____ Hearsay

        _____ Not Hearsay

        Reasoning:

5.   A testifies that in another case he had already testified, under oath, that it was hot on August 20th.

        _____ Hearsay

        _____ Not Hearsay

        Reasoning:

6.   Counsel introduces A's deposition taken in another case in which he states that "it was very hot on August 20th."

        _____ Hearsay

        _____ Not Hearsay

        Reasoning:

c.   **Hearsay Problems III**

Assume in the following problems that P is suing her landlord, L for intentional infliction of physical injury and emotional distress by not turning up the heat in her apartment on January 13th when the outside temperature stayed in the 20's for 36 continuous hours. Determine whether the following pieces of evidence amount to hearsay and whether they might be admissible under an exemption (Rule 801) or an exception (Rules 803 or 804).

1.   P testifies that on January 13th, she told her friend B, "I'm cold."

2.   P testifies that on February 12th, she told B that she had been cold on January 13th.

3.   B testifies on P's behalf that on January 13th, he overheard the following conversation between P and L in the hallway.

> P: You jerk. The heat is off in this place, I am freezing and have no feeling in my feet, and you don't seem to care.
>
> L: Something is wrong with the furnace.
>
> P: I remember this happened last winter when you turned off the heat.
>
> L: I didn't do any such thing last year and you know it. And I resent your accusations.
>
> P: I was mad then and I'm really upset now. I haven't slept for the last three nights because of the cold. It's lawsuit time."
>
> L: Look, I'll check on the furnace myself as soon as I make several phone calls.

Are these statements hearsay? Are they admissible?

4.   Assume that instead of talking to L in #3, P talked to the apartment maintenance man. Would your answers be the same?

5.   Assume that in #3, B testified on behalf of L. Would your answers be the same?

6.   The nurse in the Emergency Room who treated P, testifies that P told her: "I have no feeling in my feet. This same thing happened to me last year when it got cold. It's all because L refuses to turn up the heat. I am so angry at him and I am going to sue him for everything he has."

7.   The doctor who later treated P testifies that she told P that "You have a severe case of dehydration and frostbite. Do you have a lawyer?"

d.   Past Recollection Recorded and Present Memory Refreshed

(i)   Memo by Sheriff's Deputy

Prisoners at the local county jail have sued the local sheriff and his guards for using excessive force.   On one particularly hot summer afternoon the jail air conditioning unit failed. When the temperatures soared inside the jail, tempers did as well. Deputies used force in getting some of the prisoners back into their cells after a morning workout.

The defense counsel wishes to prove first, when he got the first call concerning the problem at the jail, and second, the names of the three deputies and the two inmates, involved.

Deputy Stevens—after investigating the incident, and confirming the details and names of the individuals involved—prepared a memo for record.

The proponent will be defense counsel for the county, who should be prepared to conduct a direct examination of Deputy Stevens to lay the foundation for admitting the following memo for record as either past recollection recorded or present memory refreshed—depending on how much Miller remembers while on the stand.

Be prepared to act as a counsel, judge, or court reporter.

MEMO FOR RECORD

RE: **AC Problems at Jail Today**
FROM: **Stevens**
DATE: **August 2, 2019**
TIME: **1900 hours**

This afternoon we had an incident at the jail. I got a call at 1245 hours from Deputy Matson that the AC had failed in unit 16-A-4.

At 1300 hours, I got another call from Matson, saying that one of the inmates, Smith (pending assault charges) was swearing at him in a loud voice. At 1410 hours I called maintenance and left a message saying that the AC problem was going to cause us major issues.

At 1412 hours, I got an e-mail from maintenance saying that it would be several hours, at least before they could fix the AC.

At 1500 hours, I went to the jail and personally observed three of our deputies, Gomez, Anderson, and Stevens, trying to subdue two inmates, Wilson and Cortez. They were finally able to subdue the inmates. At 1645 hours, the DA's office called me and said that I should immediately prepare a memo for record.

(ii) Information Regarding License Number

Following a hit and run accident, Jim Morris was able to see the license plate and quickly wrote it down, along with the make of the vehicle. Assume that you are conducting direct examination of Morris and that he cannot remember that information. Use the following piece of paper to refresh his recollection or lay the foundation for past recollection recorded.

Iowa XN5-868

Black Silverado

JM

e.   **Admissibility of Prior Testimony Under Rule 804(b)(1).**

Assume that the declarant, W, testified at a prior proceeding but is now "unavailable" under Rule 804(a). Determine whether W's prior statement/testimony is now admissible as "former testimony" under Rule 804(b) at "this" trial.

Prior Hearing, Trial, or Deposition	This Trial
<ul><li>A v. B (A sued B for personal injuries in a an auto accident resulting from B's negligence)</li><li>A calls W, a passenger in B's car to testify against B to testify that B had been drinking.</li><li>B cross-examines W.</li></ul>	<ul><li>D v. B (same auto accident; D was riding in A's car)</li><li>D offers W's (OTCD's) Prior Testimony Against B</li><li>Is W's testimony admissible in this trial?</li></ul>
<ul><li>A v. B (In a civil case, A has alleged that B defrauded A on a land deal)</li><li>A calls W to testify against B. W testifies that he saw B falsify certain records.</li><li>B cross-examines W.</li></ul>	<ul><li>A v. C (A has filed civil suit against C, B's partner in the land deal, on grounds of fraud, in the same transaction as that covered in the prior trial)</li><li>A offers W's (OTCD) prior testimony against C.</li><li>Is W's testimony admissible in this case?</li></ul>
<ul><li>A v. B (A filed a civil strict products liability suit against B, the manufacturer of a hair spray container that exploded and injured A)</li><li>A calls W to testify against B to show that the product was defective. W is a design engineer for B, who was fired earlier for providing helpful information against B.</li><li>B waives cross-examination of W.</li></ul>	<ul><li>D v. B (D has filed a negligence suit against B, on grounds of negligence for the same type of hair spray container made by B, which injured D)</li><li>D offers W's (OTCD) Prior Testimony Against B to show that the product was defective.</li><li>Is W's testimony admissible in this case?</li></ul>
<ul><li>State v. D (D has been charged with possession of crack cocaine)</li><li>State calls W, a police officer who arrested D and seized the drugs.</li><li>D cross-examines W.</li></ul>	<ul><li>State v. D (An appellate court orders a new trial for D, on the same drug charges)</li><li>State offers W's (OTCD) Prior Testimony Against D</li><li>Is W's testimony admissible in this case?</li></ul>
<ul><li>B v. C (In a civil case, B sues C for a breach of a construction contract)</li><li>B Deposes W.</li></ul>	<ul><li>A v. B (A sues B in a civil case on grounds that B defrauded A in the same construction contract involved in B's suit against C)</li><li>A offers W's (OCD) Deposition Against B</li><li>Is W's deposition testimony admissible in this case?</li></ul>

CHAPTER NINE

AUTHENTICATION AND IDENTIFICATION OF EVIDENCE

§ 9-1. Introduction

Authentication is the manner by which the proponent of a piece of evidence proves that the evidence really is what the proponent says it is. Schematically, authentication proves that X equals X and thereby indirectly proves that X does not equal Y. In a probate case for example, the proponent would authenticate May Smith's will by proving that the will which is being offered into evidence really is the will of May Smith and not the will of Sebastian Kroegor, or any other individual. Authenticity establishes the underlying logical relevance of a piece of evidence by tying that evidence directly to the facts of the case. For example, in May Smith's probate case, only the will of May Smith would be relevant. The content of Sebastian's will has no relevancy to the distributions of May's estate and should not be admitted into evidence.

As a means to establishing underlying relevancy, authentication also serves as a means of ensuring that the fact-finder considers only authentic reliable evidence in deciding a case.

Authentication has a limited scope in that it serves only to establish an item's underlying logical relevance. Even though the proponent fully authenticates an item, that item can still be excluded from evidence on other grounds such as hearsay, best evidence, or relevancy under Rule 401. Authenticity does not establish either truth or probative value.

Successfully applying Article IX requires an understanding of what items must be authenticated, and the required foundations (authenticity requirements) for the different types of evidence. These foundations often include meeting the requirements of evidentiary rules outside of Article IX.

§ 9-2. What Must Be Authenticated?

Writings (including computer printouts or other documentary proof), physical evidence (actual, substitute, and demonstrative), voices, tape recordings, photographs, slides, videotapes, motion pictures, scientific evidence, charts and diagrams all must be authenticated under Article IX.

§ 9-3. Required Foundations

§ 9-3(A). Writings

Authentication of writings is geared toward the identification of the writings' author. This may be done either through identification of the author's handwriting, or circumstantially proving the author's identity through the writings' content. A lay witness with sufficient familiarity with the author's handwriting may make the identification. Here the sponsoring witness would have to meet the competency requirements of Rule 601, and the personal knowledge requirements of Rule 602.

A handwriting expert may be used to enter an opinion that a particular document was written by a particular individual. Use of a handwriting expert requires that the witness be recognized as an expert by the court. The Article VII rules regarding expert testimony, and Rule 601's competency requirements would also apply to the expert witness. Additionally, the handwriting expert must have an authentic identified writing sample to serve as a basis for comparison.

§ 9-3(B). Business Records

Business Records (including computer printouts) are normally authenticated by a sponsoring witness with personal knowledge (Rule 602) who can testify that the document in question came directly from the place of business. Authentication of the document's author usually is not required. Certain public documents are considered self-authenticating under Rule 902, and thus require no sponsoring witness. Authenticating a business record does not make that record immune from the rule against hearsay.

§ 9-3(C). Physical Evidence

Three methods exist to authenticate (identify) actual physical evidence: readily identifiable evidence; establishing a chain of custody, or offering circumstantial (inferential) proof.

§ 9-3(C)(1). Readily Identifiable Evidence

If a piece of evidence is readily identifiable because of its distinguishing characteristics, a witness with personal knowledge (Rule 602) of those characteristics may identify (authenticate) a piece of physical evidence. Whether or not a particular piece of evidence is readily identifiable and thus authentic, remains a determination for the judge and jury under Rule 104(b).

§ 9-3(C)(2). Using A Chain of Custody

A chain of custody is normally used to authenticate physical evidence that is not readily identifiable, usually because the evidence is fungible in nature, for example, drugs. One gram of cocaine has no distinguishing characteristics to distinguish it from any other gram of cocaine. In a drug possession case, the gram of cocaine admitted at trial must be the exact same gram of cocaine that was found in the defendant's possession. Unless it is the same cocaine, admitting the drug would have no underlying logical relevance. Using a chain of custody, the proponent establishes every individual who had possession of the object and the duration of their custody. Establishing a chain of custody makes it reasonably certain that no tampering or substitution of the item has taken place. That way, the item admitted at trial is the authentic item that was originally seized. A chain of custody can also be used for a readily identifiable item where no sponsoring witness exists who has personal knowledge of the distinguishing characteristics, or for a piece of evidence whose condition at the time in question is a material issue in the case.

§ 9-3(C)(3). Circumstantial Evidence of Authenticity

Use of circumstantial evidence can be used to develop an inference that the piece of evidence in question is authentic. This requires competent witnesses with personal knowledge to develop the inference of authenticity. Suppose a prosecutor were trying to admit a pistol found at the murder scene into evidence at trial. To prove the pistol's authenticity circumstantially, the prosecution could put on the defendant's house keeper to testify that the night of the murder, the pistol was no longer above the defendant's mantel where it is normally kept. The prosecutor could next put on a weapons expert who would testify that the pistol found at the crime scene is a rare type of pistol with only one copy of it existing in the world. The prosecutor could next put on a gun shop owner to testify that he sold the defendant this rare type of pistol. These testimonies inductively prove that the pistol being offered into evidence was the defendant's pistol. It is also easy to see that circumstantial identification is the weakest form of authentication for physical evidence. The opponent could, with minimal effort, shoot holes into the prosecutor's inferences.

§ 9-3(C)(4). Demonstrative Evidence

Where a piece of physical evidence is not the actual evidence (i.e. it is not the smoking gun), or a substitute for the actual evidence (a plastic copy of the smoking gun), but rather serves as a demonstrative purpose (such as a diagram depicting a car crash), authentication is established by a sponsoring witness who through personal knowledge testifies that the demonstrative evidence serves as a fair and adequate representation of what the demonstrative evidence portrays. In addition to diagrams, demonstrative evidence also includes charts, photographs, x-rays, slides, videotapes, and motion pictures.

Furthermore, when either the actual evidence, or the demonstrative evidence has been created through the use of a technological instrument (a tape recorder, movie camera, or scientific equipment) an additional foundation must be laid. That foundation must establish that the technological instrument was properly functioning at the time the evidence was created, that the person who created the evidence (i.e. the camera operator) had the adequate training to properly operate the instrument, and that the evidence has not changed since its creation.

§ 9-3(D). Voice Identification

Voices in telephone conversations and on audio or video tapes can be identified by a witness with sufficient familiarity with a speaker's voice, inferentially by the content of the speaker's statements, or through the use of presumptions such as the telephone directory doctrine. Where a witness will serve to identify the voice, the witness must meet the competency and personal knowledge requirements of Rules 601 and 602. Using expert witnesses to identify voice prints has met with limited success, and is not recognized as a sufficient means of identification by most jurisdictions.

§ 9-3(E). Scientific Evidence

Scientific evidence must be verified as being reliable. A proponent generally must show that a qualified individual performed the scientific procedures, that the equipment used in the procedure was capable of producing an accurate result, and that the equipment was in proper working order at the time of the procedure. Formerly, proof of the procedure's acceptance by the scientific community was an essential element to authenticating scientific evidence. This, however, is no longer the standard in both Federal and Texas Courts. Now, the focus is primarily on the reliability of the scientific principles and methodology and whether the evidence will assist the jury in deciding the case. This decision is essentially a question for the trial judge under Rule 104(a) and Rule 702. Authenticating scientific evidence often requires the use of expert testimony so that the foundations for expert testimony found in Article VII must also be met. *See* Chapter Seven, *supra*.

§ 9-4. Problems

a.   Authentication of Private Writings

Students should be prepared to lay a foundation ("authenticate" or "prove up") and introduce into evidence the attached letter written by "Spencer" to "Aurelia." Assume for the purposes of the problem that neither will be available to testify at trial. Also assume that the writing is otherwise relevant to the case.

This problem is intended to provide some "hands on" experience in using the legal rules discussed in class.

You may use any recognized means of authenticating the document (*See* Rule 901). The professor will serve as your sponsoring or foundation witness. Simply inform the professor which method you want to use (e.g., witness with knowledge of handwriting) and who the professor is to portray.

Other students will be selected to serve as the reporter, the opposing counsel, and the trial judge. Those selected should be prepared to mark exhibits, object to the questioning, and rule on the objections, respectively. The problem will be conducted three or four times.

Because there are a number of ways of authenticating this letter, students should assume that a number of them will be called upon to authenticate it until the various methods have been fairly exhausted. Thus, students should be prepared to authenticate the letter by more than one method in case they are called on and that method has already been used.

This exercise will also give the students a chance to work on the 4-Step process for introducing evidence in Chapter One, *supra*. The TEXAS EVIDENTIARY FOUNDATIONS text may be helpful in framing the foundation questions.

September 9, 1994

Aurelia—

I got your letter about the problem with the AC. As I mentioned when you leaased my apartment last year, and its on page 6 of the leaase, <u>you</u> are responsible for any repairs under $100.

I called the AC contractor and she said the bill would be only $65.

So I am <u>not</u> going to be responsible for those repairs. <u>You are</u>.

Spencer—

b. **Verification of Chart and Identification of a Knife**

Students should be prepared to verify and introduce into evidence first, a chart depicting the defendant's apartment and second, a knife found at the scene. Assume that both items are relevant to the case.

Sgt. Jones arrested the defendant at his apartment, following complaints about loud noises.

The attached hand-drawn floor plan (drawn by Sgt. Jones shortly after the defendant's arrest) shows the layout of the defendant's apartment. You should be prepared to establish through the testimony of the arresting officer, Sgt. Jones, where he found the following items: (1) crack cocaine on the kitchen sink, (2) syringes found in the bathroom on a side of the bathtub, and (3) a knife allegedly used in a prior assault — found lying on the defendant's bed.

Assume that you are the prosecutor and that the professor will serve as the arresting officer, Sergeant Jones.

Before class, the professor will draw the diagram on the dry erase board without any particular identifying marks. Note that neither the attached chart nor the chart on the board will be to scale.

Do not rely on a chain of custody to lay the foundation for the knife.

Students will serve as prosecutor, defense counsel, judge, and court reporter. The defense counsel should be prepared to object to questioning and the judge will be expected to rule on those objections.

If time permits, the problem may be covered more than once.

c.   Verification of Chart of Accident Scene and Knife

Students should be prepared to verify and introduce into evidence a chart depicting an automobile accident scene and a knife found in defendant's car. The case is a civil case in which the plaintiff is claiming damages from the accident and an assault by the defendant. The plaintiff claims that after the accident, the defendant approached the plaintiff carrying a large hunting knife and waved it in her face and threatened to cut her. He then put the knife back into his car.

The accident occurred when the defendant, driving a 2017 Taurus sedan, collided with the plaintiff's 2019 Dodge truck. The defendant was arrested for DUI and during a subsequent search of the car, the investigating officer—Sgt. Hernandez—found a knife on the front seat. Assume that both the chart and the knife are relevant to this civil case.

The testimony from the officer (and other witnesses) will demonstrate that the plaintiff was headed south on Main Street, had a green light and proceeded into the intersection. The defendant, driving from the East to the West on First Street, ran a red light and t-boned the plaintiff's truck. Both vehicles came to rest in the west-bound lane of First Street.

The officer took some measurements at the scene and seized the knife.

Sgt. Hernandez drew the attached diagram of the intersection after the accident. Assume that you are representing the plaintiff and that the professor will serve as Sgt. Hernandez.

Before class, the professor will draw the diagram on the dry erase board without any particular identifying marks. Note that neither the attached chart, nor the chart on the board, will be to scale.

Do not use a chain of custody to authenticate the knife.

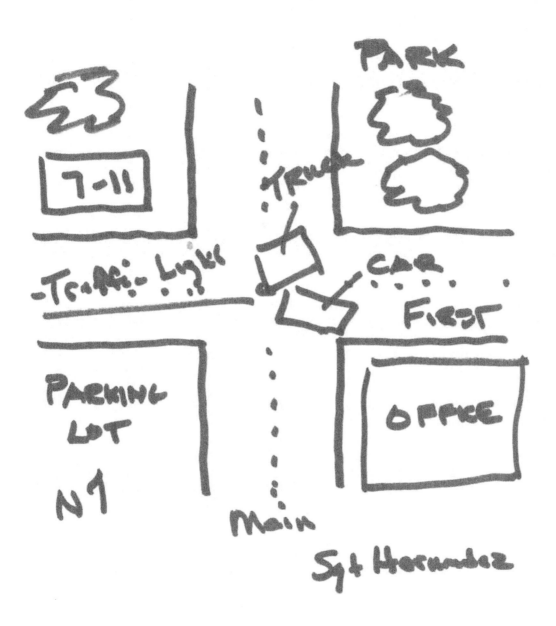

CHAPTER TEN

THE BEST EVIDENCE RULE

§ 10-1. Introduction to the Best Evidence Rule

Similar to hearsay, the evidentiary rules regarding "best evidence" rest on a presumption that certain types of evidence are inherently more trustworthy than others to prove certain disputed issues. As a more reliable source, the use of these types of evidence should be promoted. The Best Evidence rule should not be confused with the strategic concept of using the "best evidence principle," such as which eye witness would provide better testimony at trial, to prove a fact in issue.

As a rule of evidence, the best evidence rule applies *only* to writings, recordings and photographs whose contents are a material issue at trial. Where the contents are a material issue, the proponent must produce either the original document, or account for the original's unavailability. Conforming to the best evidence rule reduces the risk of inaccurate or intentionally fraudulent testimony. In practice, best evidence works more like a preferential rule rather than a rule of exclusion. Where the proponent can account for the unavailability of the original document, secondary sources at trial can be used to prove the contents of the original. When a party violates the rule of best evidence, however, no secondary evidentiary sources may be introduced by that party.

Proper use of the best evidence rule rests on counsel's ability to know:

1)   What constitutes a "document" under the best evidence rule. The definition is broader than one might expect, and includes photographs, X-rays, and video tape under both the Texas and Federal Rules.

2)   When the document's terms are in issue so that the best evidence rule applies.

3)   How the terms "original" and "duplicate" are defined under the rules.

4)   What are the acceptable excuses for non-production of the original document; and

5)   What types of evidence are admissible as secondary evidence, once an acceptable excuse for non-production of the original document has been made.

Federal Rules of Evidence 1001-1008 address these five significant areas. For the most part, the codification of the Texas and Federal Rules follow the original common law best evidence principles, although their codification prevents judges from judicially expanding the acceptable excuses for the non-production of original documents.

The best evidence rule does not work in isolation from the other rules of evidence. Simply because a piece of evidence may be admissible under the best evidence rule does not mean it is immune from other evidence rules, such as hearsay objections under Article VIII or from the authentication requirements of Article IX.

§ 10-2. "Best Evidence" Chart

The following "flow" chart demonstrates how the various rules in Article X fit together.

THE "BEST EVIDENCE" RULE

	(3) Must Produce Original (Rules 1002; 1001(d)
(1) If proffered evidence is a "writing, recording, or photograph" (Rule 1001)	OR
AND **THEN THE PROPONENT**	(4) Produce Duplicate (Rule 1003)
	OR
(2) Its contents are in issue	(5) Establish Exception (Rules 1005, 1006, 1007)
	OR
	(6) Establish Excuse for Nonproduction of Original. (Rule 1004)
	AND
	(7) Produce Secondary Evidence (No degrees)

§ 10-3. Problems and Questions

a.   In a personal injury case, the defense has discovered a photocopy of a medical report concerning the plaintiff. At trial, the defense offers the photocopy into evidence to show that the plaintiff's injuries are not as bad as she claims. The plaintiff objects on grounds of the best evidence rule. What foundation, if any, should the defendant be prepared to establish to introduce the copy?

   What if the defendant asked to see the original and the plaintiff responded that it had been lost?

b.   In a criminal case, the prosecution offers into evidence a photograph of the victim's injuries when she was admitted to the hospital. The defense objects on grounds that the photograph is not the "best evidence." The best evidence, he asserts, is the victim's testimony about the injuries, and second, the next best evidence would be the negatives of the photo. Assume you are the trial judge. What is your ruling? Why?

APPENDIX A

Federal Rules of Evidence

Appendix A consists of the official text of the Federal Rules of Evidence, as last amended on December 1, 2020.

As discussed in Chapter One, the Federal Rules served as a model for the Texas Rules of Evidence. The Texas courts often refer to the Federal Rules in interpreting similar language in the Texas Rules.

FEDERAL RULES OF EVIDENCE
FOR
UNITED STATES COURTS AND MAGISTRATES

ARTICLE I. GENERAL PROVISIONS

RULE 101. SCOPE; DEFINITIONS

(a) Scope. These rules apply to proceedings in United States courts. The specific courts and proceedings to which the rules apply, along with exceptions, are set out in Rule 1101.

(b) Definitions. In these rules:

(1) "civil case" means a civil action or proceeding;

(2) "criminal case" includes a criminal proceeding;

(3) "public office" includes a public agency;

(4) "record" includes a memorandum, report, or data compilation;

(5) a "rule prescribed by the Supreme Court" means a rule adopted by the Supreme Court under statutory authority; and

(6) a reference to any kind of written material or any other medium includes electronically stored information.

RULE 102. PURPOSE

These rules should be construed so as to administer every proceeding fairly, eliminate unjustifiable expense and delay, and promote the development of evidence law, to the end of ascertaining the truth and securing a just determination.

RULE 103. RULINGS ON EVIDENCE

(a) Preserving a Claim of Error. A party may claim error in a ruling to admit or exclude evidence only if the error affects a substantial right of the party and:

(1) if the ruling admits evidence, a party, on the record:

(A) timely objects or moves to strike; and

(B) states the specific ground, unless it was apparent from the context; or

(2) if the ruling excludes evidence, a party informs the court of its substance by an offer of proof, unless the substance was apparent from the context.

(b) Not Needing to Renew an Objection or Offer of Proof. Once the court rules definitively on the record — either before or at trial — a party need not renew an objection or offer of proof to preserve a claim of error for appeal.

(c) Court's Statement About the Ruling; Directing an Offer of Proof. The court may make any statement about the character or form of the evidence, the objection made, and the ruling. The court may direct that an offer of proof be made in question-and-answer form.

(d) Preventing the Jury from Hearing Inadmissible Evidence. To the extent practicable, the court must conduct a jury trial so that inadmissible evidence is not suggested to the jury by any means.

(e) Taking Notice of Plain Error. A court may take notice of a plain error affecting a substantial right, even if the claim of error was not properly preserved.

RULE 104. PRELIMINARY QUESTIONS

(a) In General. The court must decide any preliminary question about whether a witness is qualified, a privilege exists, or evidence is admissible. In so deciding, the court is not bound by evidence rules, except those on privilege.

(b) Relevance That Depends on a Fact. When the relevance of evidence depends on whether a fact exists, proof must be introduced sufficient to support a finding that the fact does exist. The court may admit the proposed evidence on the condition that the proof be introduced later.

(c) Conducting a Hearing So That the Jury Cannot Hear It. The court must conduct any hearing on a preliminary question so that the jury cannot hear it if:

   (1) the hearing involves the admissibility of a confession;

   (2) a defendant in a criminal case is a witness and so requests; or

   (3) justice so requires.

(d) Cross-Examining a Defendant in a Criminal Case. By testifying on a preliminary question, a defendant in a criminal case does not become subject to cross-examination on other issues in the case.

(e) Evidence Relevant to Weight and Credibility. This rule does not limit a party's right to introduce before the jury evidence that is relevant to the weight or credibility of other evidence.

RULE 105. LIMITING EVIDENCE THAT IS NOT ADMISSIBLE AGAINST OTHER PARTIES OR FOR OTHER PURPOSES

If the court admits evidence that is admissible against a party or for a purpose — but not against another party or for another purpose — the court, on timely request, must restrict the evidence to its proper scope and instruct the jury accordingly.

RULE 106. REMAINDER OF OR RELATED WRITINGS OR RECORDED STATEMENTS

If a party introduces all or part of a writing or recorded statement, an adverse party may require the introduction, at that time, of any other part — or any other writing or recorded statement — that in fairness ought to be considered at the same time.

ARTICLE II. JUDICIAL NOTICE

RULE 201. JUDICIAL NOTICE OF ADJUDICATIVE FACTS

(a) Scope. This rule governs judicial notice of an adjudicative fact only, not a legislative fact.

(b) Kinds of Facts That May Be Judicially Noticed. The court may judicially notice a fact that is not subject to reasonable dispute because it:

(1) is generally known within the trial court's territorial jurisdiction; or

(2) can be accurately and readily determined from sources whose accuracy cannot reasonably be questioned.

(c) Taking Notice. The court:

(1) may take judicial notice on its own; or

(2) must take judicial notice if a party requests it and the court is supplied with the necessary information.

(d) Timing. The court may take judicial notice at any stage of the proceeding.

(e) Opportunity to Be Heard. On timely request, a party is entitled to be heard on the propriety of taking judicial notice and the nature of the fact to be noticed. If the court takes judicial notice before notifying a party, the party, on request, is still entitled to be heard.

(f) Instructing the Jury. In a civil case, the court must instruct the jury to accept the noticed fact as conclusive. In a criminal case, the court must instruct the jury that it may or may not accept the noticed fact as conclusive.

ARTICLE III. PRESUMPTIONS IN CIVIL CASES

RULE 301. PRESUMPTIONS IN CIVIL CASES GENERALLY

In a civil case, unless a federal statute or these rules provide otherwise, the party against whom a presumption is directed has the burden of producing evidence to rebut the presumption. But this rule does not shift the burden of persuasion, which remains on the party who had it originally.

RULE 302. APPLYING STATE LAW TO PRESUMPTIONS IN CIVIL CASES

In a civil case, state law governs the effect of a presumption regarding a claim or defense for which state law supplies the rule of decision.

ARTICLE IV. RELEVANCE AND ITS LIMITS

RULE 401. TEST FOR RELEVANT EVIDENCE

Evidence is relevant if:

(a) it has any tendency to make a fact more or less probable than it would be without the evidence; and

(b) the fact is of consequence in determining the action.

RULE 402. GENERAL ADMISSIBILITY OF RELEVANT EVIDENCE

Relevant evidence is admissible unless any of the following provides otherwise:

- the United States Constitution;
- a federal statute;
- these rules; or
- other rules prescribed by the Supreme Court.

Irrelevant evidence is not admissible.

RULE 403. EXCLUDING RELEVANT EVIDENCE FOR PREJUDICE, CONFUSION, WASTE OF TIME, OR OTHER REASONS

The court may exclude relevant evidence if its probative value is substantially outweighed by a danger of one or more of the following: unfair prejudice, confusing the issues, misleading the jury, undue delay, wasting time, or needlessly presenting cumulative evidence.

RULE 404. CHARACTER EVIDENCE; CRIMES OR OTHER ACTS

(a) Character Evidence.

(1) *Prohibited Uses.* Evidence of a person's character or character trait is not admissible to prove that on a particular occasion the person acted in accordance with the character or trait.

(2) *Exceptions for a Defendant or Victim in a Criminal Case.* The following exceptions apply in a criminal case:

(A) a defendant may offer evidence of the defendant's pertinent trait, and if the evidence is admitted, the prosecutor may offer evidence to rebut it;

(B) subject to the limitations in Rule 412, a defendant may offer evidence of an alleged victim's pertinent trait, and if the evidence is admitted, the prosecutor may:

(i) offer evidence to rebut it; and

(ii) offer evidence of the defendant's same trait; and

(C) in a homicide case, the prosecutor may offer evidence of the alleged victim's trait of peacefulness to rebut evidence that the victim was the first aggressor.

(3) *Exceptions for a Witness.* Evidence of a witness's character may be admitted under Rules 607, 608, and 609.

(b) Crimes, Wrongs, or Other Acts.

(1) *Prohibited Uses.* Evidence of a crime, wrong, or other act is not admissible to prove a person's character in order to show that on a particular occasion the person acted in accordance with the character.

(2) *Permitted Uses; Notice in a Criminal Case.* This evidence may be admissible for another purpose, such as proving motive, opportunity, intent, preparation, plan, knowledge, identity, absence of mistake, or lack of accident.

(3) *Notice in a Criminal Case.* In a criminal case, the prosecutor must:

(A) provide reasonable notice of any such evidence that the prosecutor intends to offer at trial, so that the defendant has a fair opportunity to meet it;

(B) articulate in the notice the permitted purpose for which the prosecutor intends to offer the evidence and the reasoning that supports the purpose; and

(C) do so in writing before trial — or in any form during trial if the court, for good cause, excuses lack of pretrial notice.

RULE 405. METHODS OF PROVING CHARACTER

(a) By Reputation or Opinion. When evidence of a person's character or character trait is admissible, it may be proved by testimony about the person's reputation or by testimony in the form of an opinion. On cross-examination of the character witness, the court may allow an inquiry into relevant specific instances of the person's conduct.

(b) By Specific Instances of Conduct. When a person's character or character trait is an essential element of a charge, claim, or defense, the character or trait may also be proved by relevant specific instances of the person's conduct.

RULE 406. HABIT; ROUTINE PRACTICE

Evidence of a person's habit or an organization's routine practice may be admitted to prove that on a particular occasion the person or organization acted in accordance with the habit or routine practice. The court may admit this evidence regardless of whether it is corroborated or whether there was an eyewitness.

RULE 407. SUBSEQUENT REMEDIAL MEASURES

When measures are taken that would have made an earlier injury or harm less likely to occur, evidence of the subsequent measures is not admissible to prove:

- negligence;
- culpable conduct;
- a defect in a product or its design; or

- a need for a warning or instruction.

But the court may admit this evidence for another purpose, such as impeachment or — if disputed — proving ownership, control, or the feasibility of precautionary measures.

RULE 408. COMPROMISE OFFERS AND NEGOTIATIONS

(a) Prohibited Uses. Evidence of the following is not admissible — on behalf of any party — either to prove or disprove the validity or amount of a disputed claim or to impeach by a prior inconsistent statement or a contradiction:

(1) furnishing, promising, or offering — or accepting, promising to accept, or offering to accept — a valuable consideration in compromising or attempting to compromise the claim; and

(2) conduct or a statement made during compromise negotiations about the claim — except when offered in a criminal case and when the negotiations related to a claim by a public office in the exercise of its regulatory, investigative, or enforcement authority.

(b) Exceptions. The court may admit this evidence for another purpose, such as proving a witness's bias or prejudice, negating a contention of undue delay, or proving an effort to obstruct a criminal investigation or prosecution.

RULE 409. OFFERS TO PAY MEDICAL AND SIMILAR EXPENSES

Evidence of furnishing, promising to pay, or offering to pay medical, hospital, or similar expenses resulting from an injury is not admissible to prove liability for the injury.

RULE 410. PLEAS, PLEA DISCUSSIONS, AND RELATED STATEMENTS

(a) Prohibited Uses. In a civil or criminal case, evidence of the following is not admissible against the defendant who made the plea or participated in the plea discussions:

(1) a guilty plea that was later withdrawn;

(2) a nolo contendere plea;

(3) a statement made during a proceeding on either of those pleas under Federal Rule of Criminal Procedure 11 or a comparable state procedure; or

(4) a statement made during plea discussions with an attorney for the prosecuting authority if the discussions did not result in a guilty plea or they resulted in a later-withdrawn guilty plea.

(b) Exceptions. The court may admit a statement described in Rule 410(a)(3) or (4):

(1) in any proceeding in which another statement made during the same plea or plea discussions has been introduced, if in fairness the statements ought to be considered together; or

(2) in a criminal proceeding for perjury or false statement, if the defendant made the statement under oath, on the record, and with counsel present.

RULE 411. LIABILITY INSURANCE

Evidence that a person was or was not insured against liability is not admissible to prove whether the person acted negligently or otherwise wrongfully. But the court may admit this evidence for another purpose, such as proving a witness's bias or prejudice or proving agency, ownership, or control.

RULE 412. SEX-OFFENSE CASES: THE VICTIM'S SEXUAL BEHAVIOR OR PREDISPOSITION

(a) Prohibited Uses. The following evidence is not admissible in a civil or criminal proceeding involving alleged sexual misconduct:

(1) evidence offered to prove that a victim engaged in other sexual behavior; or

(2) evidence offered to prove a victim's sexual predisposition.

(b) Exceptions.

(1) *Criminal Cases.* The court may admit the following evidence in a criminal case:

(A) evidence of specific instances of a victim's sexual behavior, if offered to prove that someone other than the defendant was the source of semen, injury, or other physical evidence;

(B) evidence of specific instances of a victim's sexual behavior with respect to the person accused of the sexual misconduct, if offered by the defendant to prove consent or if offered by the prosecutor; and

(C) evidence whose exclusion would violate the defendant's constitutional rights.

(2) *Civil Cases.* In a civil case, the court may admit evidence offered to prove a victim's sexual behavior or sexual predisposition if its probative value substantially outweighs the danger of harm to any victim and of unfair prejudice to any party. The court may admit evidence of a victim's reputation only if the victim has placed it in controversy.

(c) Procedure to Determine Admissibility.

(1) *Motion.* If a party intends to offer evidence under Rule 412(b), the party must:

(A) file a motion that specifically describes the evidence and states the purpose for which it is to be offered;

(B) do so at least 14 days before trial unless the court, for good cause, sets a different time;

(C) serve the motion on all parties; and

(D) notify the victim or, when appropriate, the victim's guardian or representative.

(2) *Hearing.* Before admitting evidence under this rule, the court must conduct an in camera hearing and give the victim and parties a right to attend and be heard. Unless the court orders otherwise, the motion, related materials, and the record of the hearing must be and remain sealed.

(d) Definition of "Victim." In this rule, "victim" includes an alleged victim.

RULE 413. SIMILAR CRIMES IN SEXUAL-ASSAULT CASES

(a) Permitted Uses. In a criminal case in which a defendant is accused of a sexual assault, the court may admit evidence that the defendant committed any other sexual assault. The evidence may be considered on any matter to which it is relevant.

(b) Disclosure to the Defendant. If the prosecutor intends to offer this evidence, the prosecutor must disclose it to the defendant, including witnesses' statements or a summary of the expected testimony. The prosecutor must do so at least 15 days before trial or at a later time that the court allows for good cause.

(c) Effect on Other Rules. This rule does not limit the admission or consideration of evidence under any other rule.

(d) Definition of "Sexual Assault." In this rule and Rule 415, "sexual assault" means a crime under federal law or under state law (as "state" is defined in 18 U.S.C. § 513) involving:

(1) any conduct prohibited by 18 U.S.C. chapter 109A;

(2) contact, without consent, between any part of the defendant's body — or an object — and another person's genitals or anus;

(3) contact, without consent, between the defendant's genitals or anus and any part of another person's body;

(4) deriving sexual pleasure or gratification from inflicting death, bodily injury, or physical pain on another person; or

(5) an attempt or conspiracy to engage in conduct described in subparagraphs (1)–(4).

RULE 414. SIMILAR CRIMES IN CHILD MOLESTATION CASES

(a) Permitted Uses. In a criminal case in which a defendant is accused of child molestation, the court may admit evidence that the defendant committed any other child molestation. The evidence may be considered on any matter to which it is relevant.

(b) Disclosure to the Defendant. If the prosecutor intends to offer this evidence, the prosecutor must disclose it to the defendant, including witnesses' statements or a summary of the expected testimony. The prosecutor must do so at least 15 days before trial or at a later time that the court allows for good cause.

(c) Effect on Other Rules. This rule does not limit the admission or consideration of evidence under any other rule.

(d) Definition of "Child" and "Child Molestation." In this rule and Rule 415:

(1) "child" means a person below the age of 14; and

(2) "child molestation" means a crime under federal law or under state law (as "state" is defined in 18 U.S.C. § 513) involving:

(A) any conduct prohibited by 18 U.S.C. chapter 109A and committed with a child;

(B) any conduct prohibited by 18 U.S.C. chapter 110;

(C) contact between any part of the defendant's body — or an object — and a child's genitals or anus;

(D) contact between the defendant's genitals or anus and any part of a child's body;

(E) deriving sexual pleasure or gratification from inflicting death, bodily injury, or physical pain on a child; or

(F) an attempt or conspiracy to engage in conduct described in subparagraphs (A)–(E).

RULE 415. SIMILAR ACTS IN CIVIL CASES INVOLVING SEXUAL ASSAULT OR CHILD MOLESTATION

(a) Permitted Uses. In a civil case involving a claim for relief based on a party's alleged sexual assault or child molestation, the court may admit evidence that the party committed any other sexual assault or child molestation. The evidence may be considered as provided in Rules 413 and 414.

(b) Disclosure to the Opponent. If a party intends to offer this evidence, the party must disclose it to the party against whom it will be offered, including witnesses' statements or a summary of the expected testimony. The party must do so at least 15 days before trial or at a later time that the court allows for good cause.

(c) Effect on Other Rules. This rule does not limit the admission or consideration of evidence under any other rule.

ARTICLE V. PRIVILEGES

RULE 501. PRIVILEGE IN GENERAL

The common law — as interpreted by United States courts in the light of reason and experience — governs a claim of privilege unless any of the following provides otherwise:

- the United States Constitution;
- a federal statute; or
- rules prescribed by the Supreme Court.

But in a civil case, state law governs privilege regarding a claim or defense for which state law supplies the rule of decision.

RULE 502. ATTORNEY-CLIENT PRIVILEGE AND WORK PRODUCT; LIMITATIONS ON WAIVER

The following provisions apply, in the circumstances set out, to disclosure of a communication or information covered by the attorney-client privilege or work-product protection.

(a) Disclosure Made in a Federal Proceeding or to a Federal Office or Agency; Scope of a Waiver. When the disclosure is made in a federal proceeding or to a federal office or agency and waives the attorney-client privilege or work-product protection, the waiver extends to an undisclosed communication or information in a federal or state proceeding only if:

> **(1)** the waiver is intentional;

> **(2)** the disclosed and undisclosed communications or information concern the same subject matter; and

> **(3)** they ought in fairness to be considered together.

(b) Inadvertent Disclosure. When made in a federal proceeding or to a federal office or agency, the disclosure does not operate as a waiver in a federal or state proceeding if:

> **(1)** the disclosure is inadvertent;

> **(2)** the holder of the privilege or protection took reasonable steps to prevent disclosure; and

> **(3)** the holder promptly took reasonable steps to rectify the error, including (if applicable) following Federal Rule of Civil Procedure 26 (b)(5)(B).

(c) Disclosure Made in a State Proceeding. When the disclosure is made in a state proceeding and is not the subject of a state-court order concerning waiver, the disclosure does not operate as a waiver in a federal proceeding if the disclosure:

> **(1)** would not be a waiver under this rule if it had been made in a federal proceeding; or

> **(2)** is not a waiver under the law of the state where the disclosure occurred.

(d) Controlling Effect of a Court Order. A federal court may order that the privilege or protection is not waived by disclosure connected with the litigation pending before the court — in which event the disclosure is also not a waiver in any other federal or state proceeding.

(e) Controlling Effect of a Party Agreement. An agreement on the effect of disclosure in a federal proceeding is binding only on the parties to the agreement, unless it is incorporated into a court order.

(f) Controlling Effect of this Rule. Notwithstanding Rules 101 and 1101, this rule applies to state proceedings and to federal court-annexed and federal court-mandated arbitration proceedings, in the circumstances set out in the rule. And notwithstanding Rule 501, this rule applies even if state law provides the rule of decision.

(g) Definitions. In this rule:

> **(1)** "attorney-client privilege" means the protection that applicable law provides for confidential attorney-client communications; and

> **(2)** "work-product protection" means the protection that applicable law provides for tangible material (or its intangible equivalent) prepared in anticipation of litigation or for trial.

ARTICLE VI. WITNESSES

RULE 601. COMPETENCY TO TESTIFY IN GENERAL

Every person is competent to be a witness unless these rules provide otherwise. But in a civil case, state law governs the witness's competency regarding a claim or defense for which state law supplies the rule of decision.

RULE 602. NEED FOR PERSONAL KNOWLEDGE

A witness may testify to a matter only if evidence is introduced sufficient to support a finding that the witness has personal knowledge of the matter. Evidence to prove personal knowledge may consist of the witness's own testimony. This rule does not apply to a witness's expert testimony under Rule 703.

RULE 603. OATH OR AFFIRMATION TO TESTIFY TRUTHFULLY

Before testifying, a witness must give an oath or affirmation to testify truthfully. It must be in a form designed to impress that duty on the witness's conscience.

RULE 604. INTERPRETER

An interpreter must be qualified and must give an oath or affirmation to make a true translation.

RULE 605. JUDGE'S COMPETENCY AS A WITNESS

The presiding judge may not testify as a witness at the trial. A party need not object to preserve the issue.

RULE 606. JUROR'S COMPETENCY AS A WITNESS

(a) At the Trial. A juror may not testify as a witness before the other jurors at the trial. If a juror is called to testify, the court must give a party an opportunity to object outside the jury's presence.

(b) During an Inquiry into the Validity of a Verdict or Indictment.

(1) *Prohibited Testimony or Other Evidence.* During an inquiry into the validity of a verdict or indictment, a juror may not testify about any statement made or incident that occurred during the jury's deliberations; the effect of anything on that juror's or another juror's vote; or any juror's mental processes concerning the verdict or indictment. The court may not receive a juror's affidavit or evidence of a juror's statement on these matters.

(2) *Exceptions.* A juror may testify about whether:

(A) extraneous prejudicial information was improperly brought to the jury's attention;

(B) an outside influence was improperly brought to bear on any juror; or

(C) a mistake was made in entering the verdict on the verdict form.

RULE 607. WHO MAY IMPEACH A WITNESS

Any party, including the party that called the witness, may attack the witness's credibility.

RULE 608. A WITNESS'S CHARACTER FOR TRUTHFULNESS OR UNTRUTHFULNESS

(a) Reputation or Opinion Evidence. A witness's credibility may be attacked or supported by testimony about the witness's reputation for having a character for truthfulness or untruthfulness, or by testimony in the form of an opinion about that character. But evidence of truthful character is admissible only after the witness's character for truthfulness has been attacked.

(b) Specific Instances of Conduct. Except for a criminal conviction under Rule 609, extrinsic evidence is not admissible to prove specific instances of a witness's conduct in order to attack or support the witness's character for truthfulness. But the court may, on cross-examination, allow them to be inquired into if they are probative of the character for truthfulness or untruthfulness of:

>   **(1)** the witness; or

>   **(2)** another witness whose character the witness being cross-examined has testified about.

By testifying on another matter, a witness does not waive any privilege against self-incrimination for testimony that relates only to the witness's character for truthfulness.

RULE 609. IMPEACHMENT BY EVIDENCE OF A CRIMINAL CONVICTION

(a) In General. The following rules apply to attacking a witness's character for truthfulness by evidence of a criminal conviction:

>   **(1)** for a crime that, in the convicting jurisdiction, was punishable by death or by imprisonment for more than one year, the evidence:

>>   **(A)** must be admitted, subject to Rule 403, in a civil case or in a criminal case in which the witness is not a defendant; and

>>   **(B)** must be admitted in a criminal case in which the witness is a defendant, if the probative value of the evidence outweighs its prejudicial effect to that defendant; and

>   **(2)** for any crime regardless of the punishment, the evidence must be admitted if the court can readily determine that establishing the elements of the crime required proving — or the witness's admitting — a dishonest act or false statement.

(b) Limit on Using the Evidence After 10 Years. This subdivision (b) applies if more than 10 years have passed since the witness's conviction or release from confinement for it, whichever is later. Evidence of the conviction is admissible only if:

>   **(1)** its probative value, supported by specific facts and circumstances, substantially outweighs its prejudicial effect; and

>   **(2)** the proponent gives an adverse party reasonable written notice of the intent to use it so that the party has a fair opportunity to contest its use.

(c) Effect of a Pardon, Annulment, or Certificate of Rehabilitation. Evidence of a conviction is not admissible if:

(1) the conviction has been the subject of a pardon, annulment, certificate of rehabilitation, or other equivalent procedure based on a finding that the person has been rehabilitated, and the person has not been convicted of a later crime punishable by death or by imprisonment for more than one year; or

(2) the conviction has been the subject of a pardon, annulment, or other equivalent procedure based on a finding of innocence.

(d) Juvenile Adjudications. Evidence of a juvenile adjudication is admissible under this rule only if:

(1) it is offered in a criminal case;

(2) the adjudication was of a witness other than the defendant;

(3) an adult's conviction for that offense would be admissible to attack the adult's credibility; and

(4) admitting the evidence is necessary to fairly determine guilt or innocence.

(e) Pendency of an Appeal. A conviction that satisfies this rule is admissible even if an appeal is pending. Evidence of the pendency is also admissible.

RULE 610. RELIGIOUS BELIEFS OR OPINIONS

Evidence of a witness's religious beliefs or opinions is not admissible to attack or support the witness's credibility.

RULE 611. MODE AND ORDER OF EXAMINING WITNESSES AND PRESENTING EVIDENCE

(a) Control by the Court; Purposes. The court should exercise reasonable control over the mode and order of examining witnesses and presenting evidence so as to:

(1) make those procedures effective for determining the truth;

(2) avoid wasting time; and

(3) protect witnesses from harassment or undue embarrassment.

(b) Scope of Cross-Examination. Cross-examination should not go beyond the subject matter of the direct examination and matters affecting the witness's credibility. The court may allow inquiry into additional matters as if on direct examination.

(c) Leading Questions. Leading questions should not be used on direct examination except as necessary to develop the witness's testimony. Ordinarily, the court should allow leading questions:

(1) on cross-examination; and

(2) when a party calls a hostile witness, an adverse party, or a witness identified with an adverse party.

RULE 612. WRITING USED TO REFRESH A WITNESS'S MEMORY

(a) Scope. This rule gives an adverse party certain options when a witness uses a writing to refresh memory:

    (1) while testifying; or

    (2) before testifying, if the court decides that justice requires the party to have those options.

(b) Adverse Party's Options; Deleting Unrelated Matter. Unless 18 U.S.C. § 3500 provides otherwise in a criminal case, an adverse party is entitled to have the writing produced at the hearing, to inspect it, to cross-examine the witness about it, and to introduce in evidence any portion that relates to the witness's testimony. If the producing party claims that the writing includes unrelated matter, the court must examine the writing in camera, delete any unrelated portion, and order that the rest be delivered to the adverse party. Any portion deleted over objection must be preserved for the record.

(c) Failure to Produce or Deliver the Writing. If a writing is not produced or is not delivered as ordered, the court may issue any appropriate order. But if the prosecution does not comply in a criminal case, the court must strike the witness's testimony or — if justice so requires — declare a mistrial.

RULE 613. WITNESS'S PRIOR STATEMENT

(a) Showing or Disclosing the Statement During Examination. When examining a witness about the witness's prior statement, a party need not show it or disclose its contents to the witness. But the party must, on request, show it or disclose its contents to an adverse party's attorney.

(b) Extrinsic Evidence of a Prior Inconsistent Statement. Extrinsic evidence of a witness's prior inconsistent statement is admissible only if the witness is given an opportunity to explain or deny the statement and an adverse party is given an opportunity to examine the witness about it, or if justice so requires. This subdivision (b) does not apply to an opposing party's statement under Rule 801(d)(2).

RULE 614. COURT'S CALLING OR EXAMINING A WITNESS

(a) Calling. The court may call a witness on its own or at a party's request. Each party is entitled to cross-examine the witness.

(b) Examining. The court may examine a witness regardless of who calls the witness.

(c) Objections. A party may object to the court's calling or examining a witness either at that time or at the next opportunity when the jury is not present.

RULE 615. EXCLUDING WITNESSES

At a party's request, the court must order witnesses excluded so that they cannot hear other witnesses' testimony. Or the court may do so on its own. But this rule does not authorize excluding:

(a) a party who is a natural person;

(b) an officer or employee of a party that is not a natural person, after being designated as the party's representative by its attorney;

(c) a person whose presence a party shows to be essential to presenting the party's claim or defense; or

(d) a person authorized by statute to be present.

ARTICLE VII. OPINIONS AND EXPERT TESTIMONY

RULE 701. OPINION TESTIMONY BY LAY WITNESSES

If a witness is not testifying as an expert, testimony in the form of an opinion is limited to one that is:

(a) rationally based on the witness's perception;

(b) helpful to clearly understanding the witness's testimony or to determining a fact in issue; and

(c) not based on scientific, technical, or other specialized knowledge within the scope of Rule 702.

RULE 702. TESTIMONY BY EXPERT WITNESSES

A witness who is qualified as an expert by knowledge, skill, experience, training, or education may testify in the form of an opinion or otherwise if:

(a) the expert's scientific, technical, or other specialized knowledge will help the trier of fact to understand the evidence or to determine a fact in issue;

(b) the testimony is based on sufficient facts or data;

(c) the testimony is the product of reliable principles and methods; and

(d) the expert has reliably applied the principles and methods to the facts of the case.

RULE 703. BASES OF AN EXPERT'S OPINION TESTIMONY

An expert may base an opinion on facts or data in the case that the expert has been made aware of or personally observed. If experts in the particular field would reasonably rely on those kinds of facts or data in forming an opinion on the subject, they need not be admissible for the opinion to be admitted. But if the facts or data would otherwise be inadmissible, the proponent of the opinion may disclose them to the jury only if their probative value in helping the jury evaluate the opinion substantially outweighs their prejudicial effect.

RULE 704. OPINION ON AN ULTIMATE ISSUE

(a) In General — Not Automatically Objectionable. An opinion is not objectionable just because it embraces an ultimate issue.

(b) Exception. In a criminal case, an expert witness must not state an opinion about whether the defendant did or did not have a mental state or condition that constitutes an element of the crime charged or of a defense. Those matters are for the trier of fact alone.

RULE 705. DISCLOSING THE FACTS OR DATA UNDERLYING AN EXPERT'S OPINION

Unless the court orders otherwise, an expert may state an opinion — and give the reasons for it — without first testifying to the underlying facts or data. But the expert may be required to disclose those facts or data on cross-examination.

RULE 706. COURT-APPOINTED EXPERT WITNESSES

(a) Appointment Process. On a party's motion or on its own, the court may order the parties to show cause why expert witnesses should not be appointed and may ask the parties to submit nominations. The court may appoint any expert that the parties agree on and any of its own choosing. But the court may only appoint someone who consents to act.

(b) Expert's Role. The court must inform the expert of the expert's duties. The court may do so in writing and have a copy filed with the clerk or may do so orally at a conference in which the parties have an opportunity to participate. The expert:

(1) must advise the parties of any findings the expert makes;

(2) may be deposed by any party;

(3) may be called to testify by the court or any party; and

(4) may be cross-examined by any party, including the party that called the expert.

(c) Compensation. The expert is entitled to a reasonable compensation, as set by the court. The compensation is payable as follows:

(1) in a criminal case or in a civil case involving just compensation under the Fifth Amendment, from any funds that are provided by law; and

(2) in any other civil case, by the parties in the proportion and at the time that the court directs — and the compensation is then charged like other costs.

(d) Disclosing the Appointment to the Jury. The court may authorize disclosure to the jury that the court appointed the expert.

(e) Parties' Choice of Their Own Experts. This rule does not limit a party in calling its own experts.

ARTICLE VIII. HEARSAY

RULE 801. DEFINITIONS THAT APPLY TO THIS ARTICLE; EXCLUSIONS FROM HEARSAY

The following definitions apply under this article:

(a) Statement. "Statement" means a person's oral assertion, written assertion, or nonverbal conduct, if the person intended it as an assertion.

(b) Declarant. "Declarant" means the person who made the statement.

(c) Hearsay. "Hearsay" means a statement that:

(1) the declarant does not make while testifying at the current trial or hearing; and

(2) a party offers in evidence to prove the truth of the matter asserted in the statement.

(d) Statements That Are Not Hearsay. A statement that meets the following conditions is not hearsay:

(1) *A Declarant-Witness's Prior Statement.* The declarant testifies and is subject to cross-examination about a prior statement, and the statement:

(A) is inconsistent with the declarant's testimony and was given under penalty of perjury at a trial, hearing, or other proceeding or in a deposition;

(B) is consistent with the declarant's testimony and is offered:

(i) to rebut an express or implied charge that the declarant recently fabricated it or acted from a recent improper influence or motive in so testifying; or

(ii) to rehabilitate the declarant's credibility as a witness when attacked on another ground; or

(C) identifies a person as someone the declarant perceived earlier.

(2) *An Opposing Party's Statement.* The statement is offered against an opposing party and:

(A) was made by the party in an individual or representative capacity;

(B) is one the party manifested that it adopted or believed to be true;

(C) was made by a person whom the party authorized to make a statement on the subject;

(D) was made by the party's agent or employee on a matter within the scope of that relationship and while it existed; or

(E) was made by the party's coconspirator during and in furtherance of the conspiracy.

The statement must be considered but does not by itself establish the declarant's authority under (C); the existence or scope of the relationship under (D); or the existence of the conspiracy or participation in it under (E).

RULE 802. THE RULE AGAINST HEARSAY

Hearsay is not admissible unless any of the following provides otherwise:

- a federal statute;

- these rules; or

- other rules prescribed by the Supreme Court.

RULE 803. EXCEPTIONS TO THE RULE AGAINST HEARSAY — REGARDLESS OF WHETHER THE DECLARANT IS AVAILABLE AS A WITNESS

The following are not excluded by the rule against hearsay, regardless of whether the declarant is available as a witness:

(1) *Present Sense Impression.* A statement describing or explaining an event or condition, made while or immediately after the declarant perceived it.

(2) *Excited Utterance.* A statement relating to a startling event or condition, made while the declarant was under the stress of excitement that it caused.

(3) *Then-Existing Mental, Emotional, or Physical Condition.* A statement of the declarant's then-existing state of mind (such as motive, intent, or plan) or emotional, sensory, or physical condition (such as mental feeling, pain, or bodily health), but not including a statement of memory or belief to prove the fact remembered or believed unless it relates to the validity or terms of the declarant's will.

(4) *Statement Made for Medical Diagnosis or Treatment.* A statement that:

(A) is made for — and is reasonably pertinent to — medical diagnosis or treatment; and

(B) describes medical history; past or present symptoms or sensations; their inception; or their general cause.

(5) *Recorded Recollection.* A record that:

(A) is on a matter the witness once knew about but now cannot recall well enough to testify fully and accurately;

(B) was made or adopted by the witness when the matter was fresh in the witness's memory; and

(C) accurately reflects the witness's knowledge.

If admitted, the record may be read into evidence but may be received as an exhibit only if offered by an adverse party.

(6) *Records of a Regularly Conducted Activity.* A record of an act, event, condition, opinion, or diagnosis if:

(A) the record was made at or near the time by — or from information transmitted by — someone with knowledge;

(B) the record was kept in the course of a regularly conducted activity of a business, organization, occupation, or calling, whether or not for profit;

(C) making the record was a regular practice of that activity;

(D) all these conditions are shown by the testimony of the custodian or another qualified witness, or by a certification that complies with Rule 902(11) or (12) or with a statute permitting certification; and

(E) the opponent does not show that the source of information nor the method or circumstances of preparation indicate a lack of trustworthiness.

(7) *Absence of a Record of a Regularly Conducted Activity.* Evidence that a matter is not included in a record described in paragraph (6) if:

(A) the evidence is admitted to prove that the matter did not occur or exist;

(B) a record was regularly kept for a matter of that kind; and

(C) neither the possible source of the information nor other circumstances indicate a lack of trustworthiness.

(8) *Public Records.* A record or statement of a public office if:

(A) it sets out:

(i) the office's activities;

(ii) a matter observed while under a legal duty to report, but not including, in a criminal case, a matter observed by law-enforcement personnel; or

(iii) in a civil case or against the government in a criminal case, factual findings from a legally authorized investigation; and

(B) the opponent does not show that source of information nor other circumstances indicate a lack of trustworthiness.

(9) *Public Records of Vital Statistics.* A record of a birth, death, or marriage, if reported to a public office in accordance with a legal duty.

(10) *Absence of a Public Record.* Testimony — or a certification under Rule 902 — that a diligent search failed to disclose a public record or statement if:

(A) the testimony or certification is admitted to prove that:

(i) the record or statement does not exist; or

(ii) a matter did not occur or exist, if a public office regularly kept a record or statement for a matter of that kind.

(B) in a criminal case, a prosecutor who intends to offer a certification provides written notice of that intent at least 14 days before trial, and the defendant does not object in writing within 7 days of receiving the notice — unless the court sets a different time for the notice or the objection.

(11) *Records of Religious Organizations Concerning Personal or Family History.* A statement of birth, legitimacy, ancestry, marriage, divorce, death, relationship by blood or marriage, or similar facts of personal or family history, contained in a regularly kept record of a religious organization.

(12) *Certificates of Marriage, Baptism, and Similar Ceremonies.* A statement of fact contained in a certificate:

> **(A)** made by a person who is authorized by a religious organization or by law to perform the act certified;

> **(B)** attesting that the person performed a marriage or similar ceremony or administered a sacrament; and

> **(C)** purporting to have been issued at the time of the act or within a reasonable time after it.

(13) *Family Records.* A statement of fact about personal or family history contained in a family record, such as a Bible, genealogy, chart, engraving on a ring, inscription on a portrait, or engraving on an urn or burial marker.

(14) *Records of Documents That Affect an Interest in Property.* The record of a document that purports to establish or affect an interest in property if:

> **(A)** the record is admitted to prove the content of the original recorded document, along with its signing and its delivery by each person who purports to have signed it;

> **(B)** the record is kept in a public office; and

> **(C)** a statute authorizes recording documents of that kind in that office.

(15) *Statements in Documents That Affect an Interest in Property.* A statement contained in a document that purports to establish or affect an interest in property if the matter stated was relevant to the document's purpose — unless later dealings with the property are inconsistent with the truth of the statement or the purport of the document.

(16) *Statements in Ancient Documents.* A statement in a document that was prepared before January 1, 1998, and whose authenticity is established.

(17) *Market Reports and Similar Commercial Publications.* Market quotations, lists, directories, or other compilations that are generally relied on by the public or by persons in particular occupations.

(18) *Statements in Learned Treatises, Periodicals, or Pamphlets.* A statement contained in a treatise, periodical, or pamphlet if:

> **(A)** the statement is called to the attention of an expert witness on cross-examination or relied on by the expert on direct examination; and

> **(B)** the publication is established as a reliable authority by the expert's admission or testimony, by another expert's testimony, or by judicial notice.

If admitted, the statement may be read into evidence but not received as an exhibit.

(19) *Reputation Concerning Personal or Family History.* A reputation among a person's family by blood, adoption, or marriage — or among a person's associates or in the community — concerning the person's birth, adoption, legitimacy, ancestry, marriage, divorce, death, relationship by blood, adoption, or marriage, or similar facts of personal or family history.

(20) *Reputation Concerning Boundaries or General History.* A reputation in a community — arising before the controversy — concerning boundaries of land in the community or customs that affect the land, or concerning general historical events important to that community, state, or nation.

(21) *Reputation Concerning Character.* A reputation among a person's associates or in the community concerning the person's character.

(22) *Judgment of a Previous Conviction.* Evidence of a final judgment of conviction if:

(A) the judgment was entered after a trial or guilty plea, but not a nolo contendere plea;

(B) the conviction was for a crime punishable by death or by imprisonment for more than a year;

(C) the evidence is admitted to prove any fact essential to the judgment; and

(D) when offered by the prosecutor in a criminal case for a purpose other than impeachment, the judgment was against the defendant.

The pendency of an appeal may be shown but does not affect admissibility.

(23) *Judgments Involving Personal, Family, or General History, or a Boundary.* A judgment that is admitted to prove a matter of personal, family, or general history, or boundaries, if the matter:

(A) was essential to the judgment; and

(B) could be proved by evidence of reputation.

(24) *[Other Exceptions .]* [Transferred to Rule 807.]

RULE 804. HEARSAY EXCEPTIONS; DECLARANT UNAVAILABLE

(a) Criteria for Being Unavailable. A declarant is considered to be unavailable as a witness if the declarant:

(1) is exempted from testifying about the subject matter of the declarant's statement because the court rules that a privilege applies;

(2) refuses to testify about the subject matter despite a court order to do so;

(3) testifies to not remembering the subject matter;

(4) cannot be present or testify at the trial or hearing because of death or a then-existing infirmity, physical illness, or mental illness; or

(5) is absent from the trial or hearing and the statement's proponent has not been able, by process or other reasonable means, to procure:

(A) the declarant's attendance, in the case of a hearsay exception under Rule 804(b)(1) or (6); or

(B) the declarant's attendance or testimony, in the case of a hearsay exception under Rule 804(b)(2), (3), or (4).

But this subdivision (a) does not apply if the statement's proponent procured or wrongfully caused the declarant's unavailability as a witness in order to prevent the declarant from attending or testifying.

(b) The Exceptions. The following are not excluded by the rule against hearsay if the declarant is unavailable as a witness:

(1) *Former Testimony.* Testimony that:

(A) was given as a witness at a trial, hearing, or lawful deposition, whether given during the current proceeding or a different one; and

(B) is now offered against a party who had — or, in a civil case, whose predecessor in interest had — an opportunity and similar motive to develop it by direct, cross-, or redirect examination.

(2) *Statement Under the Belief of Imminent Death.* In a prosecution for homicide or in a civil case, a statement that the declarant, while believing the declarant's death to be imminent, made about its cause or circumstances.

(3) *Statement Against Interest.* A statement that:

(A) a reasonable person in the declarant's position would have made only if the person believed it to be true because, when made, it was so contrary to the declarant's proprietary or pecuniary interest or had so great a tendency to invalidate the declarant's claim against someone else or to expose the declarant to civil or criminal liability; and

(B) is supported by corroborating circumstances that clearly indicate its trustworthiness, if it is offered in a criminal case as one that tends to expose the declarant to criminal liability.

(4) *Statement of Personal or Family History.* A statement about:

(A) the declarant's own birth, adoption, legitimacy, ancestry, marriage, divorce, relationship by blood, adoption, or marriage, or similar facts of personal or family history, even though the declarant had no way of acquiring personal knowledge about that fact; or

(B) another person concerning any of these facts, as well as death, if the declarant was related to the person by blood, adoption, or marriage or was so intimately associated with the person's family that the declarant's information is likely to be accurate.

(5) [*Other Exceptions* .] [Transferred to Rule 807.]

(6) *Statement Offered Against a Party That Wrongfully Caused the Declarant's Unavailability.* A statement offered against a party that wrongfully caused — or acquiesced in wrongfully causing — the declarant's unavailability as a witness, and did so intending that result.

RULE 805. HEARSAY WITHIN HEARSAY

Hearsay within hearsay is not excluded by the rule against hearsay if each part of the combined statements conforms with an exception to the rule.

RULE 806. ATTACKING AND SUPPORTING THE DECLARANT'S CREDIBILITY

When a hearsay statement — or a statement described in Rule 801(d)(2)(C), (D), or (E) — has been admitted in evidence, the declarant's credibility may be attacked, and then supported, by any evidence that would be admissible for those purposes if the declarant had testified as a witness. The court may admit evidence of the declarant's inconsistent statement or conduct, regardless of when it occurred or whether the declarant had an opportunity to explain or deny it. If the party against whom the statement was admitted calls the declarant as a witness, the party may examine the declarant on the statement as if on cross-examination.

RULE 807. RESIDUAL EXCEPTION

(a) In General. Under the following conditions, a hearsay statement is not excluded by the rule against hearsay even if the statement is not admissible under a hearsay exception in Rule 803 or 804:

> (1) the statement is supported by sufficient guarantees of trustworthiness—after considering the totality of circumstances under which it was made and evidence, if any, corroborating the statement; and

> (2) it is more probative on the point for which it is offered than any other evidence that the proponent can obtain through reasonable efforts.

(b) Notice. The statement is admissible only if the proponent gives an adverse party reasonable notice of the intent to offer the statement—including its substance and the declarant's name—so that the party has a fair opportunity to meet it. The notice must be provided in writing before the trial or hearing—or in any form during the trial or hearing if the court, for good cause, excuses a lack of earlier notice.

ARTICLE IX. AUTHENTICATION AND IDENTIFICATION

RULE 901. AUTHENTICATING OR IDENTIFYING EVIDENCE

(a) In General. To satisfy the requirement of authenticating or identifying an item of evidence, the proponent must produce evidence sufficient to support a finding that the item is what the proponent claims it is.

(b) Examples. The following are examples only — not a complete list — of evidence that satisfies the requirement:

> **(1) *Testimony of a Witness with Knowledge.*** Testimony that an item is what it is claimed to be.

(2) *Nonexpert Opinion About Handwriting.* A nonexpert's opinion that handwriting is genuine, based on a familiarity with it that was not acquired for the current litigation.

(3) *Comparison by an Expert Witness or the Trier of Fact.* A comparison with an authenticated specimen by an expert witness or the trier of fact.

(4) *Distinctive Characteristics and the Like.* The appearance, contents, substance, internal patterns, or other distinctive characteristics of the item, taken together with all the circumstances.

(5) *Opinion About a Voice.* An opinion identifying a person's voice — whether heard firsthand or through mechanical or electronic transmission or recording — based on hearing the voice at any time under circumstances that connect it with the alleged speaker.

(6) *Evidence About a Telephone Conversation.* For a telephone conversation, evidence that a call was made to the number assigned at the time to:

　　(A) a particular person, if circumstances, including self-identification, show that the person answering was the one called; or

　　(B) a particular business, if the call was made to a business and the call related to business reasonably transacted over the telephone.

(7) *Evidence About Public Records.* Evidence that:

　　(A) a document was recorded or filed in a public office as authorized by law; or

　　(B) a purported public record or statement is from the office where items of this kind are kept.

(8) *Evidence About Ancient Documents or Data Compilations.* For a document or data compilation, evidence that it:

　　(A) is in a condition that creates no suspicion about its authenticity;

　　(B) was in a place where, if authentic, it would likely be; and

　　(C) is at least 20 years old when offered.

(9) *Evidence About a Process or System.* Evidence describing a process or system and showing that it produces an accurate result.

(10) *Methods Provided by a Statute or Rule.* Any method of authentication or identification allowed by a federal statute or a rule prescribed by the Supreme Court.

RULE 902. EVIDENCE THAT IS SELF-AUTHENTICATING

The following items of evidence are self-authenticating; they require no extrinsic evidence of authenticity in order to be admitted:

(1) *Domestic Public Documents That Are Sealed and Signed.* A document that bears:

　　(A) a seal purporting to be that of the United States; any state, district, commonwealth, territory, or insular possession of the United States; the former Panama Canal Zone; the Trust Territory of the Pacific Islands; a political subdivision of any of these entities; or a department, agency, or officer of any entity named above; and

(B) a signature purporting to be an execution or attestation.

(2) ***Domestic Public Documents That Are Not Sealed but Are Signed and Certified.*** A document that bears no seal if:

(A) it bears the signature of an officer or employee of an entity named in Rule 902(1)(A); and

(B) another public officer who has a seal and official duties within that same entity certifies under seal — or its equivalent — that the signer has the official capacity and that the signature is genuine.

(3) ***Foreign Public Documents.*** A document that purports to be signed or attested by a person who is authorized by a foreign country's law to do so. The document must be accompanied by a final certification that certifies the genuineness of the signature and official position of the signer or attester — or of any foreign official whose certificate of genuineness relates to the signature or attestation or is in a chain of certificates of genuineness relating to the signature or attestation. The certification may be made by a secretary of a United States embassy or legation; by a consul general, vice consul, or consular agent of the United States; or by a diplomatic or consular official of the foreign country assigned or accredited to the United States. If all parties have been given a reasonable opportunity to investigate the document's authenticity and accuracy, the court may, for good cause, either:

(A) order that it be treated as presumptively authentic without final certification; or

(B) allow it to be evidenced by an attested summary with or without final certification.

(4) ***Certified Copies of Public Records.*** A copy of an official record — or a copy of a document that was recorded or filed in a public office as authorized by law — if the copy is certified as correct by:

(A) the custodian or another person authorized to make the certification; or

(B) a certificate that complies with Rule 902(1), (2), or (3), a federal statute, or a rule prescribed by the Supreme Court.

(5) ***Official Publications.*** A book, pamphlet, or other publication purporting to be issued by a public authority.

(6) ***Newspapers and Periodicals.*** Printed material purporting to be a newspaper or periodical.

(7) ***Trade Inscriptions and the Like.*** An inscription, sign, tag, or label purporting to have been affixed in the course of business and indicating origin, ownership, or control.

(8) ***Acknowledged Documents.*** A document accompanied by a certificate of acknowledgment that is lawfully executed by a notary public or another officer who is authorized to take acknowledgments.

(9) *Commercial Paper and Related Documents.* Commercial paper, a signature on it, and related documents, to the extent allowed by general commercial law.

(10) *Presumptions Under a Federal Statute.* A signature, document, or anything else that a federal statute declares to be presumptively or prima facie genuine or authentic.

(11) *Certified Domestic Records of a Regularly Conducted Activity.* The original or a copy of a domestic record that meets the requirements of Rule 803(6)(A)-(C), as shown by a certification of the custodian or another qualified person that complies with a federal statute or a rule prescribed by the Supreme Court. Before the trial or hearing, the proponent must give an adverse party reasonable written notice of the intent to offer the record — and must make the record and certification available for inspection — so that the party has a fair opportunity to challenge them.

(12) *Certified Foreign Records of a Regularly Conducted Activity.* In a civil case, the original or a copy of a foreign record that meets the requirements of Rule 902(11), modified as follows: the certification, rather than complying with a federal statute or Supreme Court rule, must be signed in a manner that, if falsely made, would subject the maker to a criminal penalty in the country where the certification is signed. The proponent must also meet the notice requirements of Rule 902(11).

(13) *Certified Records Generated by an Electronic Process or System.* A record generated by an electronic process or system that produces an accurate result, as shown by a certification of a qualified person that complies with the certification requirements of Rule 902(11) or (12). The proponent must also meet the notice requirements of Rule 902(11).

(14) *Certified Data Copied from an Electronic Device, Storage Medium, or File.* Data copied from an electronic device, storage medium, or file, if authenticated by a process of digital identification, as shown by a certification of a qualified person that complies with the certification requirements of Rule 902(11) or (12). The proponent also must meet the notice requirements of Rule 902(11).

RULE 903. SUBSCRIBING WITNESS'S TESTIMONY

A subscribing witness's testimony is necessary to authenticate a writing only if required by the law of the jurisdiction that governs its validity.

ARTICLE X. CONTENTS OF WRITINGS, RECORDINGS, AND PHOTOGRAPHS

RULE 1001. DEFINITIONS THAT APPLY TO THIS ARTICLE

In this article:

(a) A "writing" consists of letters, words, numbers, or their equivalent set down in any form.

(b) A "recording" consists of letters, words, numbers, or their equivalent recorded in any manner.

(c) A "photograph" means a photographic image or its equivalent stored in any form.

(d) An "original" of a writing or recording means the writing or recording itself or any counterpart intended to have the same effect by the person who executed or issued it. For electronically stored information, "original" means any printout — or other output readable by sight — if it accurately reflects the information. An "original" of a photograph includes the negative or a print from it.

(e) A "duplicate" means a counterpart produced by a mechanical, photographic, chemical, electronic, or other equivalent process or technique that accurately reproduces the original.

RULE 1002. REQUIREMENT OF THE ORIGINAL

An original writing, recording, or photograph is required in order to prove its content unless these rules or a federal statute provides otherwise.

RULE 1003. ADMISSIBILITY OF DUPLICATES

A duplicate is admissible to the same extent as the original unless a genuine question is raised about the original's authenticity or the circumstances make it unfair to admit the duplicate.

RULE 1004. ADMISSIBILITY OF OTHER EVIDENCE OF CONTENT

An original is not required and other evidence of the content of a writing, recording, or photograph is admissible if:

(a) all the originals are lost or destroyed, and not by the proponent acting in bad faith;

(b) an original cannot be obtained by any available judicial process;

(c) the party against whom the original would be offered had control of the original; was at that time put on notice, by pleadings or otherwise, that the original would be a subject of proof at the trial or hearing; and fails to produce it at the trial or hearing; or

(d) the writing, recording, or photograph is not closely related to a controlling issue

RULE 1005. COPIES OF PUBLIC RECORDS TO PROVE CONTENT

The proponent may use a copy to prove the content of an official record — or of a document that was recorded or filed in a public office as authorized by law — if these conditions are met: the record or document is otherwise admissible; and the copy is certified as correct in accordance with Rule 902(4) or is testified to be correct by a witness who has compared it with the original. If no such copy can be obtained by reasonable diligence, then the proponent may use other evidence to prove the content.

RULE 1006. SUMMARIES TO PROVE CONTENT

The proponent may use a summary, chart, or calculation to prove the content of voluminous writings, recordings, or photographs that cannot be conveniently examined in court. The proponent must make the originals or duplicates available for examination or copying, or both, by other parties at a reasonable time and place. And the court may order the proponent to produce them in court.

RULE 1007. TESTIMONY OR STATEMENT OF A PARTY TO PROVE CONTENT

The proponent may prove the content of a writing, recording, or photograph by the testimony, deposition, or written statement of the party against whom the evidence is offered. The proponent need not account for the original.

RULE 1008. FUNCTIONS OF THE COURT AND JURY

Ordinarily, the court determines whether the proponent has fulfilled the factual conditions for admitting other evidence of the content of a writing, recording, or photograph under Rule 1004 or 1005. But in a jury trial, the jury determines — in accordance with Rule 104(b) — any issue about whether:

(a) an asserted writing, recording, or photograph ever existed;

(b) another one produced at the trial or hearing is the original; or

(c) other evidence of content accurately reflects the content.

ARTICLE XI. MISCELLANEOUS RULES

RULE 1101. APPLICABILITY OF THE RULES

(a) To Courts and Judges. These rules apply to proceedings before:

- United States district courts;
- United States bankruptcy and magistrate judges;
- United States courts of appeals;
- the United States Court of Federal Claims; and
- the district courts of Guam, the Virgin Islands, and the Northern Mariana Islands.

(b) To Cases and Proceedings. These rules apply in:

- civil cases and proceedings, including bankruptcy, admiralty, and maritime cases;
- criminal cases and proceedings; and
- contempt proceedings, except those in which the court may act summarily.

(c) Rules on Privilege. The rules on privilege apply to all stages of a case or proceeding.

(d) Exceptions. These rules — except for those on privilege — do not apply to the following:

   (1) the court's determination, under Rule 104(a), on a preliminary question of fact governing admissibility;

   (2) grand-jury proceedings; and

   (3) miscellaneous proceedings such as:

- extradition or rendition;

- issuing an arrest warrant, criminal summons, or search warrant;

- a preliminary examination in a criminal case;

- sentencing;

- granting or revoking probation or supervised release; and

- considering whether to release on bail or otherwise.

(e) Other Statutes and Rules. A federal statute or a rule prescribed by the Supreme Court may provide for admitting or excluding evidence independently from these rules.

RULE 1102. AMENDMENTS

These rules may be amended as provided in 28 U.S.C. § 2072.

RULE 1103. TITLE

These rules may be cited as the Federal Rules of Evidence.

APPENDIX B

SAMPLE EVIDENCE EXAMINATION

The following exam is an edited version of an evidence examination, using the multiple choice and the true-false format. Although this exam covers only a portion of the topics covered in the evidence class, it should give you a good idea of the type and length of questions you are likely to see on a final examination.

The answers to the questions follow the examination.

ST. MARY'S UNIVERSITY
SCHOOL OF LAW

Evidence II
Professor D. Schlueter

Test No. _____
Student Exam ID No. _____

INSTRUCTIONS

1.   This is a two-hour closed book examination. It consists of a total of 33 objective questions (29 multiple choice and 4 true/false). Each question is worth 3 points. Be sure that you have all 15 pages of the examination. You are free to make whatever marks, notes, comments, etc. you care to make on the examination itself.

2.   The examination consists of three parts. The first part deals with a civil case being tried in Texas. The second part deals with a criminal case being tried in Texas. The third part consists of 5 miscellaneous evidence questions. Unless otherwise stated, assume that the Texas Rules of Evidence apply.

3.   The answers to the questions must be recorded clearly on the computer scantron sheet, using a soft lead pencil. Only answers marked on the scantron sheet will be credited.

4.   Write your Student Exam ID Number on the scantron sheet in the place normally reserved for the social security number (upper left hand corner); fill in the appropriate blanks beneath the number. Also, in the place reserved for your name, write your class section (B or C) and also the examination number which appears in the top right hand corner of your examination.

5.   Your name, initials, or other identification should appear nowhere, either on the exam itself or on the scantron sheet.

6.   Please ensure that you have all pages to the examination. If you find it necessary to take the exam apart, please be sure to reassemble it in the proper order.

7.   When you turn in your examination, please be sure to place it in the box or at the place designated for your section.

PART I

The following 17 questions relate to a Texas Civil Trial in which Jones, the plaintiff, has alleged that a Mr. Smith negligently ran his delivery truck through a red light and collided with Jones' car. As a result, Jones and her daughter have sustained multiple injuries which required extensive treatment and rehabilitation. The named defendants are the Ajax company, Smith's employer (the owner of the truck) which is being sued on a theory of negligence and BigTruck, Inc., the truck's manufacturer which is being sued on a theory of strict liability. Jones is asking for $500,000 in general damages and $900,000 in punitive damages.

1. At trial, the plaintiff is questioning an eyewitness, Mr. Fiberboard, about the accident and the witness relates the fact that he overheard Smith say that he was not worried because he was covered by his company's insurance. The defense objects to the mention of insurance. Which of the following would be the most accurate statement?

    A. The objection should be sustained because the Texas courts are particularly intolerant of any mention of insurance in a civil case.

    B. The objection should be summarily overruled.

    C. The objection should be overruled if the plaintiff's counsel can convince the judge that he is offering evidence of insurance for some reason other than the fact that the defendant was negligent.

    D. None of the above statements is correct.

2. Assume that defense counsel in the Question #1 now objects that the eyewitness' testimony of what he overheard Smith say about his insurance coverage is blatant hearsay. Which of the following is the most accurate statement concerning admissibility of Smith's statement?

    A. The statement by Smith is inadmissible hearsay.

    B. The statement by Smith is inadmissible hearsay because Smith is not on the stand testifying.

    C. The statement by Smith may be admissible as an admission by a party.

    D. None of the above statements is correct.

3. Assume that the eyewitness in Question #1 is now asked by the plaintiff's counsel to relate what he saw. He testifies that he was waiting for a bus when he heard screeching breaks, looked up and saw the delivery truck hit the plaintiff's car broadside. He also states that he believed that the truck was going awfully fast at the time of the accident. The defense counsel objects on the ground of inadmissible opinion testimony. Which of the following most accurately describes the admissibility of his opinion?

    A. His opinion is inadmissible because the jury alone determines the ultimate issue of negligence and his opinion about the manner of operation of the truck goes to that ultimate issue. The opinion thus impermissibly invades the province of the jury.

    B. His opinion about speed is inadmissible unless counsel establishes that he is an expert witness and has some basis for his opinion.

C. The only thing counsel has to establish for any witness's opinion about speed to be admissible is that the opinion testimony would be helpful to the jury.

D. None of the above is an accurate statement.

4. The plaintiff's counsel also asks the eyewitness to relate what he said at the time of the accident. The eyewitness states that immediately after seeing the accident he blurted out to another bystander "That SOB in the truck just ran a red light." Defense counsel objects on grounds of hearsay. Assume that the statement is offered to prove the truth of the matter asserted, which of the following is the most correct statement?

A. The statement is admissible hearsay.

B. The statement is admissible as a statement against interest.

C. The statement is admissible as an excited utterance, a statement against interest, and as a present sense impression.

D. None of the above is an accurate statement.

5. Plaintiff's counsel calls Dr. Wellgood to the stand to testify concerning injuries to the plaintiff. The Doctor relates that he has never seen the plaintiff as a patient but that in his professional opinion she has sustained permanent injuries which will affect her ability to work. The defense counsel objects that the Doctor's opinion is inadmissible for lack of a basis. Which of the following is the most correct statement?

A. Under Texas law, the Doctor may not rely solely on hearsay statements of others in forming his opinion.

B. The Doctor may not rely on medical charts and graphs prepared by others not under the same business duty as he to report accurate findings.

C. At the minimum, for his opinion to be admissible, the Doctor must have personally examined the plaintiff.

D. None of the above statements is accurate.

6. The plaintiff's counsel offers testimony by a hospital roommate of the plaintiff's that she overheard a lawyer for the Ajax company offer the plaintiff a high-paying job if she would drop her lawsuit against the company. Defense counsel objects. Which of the following is the most accurate statement concerning the admissibility of the lawyer's offer?

A. The offer is admissible as a statement against interest.

B. The offer is inadmissible because it amounts to an offer to compromise a claim.

C. The offer is admissible as the "Mary Carter" exception to the general rule which blocks admissibility of settlement offers.

D. The offer is inadmissible because it is a privileged lawyer-client communication.

7. Plaintiff's counsel offers into evidence a medical file prepared on the plaintiff by the Mercy Forever Hospital. One of the documents is the report written by the emergency room staff. The entry reads as follows:

> "Patient complains of severe chest pains and shortness of breath. Blood pressure is 130/78. Pulse is 65. Patient appears close to shock. There are numerous lacerations on arms, legs, and neck. Friend accompanying patient indicates that injuries were caused by collision with truck at intersection of First and Main Streets at approximately 5:00 p.m."

Assuming that the entry can be authenticated and is offered to prove the truth of the matter asserted, which of the following is the most accurate statement?

A. The entire entry is admissible under the statement of bodily condition, Rule 803(4), exception to the hearsay rule.

B. The entire entry is admissible under the business records exception to the hearsay rule if the staff person who prepared the entry testifies at trial.

C. Portions of the entry are admissible under the business records exception to the hearsay rule.

D. None of the above statements is accurate.

8. Plaintiff's counsel next offers into evidence a memo written by the CEO of the company that manufactured the truck to the company's lawyer concerning the fact that (1) the lawyer is authorized to attempt to settle the case with the plaintiff and (2) he is concerned about a number of design changes that were made in the truck's brake system in response to similar accidents in other states. Which of the following is the most accurate statement?

A. The entire memo is inadmissible because it presents evidence concerning an offer to settle a disputed claim and evidence regarding subsequent repairs, both of which would be inadmissible in this case.

B. The entire memo is inadmissible as the lawyer's work product.

C. the entire memo is privileged under the lawyer-client privilege, but only the CEO could claim the privilege because it was his "communication."

D. None of the above statements is accurate.

9. Plaintiff offers the deposition testimony of the plaintiff's ex-husband (taken before their divorce and for the purpose of this case) to the effect that his wife suffered severe back pains in the months following the accident. The ex-husband has refused all attempts to obtain his testimony at trial and has indicated that he would rather go to jail than testify for his ex-wife, the plaintiff. Which of the following is the most accurate statement?

A. The deposition could be admitted for the truth of the matter asserted under Rule 801 as nonhearsay.

B. The deposition could be admitted under the former testimony exception in Rule 804 even if the court considers him to be "available."

C. The deposition can only be used as nonhearsay impeachment evidence if the ex-husband changes his mind and takes the stand to testify.

D. None of the above is an accurate statement.

10. The plaintiff offers evidence that two years ago Ajax's driver, Smith, entered pleas of guilty in Arizona to several misdemeanor counts of reckless driving and one count of manslaughter by a motor vehicle. The pleas were ultimately withdrawn, however, when the judge expressed concern about the providency of the guilty plea. In a contested trial, Smith was ultimately found guilty of only a misdemeanor charge of negligent driving. Which of the following statements is the most accurate?

A. Because this is a civil trial, evidence of Smith's pleas of guilty are admissible.

B. Evidence of Smith's pleas of guilty are not admissible.

C. Although Smith's guilty pleas are not admissible, if he had successfully entered a nolo contendere plea, it would have been admissible in this case.

D. If this were a criminal case, Smith's pleas of guilty would have been admissible.

11. During the trial, there is a dispute about whether there was a working traffic light at the intersection of First and Main at the time of the accident. The plaintiff finally asks the trial judge to judicially note that fact. Which of the following statements is the most accurate?

A. Whether a stop light existed at that intersection is not an adjudicative fact capable of judicial notice.

B. Because this is an adjudicative fact, the trial judge must take judicial notice upon request even if the plaintiff can offer no supporting information.

C. If the judge takes judicial notice of the fact, the jury is not bound to accept it and it would be error to so instruct them.

D. None of the above statements is a correct statement.

12. Assume that in the preceding question, the trial judge refuses to take judicial notice of the fact that a working stoplight existed at the intersection and the plaintiff now offers a copy of an official city record that shows that at the time of the accident, a working stoplight existed at the intersection. The defense objects on grounds of the best evidence rule. Which of the following is the most accurate statement.

A. The best evidence rule does not apply because this is an official record.

B. The best evidence rule applies but because this is an official record, it is automatically exempt from the rule under Rule 1005.

C. The best evidence rule applies but the copy of the record could be admissible if someone testified that the copy had been compared with the original and the copy was correct.

E. The best evidence is inapplicable here because that rule only applies to those documents, tapes, photographs, etc. which have independent legal significance, such as a contract or notice of a defect.

13. During its case, the defendant calls the plaintiff's ex-husband to the stand to testify that after the accident he saw his wife fall down the stairs and that later he overheard her tell her doctor that she had re-injured her back in a freak home accident but was afraid to say anything to her lawyer. Which of the following is the most accurate statement?

A. The ex-husband cannot testify as to anything he saw or heard during their marriage because it is privileged.

B. The ex-husband cannot testify to what he overheard his wife say on the phone, if she intended it to be a confidential communication to her doctor.

C. The ex-husband can testify as to what he overheard his wife say, even if she intended it to be confidential, because the communication involved a physical condition which she has raised as an issue in the trial.

D. The ex-husband can testify as to what he heard because even if his wife intended the conversation to be confidential, they are no longer married.

14. The defense counsel for Ajax calls a Ms. Wilson to the stand to testify as to the work order given to Mr. Smith for his daily truck deliveries on the date of the accident. But she is having trouble remembering exactly which locations he was supposed to visit. Which of the following is the most accurate statement.

A. The printed delivery schedule may be used either as past recollection recorded or present memory refreshed. In either case, the defense counsel could offer the document into evidence as a defense exhibit.

B. The delivery schedule may be used as present memory refreshed if Ms. Wilson indicates that looking at it might refresh her recollection. If it does, then the opposing counsel is not permitted to introduce it into evidence.

C. If the document is admissible under the past recollection record exception to the hearsay rule, the proponent (the defense counsel) is only permitted to read it to the jury.

D. In order for the defense counsel to rely on the delivery schedule to refresh his witness' memory, he must establish that the witness personally prepared the schedule while it was fresh in her mind.

15. The defense calls to the stand a Mr. Nordic who testifies that he overheard the plaintiff say to a fellow golfer at the country club that she had been only slightly injured in the accident but was going to sue Ajax anyway. Which of the following is the most accurate statement?

    A. The statement is inadmissible hearsay unless the plaintiff is willing to take the stand and be available for cross-examination.

    B. The statement is admissible as nonhearsay under Rule 801 even if the plaintiff does not take the stand.

    C. The statement is inadmissible under the Texas "eavesdropper rule."

    D. The statement is admissible under the statement of bodily condition exception to the hearsay rule, i.e., Rule 803(4).

16. A defense expert witness, Dr. Molley testifies that in his opinion the back and neck injuries allegedly sustained by the plaintiff are not permanent. On cross-examination, plaintiff's counsel attempts to question Dr. Molley about a published treatise on the topic of back and neck injuries. Defense counsel objects on grounds of hearsay. Which of the following is the most accurate statement?

    A. Plaintiff's counsel may not rely upon the treatise in any way if Dr. Molley refuses to recognize it as an authoritative source.

    B. Under the Texas Rules of Evidence "treatises" may be used either for impeachment purposes or as substantive evidence.

    C. If plaintiff's counsel can establish that the treatise is published and is reliable authority, he may offer the treatise into evidence as a plaintiff's exhibit.

    D. None of the above is an accurate statement.

17. The defense also offers the typewritten, death-bed statement dictated by a Mr. Wools, a terminally ill patient, who saw the accident and stated that it was the plaintiff, and not Mr. Smith, who had run the red light several months earlier and had caused the accident. When Wools made the statement he knew he was dying of cancer. Which of the following is the most correct statement?

    A. The statement is admissible as a dying declaration.

    B. The statement is admissible as a dying declaration only if the defense can show that the witness is now dead.

    C. The statement is not admissible as a dying declaration.

    D. The statement is not admissible as a dying statement because in Texas, such statements are admissible only in murder or wrongful death cases.

PART II

The following 12 questions relate to a Texas Criminal Trial. Unless otherwise stated, assume that the Texas Rules of Criminal Evidence apply.

Jebb Sweatt is on trial for murder of one Ned Turner. He was initially targeted by the police as the killer when as part of a drug sting operation, his home was searched for drugs and police discovered, in plain view, Turner's bloodied coat. The two men apparently had a falling out over a bad drug deal and Turner ended up with multiple gunshot wounds to his chest.

18. At a pretrial motion to suppress the coat found in Sweatt's house, an agent testifies that the house was searched because of an informant's tip that drugs were hidden in the house. The defense counsel objects that those statements are blatant and inadmissible hearsay. Which of the following is the most accurate statement?

    A. The statements of the informant are clearly inadmissible hearsay.

    B. The statements of the informant are admissible hearsay under the statement against interest exception to the hearsay rule.

    C. The statements are not hearsay.

    D. The statements are not hearsay because the agent is now on the stand available for cross-examination.

19. The defense moves to require the prosecution to identify the informant who originally tipped the police that drugs were hidden in Sweatt's home. Which of the following is the most accurate statement?

    A. The informant's identity need not be revealed unless the defense can show that the ability to cross-examine the policeman will be unduly limited.

    B. The court may require the prosecution to disclose the identity of the informant if the trial judge believes that the informant was not reliable or credible.

    C. Although the prosecution may have to disclose the identify of the informant, it is not required to disclose confidential communications that the informant may have made.

    D. The informant's privilege is held by the informant but may be claimed by an "appropriate representative of the public entity."

20. The prosecution offers into evidence the testimony of Turner's wife that on the night he was killed he said, "This is it. I am going to meet some guy named Sweatt." Which of the following is the most correct statement?

    A. Turner's statement is inadmissible hearsay.

    B. Turner's statement is admissible under the present sense impression exception to the hearsay rule.

    C. Turner's statement is admissible under Rule 803(3) (statement of existing mental, emotional, or physical condition).

D. Turner's statement is admissible under the excited utterance exception to the hearsay rule.

21. The prosecution offers into evidence the police detective's official report showing the location of Turner's body at the scene of the crime in an attempt to show just that. The defense objects that the report is hearsay. Which of the following is the most correct statement?

    A. The report is not hearsay.

    B. The report is admissible under the official records exception to the hearsay rule, Rule 803(8).

    C. The report is not admissible under the official records exception to the hearsay rule, Rule 803(8).

    D. None of the above is a correct statement.

22. The prosecution offers the testimony of the officer who searched Sweatt's apartment and located the victim's bloodied coat. The officer states he remembered that at the time he saw the coat he said to his partner that the coat looked like the one described by the victim's wife. The defense argues that the statement is inadmissible hearsay. Which of the following is the most accurate statement?

    A. The statement is inadmissible hearsay.

    B. The statement is admissible under the present sense impression exception to the hearsay rule, Rule 803(1).

    C. The statement is admissible under the past recollection recorded exception to the hearsay rule.

    D. The statement is inadmissible hearsay because the wife, who originally described the coat is not on the stand testifying.

23. The prosecution calls to the stand the former law clerk for the defense counsel who is prepared to testify that counsel asked him to interview Sweatt concerning his background and possible character witnesses. During the interview, Sweatt admitted that he had killed Turner because of a bad drug deal. He also said that he had said the same thing to Turner's widow when she confronted him shortly after he was arrested. The defense counsel objects that Sweatt's statements to the law clerk are privileged. Which of the following is the most accurate statement?

    A. Sweatt's statements are not privileged but the attorney-client privilege may only be claimed by the client himself.

    B. Sweatt's statements are probably privileged even if he made them to his counsel's law clerk.

    C. Sweatt's statements to the law clerk are not privileged under the attorney-client privilege if Sweat did not intend to keep his statements to the law clerk confidential.

    D. Sweatt's statements are not privileged because they relate to criminal activity.

E. B and C are correct statements.

24. The prosecution offers into evidence the testimony of a Dr. Williams, who works with a private drug rehabilitation program. Williams is prepared to testify that during a voluntary group therapy session for the treatment of drug abuse, Sweatt admitted to him that he had a drug problem and that he would do anything, even kill someone, to get his supply of drugs. The defense counsel objects on the grounds that Sweatt's statement is privileged. Which of the following is the most correct statement?

A. This statement would be privileged under the doctor-patient privilege.

B. Sweatt's statement would be privileged under the alcohol or drug abuser communications privilege.

C. Sweatt's statement would not be privileged under the alcohol or drug abuser privilege because under that rule, Sweatt's admission would not be confidential because it was made in a group session.

D. None of the above statements is correct.

25. The defense counsel offers the written statement of Johnny Winflit, a friend of Sweatt's, who states that he killed Turner because the latter owed him $10,000 on a gambling debt. The prosecution objects that the incriminating statement of Winflit is inadmissible hearsay. Which of the following is the most accurate statement?

A. The statement is admissible under the statement against interest exception to the hearsay rule if the defense can show that Winflit is "unavailable."

B. The statement is not admissible under the statement against interest exception to the hearsay rule because it is not against Sweatt's interest and he is the one offering the statement.

C. The statement is admissible under the statement against interest exception even if there are no corroborating circumstances which clearly indicate the trustworthiness of the statement.

D. None of the foregoing statements is correct.

26. Assume that in question #25, supra, the prosecution also objects on the grounds of the best evidence rule: The statement appears to be a photocopy. Which of the following is the most correct statement?

A. A copy which raises no questions about authenticity of the original is as admissible as an original if it would not be unfair to admit it in lieu of the original.

B. This copy would only be admissible if the defense could show that the original was not available under any of the provisions of Rule 1004 (Admissibility of Other Evidence of Contents).

C. Only the original will be admissible.

D. None of the above statements is correct.

27. In rebuttal, the prosecution offers the testimony of one Jesse Roberts who testifies that on the night in question he loaned his gun to Sweatt who said that he needed it to "settle an old score." Which of the following is the most accurate?

A. Sweatt's statement is admissible as hearsay under Rule 801 only if the prosecution can show that there was a conspiracy between Roberts and Sweatt.

B. Sweatt's statement is inadmissible hearsay.

C. Sweatt's statement is admissible as a party admission under Rule 801.

D. None of the above statements is accurate.

28. On further questioning of Jesse Roberts, supra, Roberts states that he told Sweatt, "You are out to get Turner, aren't you?" Sweatt simply looked at Roberts and left. Which of the following statements is the most accurate?

A. Sweatt's actions are inadmissible hearsay.

B. Sweatt's actions are probably admissible as a party "admission by silence" under Rule 801.

C. Sweatt's actions are not even hearsay because he did not say anything to Roberts.

D. Sweatt's actions are admissible hearsay.

29. In rebuttal the prosecution calls to the stand Rev. James Sweatt, a man who purports to be a minister of the "New Life Church: A Loving, Learning Kind of Place" and is Sweatt's step-brother. Sweatt called him when he learned that the police were after him and told him what he had done. Which of the following is the most correct statement?

A. The clergy-penitent privilege may be available in this case if Sweatt sought out his clergyman brother for spiritual purposes.

B. Sweatt's statements to his brother are not privileged because his brother is obviously not an ordained minister or similar functionary of an established, main-line religion.

C. Assuming that there is a valid privilege, only the clergyman could claim the privilege.

D. None of the above statements is accurate.

PART III

The following 4 questions are true - false questions.

30. The Texas Rules of Evidence governing privileges are based primarily upon intrinsic policy considerations.

   A. TRUE

   B. FALSE

31. Under the Federal Rules of Evidence, an implied assertion by a declarant is considered to be "hearsay" under Rule 801.

   A. TRUE

   B. FALSE

32. A main difference in Federal Rule of Evidence 410 (Inadmissibility of Pleas, etc.) and the Texas Rules counterpart is the fact that under the Texas Rules, a defendant's statements during his guilty plea providency inquiry may be admissible in a later prosecution for perjury if they were under oath, on the record, and in the presence of counsel.

   A. TRUE

   B. FALSE

33. The "Wigmore" four-pronged test for determining whether a new common law privilege should be recognized is as follows: (1) Did the communication originate in a confidence that it would not be disclosed?; (2) Is the element of confidentiality essential to full and satisfactory maintenance of the parties' relationship?; (3) Is the relationship one of the traditional ones recognized by society?; and (4) Is there any utility to the proposed privilege?

   A. TRUE

   B. FALSE

HAVE A PROSPEROUS SUMMER

ANSWERS TO SAMPLE EXAMINATION

1. C
2. C
3. D
4. A
5. D
6. B
7. C
8. D
9. A
10 B
11. D
12 C
13 C
14 C
15 B
16 B
17 C
18 C
19 B
20 C
21 C
22 B
23 E
24 B
25 D
26 A
27 C
28 B
29 A
30 B
31 B
32 B
33 B

APPENDIX C

COMPARISON CHART

The following chart is intended to provide a summary of the comparisons between the Texas Rules of Evidence and the Federal Rules of Evidence. The author is deeply indebted to Ms. Chance Wolfe for updating and formatting this chart.

Rule & Subject	Texas Rule	Federal Rule
101 Title, Scope, and Applicability of the Rules; Definitions	(a) Known as Texas Rules of Evidence	Rules govern proceedings in U.S. courts & before U.S. magistrates; subject to limitations of Rule 1101
	(b) Applies in civil and criminal proceedings (including examining trials before magistrates), but not small claims court	No Federal rule
	(c) Privilege rules applicable in all proceedings	No Federal rule
	(d)) Hierarchy from U.S. Constitution down to common law	No Federal Rule
	(e) Special rules for criminal proceedings (e)(1) Preliminary admissibility question (e)(2) Grand jury proceedings (e)(3)(a)-(f) Rules not applicable in proceedings listed:	No Federal Rule
	(f) Justice court cases	No Federal Rule
	(g) Military hearings	No Federal Rule
	(h) Definitions	(b) Definitions
Rule 102 Purpose	States purpose of rules and offers guidance on applying the rules	Same

Rule and Subject	Texas Rules	Federal Rule
103 Rulings on Evidence	(a) Error must involve substantial right (a)(1) Timely, specific objection to preserve error (a)(2) Offer of proof necessary	Generally the Same. Rule explicitly indicates that definitive ruling on objection, before or during trial.
	(b) Need not repeat objection to preserve claim of error on appeal	Same
	(c) Requires court to hear party's offer outside presence of the jury and before charge is read to the jury; court may supplement; at request of party, shall direct offer in question and answer form	Does not require court to hear offer of proof outside presence of the jury or before jury charge read; court may make any statement about evidence, objection, and ruling; court may direct offer in question and answer form.
	(d) Conduct proceedings to avoid jury's exposure to inadmissible evidence	Same
	(e) Fundamental error-- court not precluded from taking notice of fundamental error.	Same except substitutes "plain error" for "fundamental error"

Rule & Subject	Texas Rule	Federal Rule
Rule 104 Preliminary Questions	(a) Determined by the court, subject to (b); not bound by rules of evidence except for privileges	Same
	(b) Conditional submission of evidence based on later factual showing of relevancy	Same
	(c) Preliminary matters discussed outside jury's presence when justice requires or accused is witness including hearings concerning admissibility of confessions	Same
	(d) Testimony of accused, out of hearing of jury, does not subject accused to cross-examination	Same, except omits phrase "out of hearing of the jury"
	(e) Jury hears evidence relevant to weight and credibility	Same
Rule 105. Evidence that is Not Admissible Against Other Parties or for Other Purposes	(a) Court, upon request, restricts evidence to one party or one purpose and so instructs jury	Same
	(b)Preserving a Claim of Error (b)(1) An error to evidence admitted without restriction is preserved only if instruction is requested (b)(2) Evidence excluded in (a) must be offered by proponent for proper limited purpose to allow complaint on appeal	No Federal rule

Rule & Subject	Texas Rule	Federal Rule
106 Remainder of or Related Writings or Recorded Statements	Adverse party may introduce other parts of writings, recordings, or depositions contemporaneously with proponent's introduction	Adverse party may require opponent to introduce remainder of writing, recording, or deposition
107 Rule of Optional Completeness	When part of an act, declaration, conversation, writing or recorded statement is given, other party may inquire into remainder	No Federal Rule

Rule & Subject	Texas Rule	Federal Rule
201 Judicial Notice of Adjudicative Facts	(a) Scope limited to adjudicative facts	Same
	(b) Judicially noticed fact must be (1) generally known in court's territorial jurisdiction or (2) capable of accurate verification	Same
	(c) Judicial notice discretionary in trial court	Same
	(d) Judicial notice may be taken at any time	Same
	(e) Party has opportunity to be heard as to propriety of judicial notice upon request; judicial notice mandatory if court is supplied with necessary supporting information	Same
	(f) Civil cases: judicially noticed facts must be accepted as conclusive; Criminal cases: judicially noticed facts may be accepted as conclusive	Same

Rule & Subject	Texas Rule	Federal Rule
202 Judicial Notice of Other States' Law	Court, on its own motion or motion of any party, must take judicial notice of constitutions, public statutes, etc. of any U.S. jurisdiction; sufficient information and notice required; party has opportunity to be heard re propriety of judicial notice; notice can be taken at any time in proceedings; court's ruling subject to review as question of law	No Federal rule
203 Determining Foreign Law	Notice required in pleadings or written form, 30 days prior to trial, to all parties including necessary information; necessary translations required; court may consider any material or source; court's determination subject to review as question of law	No Federal rule
204 Judicial Notice of Texas Municipal and County Ordinances, Texas Register Contents, and Published Agency Rules	Court, on own motion or motion of any party, must take judicial notice; sufficient information and notice required by proponent; party has opportunity to be heard re propriety of judicial notice; court's ruling subject to review as question of law	No Federal rule

Rule & Subject	Texas Rule	Federal Rule
301 Presumption in Civil Cases	No Texas rule	In all civil cases, except as otherwise provided, presumption creates burden of going forward with evidence, but does not shift risk of non-persuasion
302 Applicability of State Law in Civil Actions and Proceedings	No Texas rule	Presumptions for fact regarding elements of a claim/defense governed by state law

Rule & Subject	Texas Rule	Federal Rule
401 Test for Relevant Evidence	Any tendency to make the existence of a consequential fact more or less probable than if no evidence	Same
402 Generally Admissibility of Relevant Evidence	All relevant evidence admissible unless prohibited by law; non-relevant evidence inadmissible	Same, but includes reference to the Supreme Court of United States
403 Excluding Relevant Evidence for Prejudice, Confusion, or Other Reasons	Relevant evidence inadmissible when substantially outweighed by unfair prejudice, issue confusion, misleading the jury, undue delay, or needless presentation of cumulative evidence	Includes "waste of time" as grounds for exclusion

Rule & Subject	Texas Rule	Federal Rule
404 Character Evidence; Crimes or Other Acts	(a)(1) Character evidence generally not admissible except:	(a)(1) Same
	(a)(2)(A) Pertinent character trait of defendant in criminal case	(a)(2)(A) Same
	(a)(2)(B) Character of party in civil case accused of conduct involving moral turpitude	No Federal rule
	(a)(3)(A) In a criminal case and subject to Rule 412, accused may introduce evidence of pertinent character trait of victim; state may rebut;	(a)(2)(A) Same except that rule permits prosecution to present character evidence regarding accused, if accused attacks character of victim under Rule 404(a)(2);
	(a)(3)(B) State may introduce evidence of peaceable character of victim in homicide case where victim alleged to have been aggressor;	Same
	(a)(3)(C) In civil case, violent character of victim of assaultive conduct admissible by accused party and by opponent to rebut same	No Federal Rule
	(a)(4) Character of witness; as provided in Rules 607, 608, and 609	Same
	(b)(1) Evidence of prior bad acts (including crimes) not admissible to prove conduct	Same,
	(b)(2) Acts may be admitted to prove something other than character; in criminal case, pre-trial notice must be given to accused upon timely request, for acts to be offered in case-in-chief	(b)(2) is the same The notice provision in (b)(3) varies from Texas Rule; prosecution is required to provide pretrial notice, without request from defense; must be in writing.

Rule & Subject	Texas Rule	Federal Rule
405 Methods of Proving Conduct	(a) Where admissible, provable by opinion or reputation; in criminal cases, during guilt stage of trial, witness must be familiar with accused or reputation of accused before date of offense; on cross, inquiry allowable into relevant specific instances of conduct	Same, except no timing requirement
	(b) When character is an essential element of charge, claim, or defense, provable by specific instances	Same
406 Habit; Routine Practice	Habit, regardless of corroboration, is relevant to prove act in conformity with habit	Same
407 Subsequent Remedial Measures; Notification of Defect	(a) Subsequent remedial measures not admissible to prove negligence, culpability, defect in design, or need for a warning; admissible to impeach, or, if disputed, to prove ownership or control, or feasibility of such measures.	Same
	(b) Notice by manufacturer as to product defect admissible	No Federal rule

Rule & Subject	Texas Rule	Federal Rule
408 Compromise Offers and Negotiations	Settlements or compromises not admissible generally; however, admissible to prove bias, prejudice, interest of witness or party, to negate contention of undue delay, or efforts to obstruct investigation	Same, except includes admissibility in criminal cases of claims by public office within scope; excludes words "interest" and "party"
409 Offers to Pay Medical and Similar Expenses	Evidence of promise to pay medical expenses not admissible to prove liability	Same
410 Pleas, Plea Discussions, and Related Statements	(a) Following not admissible: (1) guilty plea later withdrawn; (2) in civil cases, *nolo contendere* plea; in criminal cases, *nolo contendere* plea later withdrawn; (3) Rule 11 statements or pleas or similar pleas; in civil cases, also guilty pleas later withdrawn or *nolo contendere* pleas; in criminal cases, also guilty and *nolo contendere* pleas later withdrawn; (4) statement for negotiation purposes. --- (b) Exception for statements described in (3) and (4), when optional completeness is fair	(a) Does not apply to withdrawn *nolo contendere* pleas; Statements made during plea negotiations may also be admissible in criminal perjury prosecution --- Same; includes perjury and false statement exception if defendant made statements under oath with counsel present
Rule 411. Liability Insurance	Evidence of liability insurance is generally not admissible, except as provided in nonexhaustive list of exceptions in rule.	Generally the same.
412 Evidence of Previous Sexual Conduct in Criminal Cases	(a) In sexual assault case, opinion or reputation of victim's prior sexual conduct not admissible --- (b) Specific instances of prior sexual conduct are not admissible unless specified protective procedures are followed, and evidence is necessary to rebut scientific or medical evidence,	(a) Excludes evidence, in criminal *and* civil cases, that victim (1) engaged in other sexual acts or (2) had sexual predisposition --- (b)(1) Criminal; evidence of specific sexual acts admissible (A) to prove that another was source of semen, injury or other physical evidence, (B) to prove prior intimacy with accused to show

	concerns past intimacy with the accused to show consent, concerns victim's motive or bias, is admissible under Rule 609, or is constitutionally required, and probative value outweighs unfairly prejudicial effect Applies only in criminal cases	consent, and (C) where constitutionally required; (b)(2) Civil cases: evidence of sexual propensity admissible if otherwise admissible and probative value substantially outweighs harm to victim and unfair prejudice to party. Reputation evidence re victim admissible if victim raises
	------------------------------------ (c) Defense must notify court of intent to offer evidence; court must hold an in camera hearing	------------------------------------ Slightly different procedure from Texas
	------------------------------------ (d) Record of in camera hearing is sealed for appellate review	------------------------------------ No Federal rule; required sealing of record covered in (c).
	------------------------------------ (e) Definition of victim	------------------------------------ (d) Same
Rule 413 Evidence of Similar Crimes in Sexual Assault Cases.	No Texas Rule of Evidence. But see Article 38.37 CCP	Rule permits the prosecution in a federal criminal case involving sexual assault to introduce defendant's prior acts of sexual assault. Rule provides procedural guidance re notice, etc.
Rule 414. Evidence of Similar Crimes in Child Molestation Cases.	No Texas Rule of Evidence. But see Article 38.37 CCP	Rule permits prosecution in federal criminal case, where defendant is charged with child molestation, to introduce defendant's prior acts of child molestation. Rule provides procedural guidance re notice, etc.
Rule 415. Evidence of Similar Acts in Civil Cases Concerning Sexual Assault or Child Molestation.	No Texas Rule of Evidence	In federal civil case where damages are sought for child molestation or sexual assault, party may introduce evidence of prior acts of child molestation or sexual abuse under Rules 413 or 414.

Rule & Subject	Texas Rule	Federal Rule
501 Privileges in General	Unless provided by law, no person can refuse to (1) be a witness (2) disclose any matter (3) produce object or writing (4) prevent another witness from disclosure	Not analogous—provides that common law privileges be applied in light of reason and experience; where state law provides rule of decision, state law privilege applies
502 Required Reports Privileged by Statute	No disclosure of reports protected by law; no privilege for perjury, fraud, or failure to comply with the law	**502 Attorney-Client Privilege and Work Product; Limitations on Waiver** (a) Disclosure in a federal proceeding or to a federal officer wavier privilege -- (b) Privilege not waived if inadvertent disclosure occurs a federal proceeding or to a federal officer -- (c) Disclosure in a state proceeding, subject to a court order, does not waive privilege -- (d) Disclosure is not waived if there is a federal court order -- (e) Agreement on disclosure in a federal proceeding is binding between parties -- (f) Rule is applicable to all proceedings subject to rules 101, 1011 and 501

Rule and Subject	Texas Rule	Federal Rules
503 Lawyer-Client Privilege	(a) Definitions -- (b) Confidential statement between client, lawyer, representatives of each or any combination thereof protected -- (c) Privilege claimed by client, any legal representative or attorney for client -- (d) Does not apply for (1) furtherance of crime or fraud (2) claimants through deceased client (3) breach of duty by either party (4) document attested to by attorney (5) joint clients	No Federal rule
504 Spousal Privileges	(a) Confidential communication privilege (a)(1) Definition (a)(2) Privilege extends to confidential statements made during marriage (a)(3) Claimed by either spouse or representatives (a)(4) No privilege for (A) furtherance of crime or fraud (B) proceedings between spouses in civil cases (C) crime against spouse or minor child (D) commitment proceedings (E) proceeding to establish competence -- (b) Testimonial Privilege in criminal case (b)(1) Accused's spouse has privilege not to be witness for state; however, may voluntarily testify for state even over accused's objection; if testifying, subject to cross-examination per Rule 611(b) (b)(2) counsel may comment on accused's failure to call spouse (b)(3) privilege claimed by spouse;	No Federal rule

	(b)(4) Exceptions for certain crimes and proceedings, crime against other spouse, any member of household of either spouse or crime against any minor child or bigamy; or matters occurring before marriage	
505 Privilege for Communications to Clergy Member	Privilege for communications to clergy member	No Federal rule
506 Political Vote Privilege	Political vote confidential unless cast illegally	No Federal rule
507 Trade Secrets Privilege	Trade secrets protected unless privilege works fraud or injustice; judge takes protective measures	No Federal rule
508 Informer's Identity Privilege	(a) Privilege held by government entity -- (b) Appropriate government representative can claim; in criminal case, State may object and not allow the use of privilege -- (c) Exceptions (1) voluntary disclosure (2) testimony on merits in civil and criminal cases (3) legality of obtaining evidence	No Federal rule

Rule & Subject	Texas Rule	Federal Rule
509 Physician-Patient Privilege	(a) Definitions (b) No privilege in criminal proceeding except for communications made by person in treatment for drug or alcohol abuse (c) Confidential communications between physician and patient are privileged; privilege also applies to records of identity, diagnosis, evaluation, or treatment. (d) Privilege claimed by doctor through patient; patient can claim on own behalf (e) Exceptions in a civil case: (1) proceedings against doctor (2) written consent (3) evidence of medical claim (4) communication or record relevant to patient's physical, mental, or emotional condition, when such condition relied upon as part of claim or defense (5) disciplinary acts against doctor or registered nurse (6) involuntary civil commitment (7) abuse or neglect (f) Consent for release	No Federal rule

Rule & Subject	Texas Rule	Federal Rule
510 Mental Health Information Privilege in Civil Cases	(a) Definitions -- (b) Confidential communications between professional and patient are privileged; privilege extends to records of identity, diagnosis, evaluation, or treatment; -- (c) Privilege claimed by professional on client's behalf or patient can claim -- (d) Exceptions: (1) proceedings against the professional (2) right waived in writing (3) to substantiate a claim (4) court-ordered exam (5) communication or record relevant to patient's physical, mental, or emotional condition, when condition relied upon as part of claim or defense (6) abuse or neglect of institution resident	No Federal rule

Rule & Subject	Texas Rule	Federal Rule
511 Waiver by Voluntary Disclosure	(a) Privilege may be waived by (1) voluntary disclosure, (2) calling person to whom disclosure made to testify as character witness to extent such is relevant --- (b) Attorney-Client Privilege and Work Product; Limitations on Waiver (b)(1) Privileged waived if disclosed in a federal or state proceeding or to a state official (b)(2) Inadvertent disclosure not waived in state civil proceedings (b)(3) Court order prevents waiver of disclosure in federal and state proceedings (b)(4) Agreement on disclosure in a federal proceeding is binding between parties	(a) No Federal rule --- (b) Federal Rule 502 is similar to Texas Rule 511(b)
512 Privileged Matter Disclosed Under Compulsion or Without Opportunity to Claim Privilege	Privilege not defeated by (1) erroneous compulsion to disclose, (2) disclosure made without opportunity to claim privilege	No Federal rule

Rule & Subject	Texas Rule	Federal Rule
601 Competency to Testify in General; "Dead Man's Rule"	(a) Everyone competent to be a witness except (1) insane persons and (2) children and others who lack sufficient intellect to testify ------------------------------------- (b) "Dead Man's Rule" in civil actions: very limited; judge must instruct jury in appropriate instances	Unless otherwise provided, all persons competent to testify—provided that in civil proceedings where issue controlled by state law, competency also so controlled Rule does not include "dead man's" provision
602 Need for Personal Knowledge	Witness must have personal knowledge; such may be established by witness' own testimony; subject to Rule 703	Same
603 Oath or Affirmation to Testify Truthfully	Oath or affirmation required	Same
604 Interpreters	Qualify as experts and take oath	Same
605 Judge's Competency as a Witness	Trial judge not a competent witness; no objection needed	Same

Rule & Subject	Texas Rule	Federal Rule
606 Juror's Competency as a Witness	(a) Juror cannot be witness in that trial; objection made outside presence of jury	(a) Same
	(b)(1) Jurors may not testify or present other evidence concerning statements, internal processes, or other matters occurring during deliberations. (b)(2) Exceptions: (a) outside influences (b) rebut claim that juror not qualified to serve	(b) Juror may testify as to outside influence or extraneous prejudicial information
607 Who May Impeach a Witness	Credibility of any witness may be attacked by any party	Same
608 A Witness's Character for Truthfulness or Untruthfulness	(a) May impeach or rehabilitate character for truthfulness by opinion or reputation	(a) Same
	(b) No attack on witness's character for untruthfulness by showing specific instances of conduct, except convictions	(b) Adds that court may permit cross-examination on specific acts affecting veracity; such testimony does not waive privilege against self-incrimination. Rule clarifies that prohibition against proof of SIC's by extrinsic evidence only relates to acts involving witness's character.

Rule & Subject	Texas Rule	Federal Rule
Rule 609 Impeachment by Evidence of a Criminal Conviction	(a) Impeach with evidence of prior felony conviction or crime involving moral turpitude if probative value outweighs prejudice	(a) Impeach with prior conviction of crime (1) punishable by death or imprisonment of more than 1 year (different balancing tests for accused and witnesses) or (2) involving dishonesty
	(b) Time limit: 10 years unless probative value substantially outweighs prejudice	(b) Includes notice requirement for use of convictions more than 10 years old
	(c) Inadmissible if (1) rehabilitation & no subsequent conviction of felony or moral turpitude offense; (2) probation completed & no subsequent conviction of felony or crime involving moral turpitude; (3) finding of innocence	(c) Inadmissible if (1) finding of rehabilitation if no subsequent conviction of crime punishable by death or imprisonment in excess of 1 year; (2) same as Texas Rule 609(c)(3)
	(d) Juvenile adjudications inadmissible, except in proceedings conducted pursuant to Family Code, in which witness is party, unless constitutionally required	(d) Juvenile adjudications generally inadmissible; may be admissible as to credibility of witness other than accused if necessary for fair determination of guilt or innocence
	(e) Convictions must be final	(e) Conviction on appeal and fact of appeal admissible
	(f) On request, must give notice of intent to impeach	(f) No Federal Rule

Rule & Subject	Texas Rule	Federal Rule
610 Religious Beliefs or Opinions	Beliefs or opinions regarding religion not admissible to bolster or attack credibility	Same
611 Mode and Order of Examining Witnesses and Presenting Evidence	(a) Court exercises reasonable control	Same
	(b) Scope of cross-examination permitted regarding any relevant matter	Cross-examination limited to subjects raised on direct and credibility, unless court permits inquiry as on direct
	(c) No leading questions on direct except as may be necessary to develop testimony; may use leading questions on cross-examination or on direct examination of hostile witness, etc.	Same
612 Writing Used to Refresh a Witness's Memory	Provides for inspection by opposing counsel of writings used by witness before or during trial to refresh memory; right to inspect if witness uses during testimony or has reviewed before trial in criminal case; discretionary if witness in civil case reviews during testimony; rule includes provision for redactions and sanctions, including mistrial	Same, except refers to Jencks Act

Rule & Subject	Texas Rule	Federal Rule
613 Witness's Prior Statement and Bias or Interest	(a) Must lay foundation regarding contents, time, place of prior inconsistent statement, and let witness explain or deny; extrinsic evidence of statement not admissible if witness unequivocally admits making statement	Examination permitted re prior statement (not modified by "inconsistent") without necessity for production of statement or disclosure of contents; opposing counsel entitled to production or disclosure upon request
	(b) Witness must be informed of circumstances or statements that demonstrate bias and be given opportunity to explain	Not analogous; extrinsic evidence of prior inconsistent statement inadmissible unless witness given opportunity to explain or deny and opposing counsel given opportunity to interrogate, or if justice requires
	(c) No prior consistent statements unless qualified per Rule 801(e)(1)(B)	No Federal Rule
614 Excluding a Witness	Court may exclude witnesses except: (1) natural person who is a party, and spouse of that person in civil cases; (2) representative of non-natural party; (3) person whose presence is essential; (4) victim may be permitted to remain in criminal case	Federal counterpart to Texas Rule 614 is Federal Rule of Evidence 615. It is similar to Texas rule, except no provision made for spouses; states that Congress may provide for additional exceptions, e.g., victims Federal Rule 614 provides for court calling and questioning witnesses

Rule & Subject	Texas Rule	Federal Rule
615 Producing a Witness's Statement in a Criminal Case	(a) Opposing counsel may request production of statements of witness relating to witness' testimony that is possession of counsel, relates to subject matter of testimony, and that has not already been produced	No analogous rule. But see Fed. R. Evid. 612 which cites Jencks Act (18 U.S.C. § 3500)

	(b) Entire contents may be required to be produced	Federal Rule of Evidence 615 provides for "Exclusion of Witnesses," a topic covered in Texas Rule 614.

	(c) Material may be excised out of statement, during in camera inspection, and remainder turned over to requesting party	

	(d) Requesting party given reasonable time to examine statement; court may call recess	

	(e) Failure to comply with court order to produce statement can lead to testimony of witness being stricken, or, if State fails to comply, judge may declare mistrial	

	(f) Definition of "Statement" of a witness	

Rule & Subject	Texas Rule	Federal Rule
701 Opinion Testimony by Lay Witnesses	Testimony must be rationally based on witness' perception and helpful to trier of fact, and is not testifying as an expert	Same except that rule adds provision that the lay opinion testimony is not based upon scientific, technical, or other specialized knowledge.
702 Testimony by Expert Witnessses	Person with specialized knowledge may testify if qualified as expert and helpful to trier of fact; testimony may be in form of opinion or otherwise	Same except that rule adopts *Daubert* and requires that expert testimony be based upon sufficient facts or data, is the product of reliable principles or methods and the expert has applied those principles or methods in a reliable fashion to the facts in the case.
703 Bases of an Expert's Opinion Testimony	Facts or data perceived by/reviewed by/made known to expert at or before hearing; if of type reasonably relied upon by experts in forming an opinion, the facts or data need not be admissible into evidence	Same except that court may not disclose otherwise inadmissible data to jury unless court decides that probative value substantially outweighs prejudicial effect.
704 Opinion on Ultimate Issue	Testimony not objectionable because it embraces an ultimate issue to be decided by trier of fact	Generally the same. Rule 704(b) bars testimony by expert on mental state or condition of criminal defendant as it relates to element of offense or a defense

Rule & Subject	Texas Rule	Federal Rule
705 Disclosing the Underlying Facts or Data and Examining an Expert About Them	(a) Not necessary to disclose basis on direct examination unless required by court; may be required to disclose basis on cross-examination	Similar
	(b) Opponent allowed to voir dire expert, regarding basis of opinion, out of presence of jury	No Federal rule
	(c) Opinion inadmissible if expert lacks sufficient basis unless sufficient facts or data presented	No Federal rule
	(d) If basis inadmissible, other than to explain opinion, balancing test required; revealed inadmissible facts must be accompanied by instruction to jury	No Federal rule
706 Audit in Civil Cases	Verified report of court-appointed auditors is admissible notwithstanding other Rules	No comparable Federal rule. Federal Rule 706 covers court appointment of expert witness--(a) Court may appoint expert witness; (b) Court informs expert of his or her duties; expert must advise parties of findings, be available for deposition, be available to testify and cross-examined; (c) expert entitled to reasonable compensation (d) Court may authorize disclosure to jury that witness was appointed; (e) Rules does not bar parties' ability to call own experts

Rule & Subject	Texas Rule	Federal Rule
801 Definitions That Apply to This Article; Exclusions From Hearsay	(a) Statement—Oral or written verbal expression; nonverbal conduct if intended as substitute for verbal expression	Statement- Oral or written assertion; nonverbal conduct intended as an assertion (omits "verbal" in both clauses)
	(b) Declarant—a person making a statement	Same
	(c) Matter asserted—Matter explicitly asserted or implied by "statement" if its probative value "flows from declarant's belief"	Same as Texas Rule 801(d) except "matter asserted" does not extend to matters flowing from belief of declarant
	(d) Hearsay—Out of court statement offered to prove the truth of the "matter asserted"	Same as Texas Rule 801(c)
	(e) Statements which are not hearsay: (e)(1) Prior statement by witness, except statements made under oath during grand jury proceedings and depositions in criminal cases. Also includes statements made in accordance with Tex. Code Crim. Proc. art. 38.071 (e)(2) Statements by party opponents (e)(3) Depositions taken in same proceeding in civil cases; unavailability of deponent not requirement for admissibility	Federal Rule 801(d)(1) and (2) are same as Texas Rule 801(e)(1) and (2); no provision regarding depositions

Rule & Subject	Texas Rule	Federal Rule
802 The Rule Against Hearsay	Hearsay not admissible except as provided by statute, Rules, or law; hearsay alone will now support a verdict	Substantially similar, except omits sentence concerning hearsay in support of verdict
803 Exceptions to the Rule Against Hearsay— Regardless of Whether the Declarant is Available	The following are not excluded by the hearsay rule, even though declarant is available as witness: (1) Present sense impression	Same
	(2) Excited Utterance	Same
	(3) Then existing mental, emotional, or physical condition	Same
	(4) Statements for purposes of medical diagnosis or treatment	Same
	(5) Recorded recollection	Same, except does not require "personal" knowledge; omits clause regarding trustworthiness
	(6) Records of regularly conducted activity; including affidavit which complies with Rule 902(10)	Same, except provides narrower definition of "business"; includes reference to self-authentication rules
	(7) Absence of entry in records kept in accordance with the provisions of paragraph (6)	Same

Rule & Subject	Texas Rule	Federal Rule
803 Continued	(8) Public records exception, excluding police reports in criminal cases	Same
	(9) Records of vital statistics	Same
	(10) Absence of public record or entry	Same
	(11) Records of religious organizations	Same
	(12) Marriage, baptismal, and similar certificates	Same
	(13) Family records	Same
	(14) Records of documents affecting an interest in property	Same
	(15) Statements in documents affecting an interest in Property	Same
	(16) Statements in ancient documents	Only applies for documents prepared before January 1, 1998

Rule & Subject	Texas Rule	Federal Rule
803 Continued	(17) Market reports, commercial publications	Same
	(18) Learned treatises	Same
	(19) Reputation concerning personal or family history	Same
	(20) Reputation concerning boundaries or general history	Same
	(21) Reputation as to character	Same
	(22) Judgment of previous conviction; different rule for criminal cases	Substantially similar, except excludes pleas of *nolo contendere*; applies to crimes punishable by death or imprisonment in excess of 1 year
	(23) Judgment as to personal, family, or general history, or boundaries	Same
	(24) Statement against interest. Also requires corroboration of statements tending to expose the declarant to criminal liability	Not applicable. Former "catch-all" provision has been relocated in new Federal Rule of Evidence 807

Rule & Subject	Texas Rule	Federal Rule
804 Hearsay Exceptions to the Rule Against Hearsay— When Declarant is Unavailable as a Witness	(a) Unavailable declarant is one who (1) is exempted by privilege (2) refuses to testify (3) has lack of memory (4) is dead or ill (5) is absent from hearing, unless due to actions of proponent	Same
	(b) Hearsay exceptions (b)(1) Former testimony. Includes deposition testimony in civil cases; in criminal cases, deposition testimony controlled by Tex. Code Crim. Proc. ch. 39.	Same, except requires prior opportunity and similar motive to examine testimony on part of opposing party or "predecessor in interest" in civil cases, or opposing party in criminal cases
	(b)(2) Dying declarations	(b)(2) Same, except limited to civil actions and homicide prosecutions
	(b)(3) Statement of personal or family history	(b)(3) Not analogous to Texas Rule; statement against interest— similar to Texas Rule 803(24), except excludes social interest (object of hatred, ridicule, or disgrace); requires corroborating evidence for inculpatory statements of others offered to exculpate accused (b)(4) Same as Texas Rule 804(b)(3) (b)(5) Catch-all exception deleted and moved to new Federal Rule 807, the residual hearsay exception
		(b)(6) Exception that provides for "forfeiture by wrongdoing". No Texas counterpart.

Rule & Subject	Texas Rule	Federal Rule
805 Hearsay Within Hearsay	If hearsay upon hearsay, admissible if each part is independently admissible under exception or exclusion	Same
806 Attacking and Supporting the Declarant's Credibility	Hearsay declarant's credibility may be attacked; no requirement for declarant opportunity to deny or explain; if declarant called as a witness, subject to cross-examination	Same
Rule 807. Residual Hearsay Exception	There is no Texas counterpart to Federal Rule of Evidence 807	Rule provides hearsay exception in cases where (1) statement is supported by sufficient guarantees of trustworthiness, after considering the totality of circumstances under which it was made and evidence, if any, corroborating the statement; and (2) statement is more probative on the point for which it is offered than any other evidence that the proponent can obtain through reasonable efforts. Proponent must give notice to adverse party.

Rule & Subject	Texas Rule	Federal Rule
901 Authenticating or Identifying Evidence	(a) Authentication (condition precedent re admissibility) satisfied by evidence to support finding that matter in question is what proponent claims	Same
	(b) Illustrations: (1) Testimony of witness with knowledge	Same
	(2) Non-expert opinion on handwriting	Same
	(3) Comparison by trier or expert witness	Both known and unknown samples must be authenticated for jury's determination
	(4) Distinctive characteristics and the like	Same
	(5) Voice identification	Same
	(6) Telephone conversations	Same
	(7) Public records or reports	Same
	(8) Ancient documents or data compilation	Same

Rule and Subject	Texas Rule	Federal Rule
Rule 901 continued	(9) Process or system	Same
	(10) Methods provided by statute or rule	Recognizes that Congress may indicate that certain matters may be presumptively genuine
902 Evidence That is Self-Authenticating	Extrinsic evidence of authenticity not needed: (1) Domestic public documents under seal	Same
	(2) Domestic public documents not under seal	Same
	(3) Foreign public documents	Does not include sentence re coverage where there is a treaty
	(4) Certified copies of public records	Slight difference of wording
	(5) Official publication	Same
	(6) Newspapers and periodicals	Same
	(7) Trade inscriptions and the like	Same

Rule and Subject	Texas Rule	Federal Rule
Rule 902 continued	(8) Acknowledged documents	Same
	(9) Commercial paper and related documents	Same
	(10) Business records accompanied by affidavit	Federal Rule 902(10) compares to Texas Rule 902(11). Federal Rule 902(11) is comparable, however
	(11) Presumption under statutes or other rules	Federal Rule 902(11) covers authentication by use of business records by certificate
	(12) No Texas provision	Federal Rule 902(12) permits self-authentication of foreign business records—in civil cases—by certificate
Rule 903. Subscribing Witness's Testimony	Not necessary to call attesting witnesses	Same

Rule & Subject	Texas Rule	Federal Rule
1001 Definitions That Apply to This Article	(a) "Writings and Recordings:" Letters, words or their equivalent, set down by handwriting, typewriting or other form of data compilation	Same
	(b) "Photographs:" Includes still photos, x-rays, videotapes, and motion pictures	Same
	(c) "Originals:" Writing or recording itself or counterpart intended to have same effect	Same
	(d) "Duplicate:" Counterpart produced by same impression as original or some other accurate reproduction of the original	Same
1002 Requirement of the Original	Original needed to prove its contents except as otherwise provided in the rules or law	Same
1003 Admissibility of Duplicates	Duplicate admissible to same extent as original except if authenticity questioned or unfair to admit	Substantially similar wording

Rule & Subject	Texas Rule	Federal Rule
1004 Admissibility of Other Evidence of Content	"Original" not required to prove contents if: (a) Original lost or destroyed	Same
	(b) Original not obtainable	Same
	(c) Original outside the state	No Federal rule
	(d) Original in possession of opponent	Same as Texas Rule 1004(c)
	(e) Collateral matters	Same as Texas Rule 1004(d)
1005 Copies of Public Records to Prove Content	Prove by certified copy or by witness who has compared record or document with original; if above not possible, other evidence of contents may be given	Same
1006 Summaries to Prove Content	Voluminous writings, recordings, or photos may be presented in form of a chart, summary, or calculation if convenience will be furthered	Same

Rule & Subject	Texas Rule	Federal Rule
1007 Testimony or Statement of a Party to Prove Content	Contents may be proved by testimony or deposition of party against whom offered or by written admission	Same
1008 Functions of the Court and Jury	Admissibility conditioned on fact question determined by court order Texas Rule 104; but, if question as to whether writing ever existed, writing is an original or whether other evidence correctly reflects contents, then jury decided	Same
1009 Translating a Foreign Language Document	(a) Translations: Are admissible with affidavit setting forth translator's qualifications and accuracy of translation; documents must be served 45 days prior to trial --- (b) Objections: objections to translation must be made at least 15 days prior to trial --- (c) Effect of Failure to Object or Offer Conflicting Translation: Court will admit translation submitted under paragraph (a) and opposing party cannot object at trial	No Federal Rule

Rule & Subject	Texas Rule	Federal Rule
Rule 1009 continued	(d) Effect of Objections or Conflicting Translation: Court will determine if there is a genuine issue of material fact to be resolved by trier-of-fact ------------------------------------- (e) Expert Testimony of Translator: Except as provided in paragraph (c), testimony is admissible ------------------------------------- (f) Varying of Time Limits: Discretion of court to vary time limits ------------------------------------- (g) Court Appointment: Court may appoint qualified translator	

Rule & Subject	Texas Rule	Federal Rule

1101 Applicability of Rules	There is no Texas Rule 1101. Texas Rule 101 is comparable, however.	(a) Rules applicable in Federal courts
		-- 	
		(b) Rules apply in both civil and criminal hearings
		-- 	
		c) Privileges apply at all stages of proceedings
		-- 	
		(d) Rules inapplicable in:
		     (1)preliminary questions of fact
		     (2)grand jury proceedings
		     (3) miscellaneous proceedings (extradition, sentencing, bail, warrants, and preliminary examinations in criminal cases)
		-- 	
		(e) Rules applicable in part—details numerous federal proceedings

Made in the USA
Coppell, TX
20 April 2021

54099908R00164